BLACK TRUTH:
The Last Days of Gotti

BLACK TRUTH:
THE LAST DAYS
OF GOTTI

MARK D. BLACK

Disclaimer

The author assumes no responsibility or liability for any errors or omissions, or for changes made in any of the references or links in this book. All links were checked and in working order as of the date of publication. Since the links are not under the control of the author and are provided as a convenience, the author is not responsible for their availability. All information in this book is provided on an "as is" basis with no guarantees of completeness, accuracy, usefulness, timeliness, or results to be obtained from the use of this information.

This book is dedicated to John Gotti, Greg DePalma, Sammy Cagnetti, and all men who respect the honor of loyalty among friends and never sold their friends out to receive a lighter sentence.

As always, Steve and I also dedicate this book to our moms, Joy Black and Llawana Hoel, and to all other good mothers who never gave up on their children.

TABLE OF CONTENTS

"Never was anything great achieved without danger."

— Niccolò Machiavelli

FORWARD AND SYNOPSIS

In *Black Truth: Medicated in America: The Mark Black Story*, I wrote a few chapters regarding my incarceration in the federal penitentiary at Springfield, Missouri, and my encounters there with John Gotti, Greg DePalma, and Sam Cagnina III. My chance encounter with Greg DePalma led to a symbiotic friendship with him, Sam, and John. Because of the subject matter in my last novel and the fact that these men were still incarcerated in that prison, I didn't want to write anything that would compromise that book's message or adversely affect Greg, Sam, or John's welfare while they remained incarcerated or in the court system. During my last few weeks in the penitentiary at Springfield, I was caught in a situation that extended within and beyond the prison's walls into the struggle between law enforcement and organized crime figures, highlighting the dark qualities shared by each group along with some of the unexpectedly endearing qualities exhibited by those often condemned in the press.

ACKNOWLEDGMENTS

Special Thanks To:

Bill Black & Jin Black for allowing me the
time to write this novel and
follow my dreams.

Steven B. Hoel, DO, JD. for his undying friendship
and help editing this book.

Ryan A. Brandt and Don Givelos for their friendship,
help, suggestions, insights,
and for always being there.

John Gotti, Greg DePalma, and Sammy Cagnina for their
friendship and for saving my life.

PROLOGUE

My long, nightmarish road leading to meeting the Mafioso legends John Gotti, Greg Depalma, Sammy Cagnina, and drug kingpin José Reyes was an unintended journey. It began with a runaway train of incompetent psychiatrists' prescriptions of a litany of psychotropic medications from my adolescence into adulthood, which eventually drove me clinically insane. Thrown onto a pathway of psychotic madness, eventually, I found myself on a darkened highway with a police officer's gun in my face. Once jailed, my bond was denied on grounds that I was a danger to myself and the public. Fast forward one year later, and I'm sentenced to seven years between state and federal prisons for a variety of drug, explosives, and gun charges.

Once incarcerated, I mustered the presence of mind to refuse all medications over the objections of prison psychiatrists, and then, to their surprise, I miraculously regained my sanity, requiring them reluctantly to find me no longer a danger to myself or others. After completion of the state portion of my sentence, I was transferred to the custody of the Federal Bureau of Prisons (FBOP). After my sanity was cleared by the FBOP psychiatrists, prison officials eventually transferred me via federal marshals to the concrete jungles of The United States Medical Center for Federal Prisoners (MCFP Springfield) in Springfield, Missouri. There I was assigned to work as a hospital orderly, caring for federal prisoners who were sick or dying. That is where I met John Gotti, and my unforeseen relationship with him and his Mafia friends began.

For the full story regarding my psychiatric odyssey, please visit "Black Truth" at https://www.facebook.com/blacktruthstory/

CHAPTER 1

Date: March 2000.

Place: MCFP (United States Medical Center for Federal Prisoners): Springfield, Missouri.

Under cold, bleak, gray skies, Axel Rose wails over a prison transport van's speakers as a psychotic inmate screams while strapped in a specialized fiberglass chair in the back of a white van—each designed for use in transporting the criminally insane. The van's engines and the inmate roar are in unison as it makes its way down a blacktop street lined with neatly trimmed but leafless bushes. Looming ahead, the oppressive, monumental, red and white multi-story facade of Springfield's federal penitentiary comes into view. A prison guard stands next to a colossal guard tower to the right. He points towards a sign that reads: "Arrival and Receiving. No Public Access." The two federal marshals sitting in the van's cab salute the guard in comradery and understanding as the driver guns the unmarked van's engine and arcs it sharply to the left. The van races down the gravel road at the prison's perimeter, throwing rock and dust into the crisp November air. Chain-link fences, coiled razor wire, and intermittent guard towers flash before the marshals' determined eyes. The U.S. Marshal riding shotgun cranks the music louder in an attempt to drown out the unhinged inmate's hysterical shrieks. But even Slash's pulse-pounding solo is no match for the prisoner's raucous, ear-piercing screams of obscenities and demonic howls.

Glancing back at the inmate strapped in the specialized chair, the driver shakes his head, "Jesus Christ! Will you shut the fuck up?" Oblivious to his pleadings, the inmate continues the high-pitched wails unabated as the van swerves into the receiving area of MCFP. A prison guard with a worried look on his face stands in front of a gray concrete building near a reinforced steel door where all inmates are received into the confines of Springfield's penitentiary.

Inside the receiving room, I stand in a holding cell next to a burly inmate, each of us waiting to be processed into MCFP. A few guards are milling around the room when everyone inside hears the muffled rhythm of "Welcome to the Jungle" as the van door is opened. A psychotic scream then penetrates the steel door's entryway as the music ends abruptly, leaving as the only sound an eerie maniacal laughter building in intensity. Without warning, the massive door then implodes open, followed by one of the federal marshals. His steely gaze immediately commands the attention of everyone in the room. He yells with urgency, "Is it clear?" There is a brief interlude of calmness; then the shit hits the fan.

The shrill, malicious, demonic screams coming from outside rise to a crescendo. Above the chaos, the marshal roars again, "I said, is it fucking clear?!" From inside our barred, concrete reinforced holding cell, the stocky inmate and I both stand at attention. Glancing nervously at each other and our surroundings, we no longer feel safe—neither do the guards.

One of the guards inside the room finally stutters, "Yeah, yeah...it's clear!" He scrambles for a wall dedicated to devices for use on unruly inmates and quickly chooses a Taser and restraints while his partner, who was sitting at a desk, bellows into a phone demanding a nurse. Through the entryway, two marshals roll in the screaming, hysterical prisoner, who is strapped from head to toe in the molded fiberglass chair. The figure strains violently against the heavy nylon straps, and he is covered in puke and spit.

A modified hockey mask covers his face, which prevents him from biting or spitting on his captors. From beneath the glazed mask, an inhumane face glares with protruding eyes. As he howls in a nonhuman language, I feel the hair stand up on the back of my neck. I step back from the bars as my mind goes into a fight or flight mode but with nowhere to run. The inmate beside me mutters, "He's crazy." Frozen with fear, I'm dumbstruck and can't respond as I stare at something straight out of an exorcism gone horribly wrong.

The monstrosity growls beneath its mask, "Fuck you, you motherfuckers. I'll rip your eyes out and skull fuck you. You fuckin' pigs! I'll kill you. I'll fuckin' kill you!" His entire body convulses violently as his muscles bulge and strain against the constrictive bonds. The guard with the Taser points it at the man's chest with one of the marshals yelling over the confusion, "Hit him!" The guard's Taser comes alive with the sound of electricity as he holds it to the man's chest with seemingly no effect.

Then from behind, a nurse runs out of an open door and towards the man, jabbing a syringe into an exposed area on the man's arm. His head nearly instantly rolls back, then snaps upright to reveal his glazed eyes. His voice hisses, "Ivan's not here right now. Can you please leave a fuckin' message? I'll kill you...I'll thrill you...I'll..."

After uttering his last words of arcane gibberish, his head rolls to the side with his face in a frozen grimace. The nurse briefly hovers over the sedated prisoner. Apparently satisfied, she then places a cap over the needle and barks orders to the guards surrounding the man, "Get his ass on the psych ward now, and tie that son-of-a-bitch to the bed before he wakes up!" With the urgency of handling a ticking time bomb, the guards quickly wheel him out of view.

The inmate beside me turns toward me with an edgy grin on his face. "Wow! Ivan the Terrible even scares the fuck outta me, and I've kicked more ass and banged more muff than anybody in this building." He belly laughs, sticking out his scarred-knuckled hand to introduce himself, "Hi, the name's Rick. Sergeant Rick Randall." I grasp Rick's calloused hand, and we shake with anticipated friendship.

"Hi. I'm Mark Black."

Rick and I quickly bond as the guards process us into prison. While we wait for our Photo IDs, Rick goes into further details about how battalions of soldiers are being phased out of the aging military prison at Leavenworth, Kansas and integrated into the federal civilian penitentiaries. With a grin, Rick boasts with a wager, "Heck, I bet you a book of stamps some of my brothers are here now." He lightly hits my arm while smiling. "If they are, we don't have a thing to worry about. Not even against that crazy fuck," Rick assures as he thumbs at the door through which Ivan the Terrible had just made his exit.

The guard informs us that we will be assigned to the same unit, once processed and dressed in our military khakis. Reaching under his desk, he presses a button that retracts a bolt with an electric buzz, unlocking a battleship gray steel door. He points to the open door, indicating that this is the end of the line, as Rick and I walk through its entrance into our new home.

True to Rick's word, many of his brothers-in-arms from the military have already arrived, and they have his back. A huge black guy with arms as big as anacondas stops in the hallway with a look of surprise. He smiles broadly as he points with both hands as if firing pistols at Rick. "Hey! It's Rick Rambo!" Another one yells out, "Hey Sarge, if you need anything, come see me!" With high-fives and salutes acknowledging respect for my new friend, our entourage grows until we reach our unit. It's here that I first understand the deep respect and fear that the military inmates wield at Springfield.

Our new home is in an area for newbies, fresh meat, FNG's (Fucking New Guys), or whatever you want to call newly incarcerated inmates. At MCFP, rather than individual cells, we are all housed in one large room lined with bunk beds and lockers. As we step across the threshold, sixty eyeballs turn in our direction, assessing the new cuts of meat. Usually, the first thing that happens when you walk into any prison is that the other inmates test your steel to see if you're a punk, but not today. Today, Rick has a pack of killers who have his back and, by proxy, mine. His dogs of war return their glares with malice and resolve.

For a few seconds, the fear and tension in the room are palpable...then, the inmates slowly look away and return to their previous business as Rick's army buddies walk in like they own the place and start helping him settle in. I settle into my assigned bottom bunk, which is directly across from Rick, between two black guys on either side. One gives me the heads-up while the other ignores me, absorbed in tomorrow's football numbers racket. After I make my bunk, I lay there watching Rick, and his army buddies loudly reminisce about fighting in Iraq and kicking ass in different hellholes around the world. These ex-military convicts are a totally different breed of an inmate in the prison system. There is a clear understanding—military inmates are not to be fucked with. They are respected and feared like any other prison gang...and for good reason. Their loyalty is, for the most part, unconditional, having been forged in the fires of war where they honor a military code that doesn't fight for money, street creed, or other egotistical dogma. Many of them have specialized combat training, making them one of the deadliest gangs within the prison system. If you attack one, you attack them all, and it's like hitting a hornet's nest—you're going to pay.

Another reason military inmates are feared and respected by other gang leaders is that gang leaders usually will not fight their own personal wars in prison or on the streets. Instead, they will send a few flunky, teenage gang members who relied on guns while on the streets with knives to settle prison debts. When these fights occur in prison, it's typically a skinny gangbanger with a mouth and something to prove in hand-to-hand combat against a very pissed-off Navy Seal, Ranger, or grunt. This matchup results in a fucking slaughter, and everyone expects it. To add insult to injury, the military prisoners then go in force after the gang leader who sent the skinny kid, who then joins him with a one-way ticket to the hospital. For now, with Rick as my friend, I'm relatively safe in the deadly confines of MCFP.

CHAPTER 2

After settling in, I receive my work assignment by an expressionless older Afro-American guard called "Bart the Blackheart." His real name is Bartholomew, but he earned his nickname by sitting most of the day in a 9' x 8' windowless room converted into an office. Essentially, Bart's doing time just like the rest of us—he's been doing so for decades, which is reflected in his soulless eyes. And he's one of the guards that has a hard-on for every inmate—today is no exception.

With a contemptuous scowl, he barks an order, "Inmate 144577! Congratulations, you're a fucking orderly. Here's your work order. Have fun cleaning toilets and taking care of the sick."

Examining the crumpled piece of paper, I see a number with a letter scribbled on its surface that identifies a unit somewhere in the prison. Looking up into the unfeeling eyes, I ask how to find this area. I wasn't trying to be insubordinate or a smart-ass. Answering my question with a grunt, he pointed his finger to the door and sent me out of his life. Obviously, he didn't care about my dilemma. MCFP is a huge place with acres of maze-like underground tunnels leading to different areas of the prison. This is topped by a four-story building with various restricted areas which, if trespassed, can get a prisoner thrown in the hole for weeks.

As I aimlessly wander the prison's underground halls, I run into the old black man who was playing the numbers game beside my bunk. I walk towards him and pull the wrinkled paper from my pocket as he mops the floor. "Hey buddy, do you think you can help me out here? Bart the Blackheart sent me to my new job but didn't give me directions."

Looking a marginally less irritated than Bart the Blackheart, he stops mopping the floor. "That's one mean-ass nigger. You'd think he'd have some love for a brother, but he has it in for all of us."

The old black man motions for me to give him the crumbled piece of paper. Looking down at the paper, he nods his head towards an elevator hidden in a corridor. Above its highly polished stainless-steel doors is a stenciled sign with the same number and letter written on the paper. I thank him, walk over and press the elevator's up button, then enter the brightly lit interior. When the elevator opens on the ground floor, a guard is collecting food trays from the inmates after lunch. His head snaps my way.

"You're late. Get your ass over here and help me out."

As I rush to his side, he blurts out, "The name's Mike. Look, I'm not a hard ass unless you play me. If you do your job, I won't bust your balls."

I extend my hand. "Sorry, I'm new here and got lost. The name's Mark, and it won't happen again."

Mike grips my hand while stating the obvious, "Shit happens. Collect the rest of these food trays and come see me when you're finished."

I nod my head affirmatively and finish the job as Mike meanders behind me and into his office. As I'm putting up the last dinner tray, a medium-sized elderly man with his bathrobe flapping behind him comes bounding down the hall. "Hey! Hey, you!"

I look around. "Me?"

"Yeah, you. I've seen you at mass. You Catholic?" he asks with a heavy Brooklyn accent.

Except for his huge prizefighter-sized hands, he reminds me of an older gentleman with a bad comb-over whom you may see sitting benignly in Central Park, feeding the pigeons. Studying his currently jovial face, I determine that he's not a physical threat. I give an affirmative answer, "Yeah, I am."

The man replies warm-heartedly, "Would you mind wheeling me down to Mass on Sunday?"

"Nah, I wouldn't mind. Let me check with the guard."

I knock on Mike's office door, and Mike responds through the closed door, "Yes, what is it?"

"Hey, Mike. A guy is asking if I can push him in his wheelchair to Mass on Sunday."

Mike scratches the side of his temple. "You don't have to do that. It's your day off, but if you want...sure."

I give Mike the thumbs up before I turn and give the same gesture to the elderly man.

The inmate sticks his hand out to introduce himself. His rough hand almost completely envelopes mine. "I knew you was a good kid. See you tomorrow around 9:45 a.m., and the name's Greg. Greg DePalma."

"Mark Black. Nice to meet you."

He releases my hand and saunters back up the darkened hallway while waving goodbye. "I know who you are. See you tomorrow morning at 9:45, Mark Black."

As I turn around to place the last tray in the food carrier, Mike comes out of his office to start his sentry duties. He stops in front of me and puts his thumbs in his belt, "Come see me after you take those trays back to the cafeteria. I would like a word with you."

I was taken back, yet still smiled. "Sure, Mike. Am I in trouble?"

Walking down the hall jangling his oversized guard keys, he throws up a hand. "Nah, I just need a word with you and to show you a few other things on the unit."

After returning from delivering the food carrier to the cafeteria, I knock on Mike's office door. "Did you want to see me?"

Mike sits back in his office chair with an elfish appearance. "Look, I don't mind if you want to help these guys out. It's commendable, but beware—Greg DePalma is Mafia. So, tread lightly."

Dumbfounded, I stutter, "W-W-What?"

Mike waves his hand as he expounds, "He's a capo in the Gambino crime family. And, although he may look like your kindly grandfather, he's not." Pushing his nose to the side, he slips into a Brooklyn accent, "You know John Gotti and those guys?"

Not really hip to all the Mafia lore or old-time gangster movies, I laugh and wave off his warning. "I've never heard of him. I'm sure it won't be a problem."

"I'm serious," Mike quips. "Be careful. I get the feeling you're a good guy, but you don't have to help DePalma out on your day off." Then he stands up. "Let's take a walk."

As we walk down the hallway, Mike describes my chores and what's expected from me on this unit, which consists mostly of mopping and buffing floors. As he talks and shows me where the utility closet is, I think back to my teen years when I was naïve, stupid, and incarcerated at this very same prison. At that time, I befriended a black guy named Snake, who then tried to rape me. Prison has an ironic way of taking the mundane and flipping it into a real life-and-death situation. Mike points down a darkened hallway whose entryway is painted circumferentially with a wide and foreboding yellow line. Beside the line on the wall is a bright red stop sign with a warning printed below:

RESTRICTED AREA!
NO INMATE PAST THIS LINE
UNLESS ESCORTED BY AN OFFICER.

At the other end of the hallway, palely-painted prison bars are evident, illuminated by a harsh downward-directed light. Behind the bars is a small rectangular space that holds two steel doors embedded into the walls on either end of the small room.

Mike's voice becomes firm. "That is solitary confinement. Never go down there without me. Is that clear?"

"Yes, sir."

"Well then, that's about it for your job description, and I need to do my rounds."

Mike shows me a key. "If I don't plug this into a machine at both ends of this unit, I get dinged by my superior. See? Even I have to answer to the man." He then laughs at his own joke. "We'll talk later, and don't forget what I said about DePalma." Mike then turns and walks down the hallway, leaving me a little dumbfounded.

Once finished with work, I head back to my unit to ask Rick his thoughts on my situation. As soon as he hears the word "Mafia," he rails against any involvement with DePalma. "Fuck those guys. You do them a favor, they do you a favor, and all of the sudden, you owe them." Before I can offer a rebuttal, he ends the conversation with his hand in my face and an ominous warning, "Watch out for those guys. I don't trust them. But if you do run into trouble, you come to me first."

"Thanks, Rick. I really appreciate it."

Later that night, while lying in bed, I reflect on Mike's and Rick's warnings and think about all the crazy people I'd met in prison. Heck, I'd never even heard of Greg DePalma before today, and the Gotti media coverage happened while I was incarcerated, so I knew little about that, either. Besides, while incarcerated, I'd known some of the most dangerous inmates in the penal system. If you really think about it, the Mafia is just another, albeit powerful, prison gang that is far from being the craziest or most dangerous.

During my recent years of incarceration, I worked and lived with armored car takedown artists, bank robbers, and members of the Mexican Mafia and various other cartels, with their tales of torture and mutilation of rival gang members. I even knew the DC Boys, who are mostly crazy crack babies but, collectively, are now one of the most feared black gangs within the system.

These dangerous malcontents, along with the Crips, Bloods, Aryan Brotherhood, and the rest of the list of hard-boiled inmates, would end your life on a whim or due to a meaningless misunderstanding.

Frankly, compared to most of the maniacs I'd met, Greg was an old man who seemed likely to be a relic from a bygone era of Tommy guns, bootleg liquor, and old gangster movies. He would prove me wrong, but by the time I fell asleep, I decided—I'm taking the old man to Mass.

CHAPTER 3

Bright and early Sunday morning, the elevator door opens to reveal a jovial Greg DePalma sitting in his wheelchair, grinning like the Cheshire Cat.

"Hey, Mark! I'm glad you could make it. I was wondering if you was gonna come or not. Most of these fucksticks around here can't be counted on for shit." He shakes his big index finger at me. "I knew you was a good one."

Smiling, I dig him back, "I try to keep my word, especially when Jesus is involved."

As I push him into the elevator and we both laugh, Greg proposes a basic rule. "Listen, Mark. If you keep your word with me, I'll always do the same with you. It's as simple as that."

Greg's words of integrity are appreciated and carry significant weight in this world, where associating with various bad elements can easily result in more time, drama, or even a murder charge. As we ride to the ground floor, my mind drifts back as I recall learning this invaluable lesson while incarcerated in the federal penitentiary in El Reno, Oklahoma. I feel like I'm back there, standing on the seven-foot run outside my second-floor cell. As I lean against the safety rail, I watch several inmates mill around in a common living area two stories below. The noonday sun's rays are gently shining through the enormous tinted skylights when an argument ensues in an adjacent cell.

Instinctively, I know the dispute is over a card game to which I'd been invited but declined because the game's host is a squirrely, skinny, young, white dude named Mitch who is down on a six-month probation violation for pissing in a National Forest. Although Mitch lives in the next cell to mine, I keep my distance. His intellect is comparable to that of the dullest garden tool, and his word is shit—two qualities to avoid at all costs in prison and out on the streets. Today seems to be no exception for Mitch, as he backs out of his cell screaming, "Fuck you, mother fucker! I didn't cheat!"

Jack, an older white guy, doing a five-year sentence for robbing a bank with a toy gun, had just befriended Mitch a few days ago. Now, he emerges from Mitch's cell, ready to fight over a bet consisting of either stamps or cigarettes.

Mitch's back is against the safety rail, and he has no route for escape. Jack grins maliciously as he barrels straight at Mitch like a heat-seeking missile on a mission of destruction. "What the fuck did you call me, you bitch? I'm gonna..." Mitch's extended fist punctuates the end of Jack's sentence. Its impact snaps Jack's head back and spins him around as his momentum carries him backwards over the steel safety rails encircling our seven-foot run. Jack's blood-curdling scream reverberates through the dorm as he plummets headfirst towards the bottom floor. Everyone turns towards the screams and, thus, their attention is on the falling man as his head slams into the concrete floor below with a sickening pop, abruptly ending the screaming. His body violently jackknifes into the floor before crumpling onto it like a discarded ragdoll.

A guard rushes toward Jack's body while yelling, "GET IN YOUR FUCKING CELLS!"

We all know Jack is beyond help as blood oozes from beneath his head, creating a rapidly expanding pool of blood. The guard steps back to avoid getting blood on his shoes as his face arches skyward to stare at Mitch's shocked face. Mitch gags, then runs into his cell and vomits into the stainless-steel toilet, heaving in short breaths, "Oh my God! Please don't let this happen! Please, God. I didn't mean to do it." But prison officials and God are indifferent to his pleas. This incident will cost Mitch another 20 years in maximum security for second-degree murder to atone for this sin.

The elevator door opens, snapping me out of my daydream, and we wind our way through the basement's labyrinth. My footsteps echo down its cold concrete halls as Greg reveals that his old friend from New York named Tony will be meeting us. Somewhere in the bowels of the penitentiary, we arrive at our destination and enter the 60' x 60' whitewashed room used for inmates' religious activities. Wheeling Greg through the door, I notice a group of men is already moving through the aisles of steel gray folding chairs to find seats. In front of the congregation is a simple wooden podium from which the priest will deliver Catholic mass to his parishioners. In the back, a small, elderly man with a blanket draped across his legs for warmth sits alone in a wheelchair. Greg motions me towards the small, frail man. "Push me over there, Mark."

I move a couple of the steel chairs to the side to make room for Greg's wheelchair, then place him next to the old man. They shake hands as their facial expressions light up in acknowledgment of their friendship. Greg introduces me like I'm family, "Mark, this is Tony. We fucking go way back." Tony wearily nods his head and gives me a weak smile as I shake his frail hand. I will later learn that Tony's full name is Antonio Coralli, who is also known as Tony Ducks.

After the introduction, Greg points to himself and Tony. "I got a little business to attend with Tony. You mind?"

Catching his drift, I excuse myself to give Greg the requested space. "No problem. I'll pick you up on the way out."

Greg smiles warmly. "Thanks, Mark."

He then turns back to Tony.

As I sit strategically away from the men, the priest comes to the podium, and everyone falls silent – except for Greg and Tony. Throughout the entire Mass, Greg and Tony talk incessantly. The priest and other inmates ignore their hushed conversation. Occasionally, I glance at Greg and see that he is completely indifferent to the setting. His hand gestures punctuate and accent his dialogue with Tony, who nods, smiles, and pats Greg's leg.

I would find their behavior disrespectful on the outside world, but this world is no longer ruled by social mores and non-incarcerated ethics. The present reality is a chaotic configuration to those unfamiliar with the penal system, where life is uncertain, and aged offenders are destined to die alone and away from their loved ones. Contrary to media portrayal, convicts' pervasive fear isn't getting stabbed or raped in prison—instead, it is to die alone in this godforsaken place without ever seeing the outside world again. Unfortunately for Tony, this appears to be his endgame.

The priest ignores the disrespect of the convicts' conversation with saintly patience. I join in ignoring their social transgression because I'm a convict with experience. Also, I heard that Greg and I were in here under similar circumstances—we didn't snitch on our friends and take the easy way out to a lighter sentence, which seems to be the growing trend among new-age gangsters. The blacks in prison have a saying: "I'm going to get what's mine," meaning that they will cut anyone's throat or shoot anyone in the back in order to get ahead. In a world where people increasingly have no loyalty and only look out for themselves, I respect Greg's old school traditions.

I stand and move to celebrate the Eucharist, but I notice that Tony and Greg don't come forward. Most old-timers won't partake in the body of Christ if they haven't confessed their sins to a priest or if they think they already have one foot in hell. Obviously, I am in no position to judge others or question their motives as I participate in the Eucharist. From what I've seen, God doesn't need hell for condemnation—I've seen hell here on Earth. Greg and Tony continue their secret conversation unabated until Mass ends.

As I push Greg back to his unit, he apologizes, "Sorry for any racket during Mass. It's just... Tony's probably not going to make it much longer, and I can't see him on his unit. Fucking Feds have no heart. Fuck the Feds."

He was correct. Most inmates don't have access to other units like inmate orderlies. I stop in the sporadically lit hallway and pat Greg on the shoulder. "No need to apologize. Fuck the Feds." I then snicker as I reflect on an endearing epitaph I once saw.

Greg glances down at his privates. "What's so funny? My dick hanging out?"

"Nah, the phrase "Fuck the Feds" made me remember a funny story

Greg eggs me on, "Well, come on. Let's hear it."

"Well, when I first came into the Feds, they thought I was completely crazy." Greg jerks around, trying to look in my face. "You? Crazy? Get the fuck outta here!"

Coming around to his side, I nod my head. "I'm serious. I was whacked out on psych pills."

"You mean headshrinker pills?" Greg inquires.

"Yeah," I quip.

Greg shook his head. "I don't trust those fuckers. Always trying to get you to talk about your feelings. Go get yourself laid already. Am I right?"

Laughing, I fist-bump Greg's extended fist. "You got that right."

Greg looks at me quizzically. "Well, what the fuck happened?"

"Before the Feds picked me up, I did a three-year stint in Oklahoma, where a prison psychiatrist finally discovered I'd been driven clinically insane with pills prescribed by previous psychiatrists."

"See!" Greg points his thick finger at me. "You can't trust those head doctors. I've known a few celebs in my day that went down hard because of those pricks. They love to prescribe those pills, take your money, and then tell you you're crazy. What a fuckin' racket. And they call me a crook." Greg snorts and then looks at me with concern. "But you're okay now, right?"

"Yeah, I'm okay now, but at the time, I was bat-shit crazy, thinking everyone was after me, including aliens."

Greg shakes his head. "Jesus..."

"I know, right? Anyway, after the marshals picked me up from state prison, they flew me via Con Air to their Federal holding facility in Oklahoma City. Once there, I was handcuffed, shackled, and flanked by three guards who took me straight to a psychiatrist, who was holding my extensive psychiatric records in his hand. He stared at me like I was a bug and emphatically stated, 'I'm sorry, Mr. Black. We've deemed you too violent for general population.'"

Greg grins. "I like violence."

"Well, apparently, the Feds frown upon bat-shit, straight-jacket craziness. Even though I'd been off medications for nearly four years, once this shrink saw my records, he wanted to re-medicate me back into oblivion. When I refused the good doctor's medications, he throws me into solitary confinement. And guess what's waiting for me when I walk into my cell?"

Greg throws up his meaty paws. "Beats me."

"As soon as they open my cell door, I see a humongous dick drawn on the wall with **'Fuck the Feds!'** printed on the shaft in big, bold letters. I stared at the huge dick and gave the guard a thumbs-up. He shoved me into the cell before informing me that I'd better not cause any trouble or that 'they have something for me.'"

Greg started laughing.

"When I walk up, face to face with the big dick, I see written below in tiny letters, the name 'John Gotti!'"

Greg snorts, "John's got that right. That guy fucking cracks me up!"

Greg's demeanor suddenly turns quizzical. "You really don't know who the fuck I am, do you?"

Mimicking his same quizzical look, I smile. "Should I?"

Greg chuckles. "Get the fuck outta here!

CHAPTER 4

During work breaks, I hang out with another orderly in a small, desolate, whitewashed communal lounge. An oversized, overpainted, metal-framed picture window dominates the room, perfectly framing an azure blue sky restricted by crisscrossed heavy steel cables designed to discourage helicopter escapes. Beneath the window, sitting on a dismal gray metal stand is a small color TV with horrible reception. Against two of the room's walls rests a massive L-shaped wooden bookshelf sparsely filled with outdated library books. In the middle of the floor, a well-worn card table surrounded by several uncomfortable gray-metal folding chairs sits uninvitingly.

The window affords a view below of an enormous, desolate, U-shaped field that sweeps across the killing zone. Its deadly boundaries are bordered with double rows of chain-link fence, covered from top to bottom in endless coils of razor wire, which glisten in the noonday sun. Behind the gleaming sea of serpentine razor wire, strategically placed guard towers protrude out of the ground like juggernauts, emphasizing the futility of attempted escape.

During orientation, every warden admonishes newly arrived inmates that his guards "will shoot your ass" if any one of them try to run for the fence. Although getting shot and/or cut to ribbons seems, to those outside the penal system, sufficient to curb an inmate's desire to attempt escape, these disincentives are often no match for hopelessness and desperation. During the Y2K scare, a bunch of paranoid jailhouse preachers in the El Reno prison began prophesying certain death for inmates upon commencement of the New Year, in conjunction with the preachers' end-of-the-world scenarios associated with the onset of the new Millennium. The genesis of these prophesies, and their "final protocol" progeny are from studies concluding that, should bands of convicts escape with no resources, they would more than likely form into roving gangs of killers, terrorizing the communities that incarcerated them. The final protocol rumor holds that the Bureau of Prisons plans to kill us in our cells before leaving the prison unguarded, rather than jeopardize the surrounding community.

I recall walking by a darkened smoking area at El Reno on that New Year's Eve, where five black men were listening to a black guy who could have been a TV evangelist. He whips up his captivated audience into an apocalyptic frenzy: "Listen my brothers, and as the Lord Jesus is my witness, just before twelve midnight, the prison guards are going to lock us in our cells and then gas us like the Jews in Nazi Germany! But we're not going to let that happen, brothers! Instead, we're going to meet our Lord and Savior Jesus Christ, who's going to take us home tonight!" As he continued his conspiracy rant, a few "Hallelujahs!" and a "Praise Jesus!" echoed past me as I walked away.

I'm no stranger to various rumors running through American prisons regarding the possible scenarios should an end-of-the-world type cataclysm occurs, creating mass chaos across the streets of America. My feeling is that the chances are much more likely that the prison guards will not be gassing us in our cells and will, instead, immediately abandon their posts to go home to protect themselves and their families, leaving millions of unattended inmates to their own devices. Prisons are not, however, hotbeds of sanity, and fear of the unknown, sprinkled with a little apocalyptic fervor across a largely uneducated population, sends some inmates willing to listen right over the edge. Several inmates, led by this jailhouse preacher, determine to make their escape.

As the clock ticks down to midnight, armed with faith and carrying bed mats over their heads to help traverse the spirals of razor wire atop the eight-foot chain-link fence, they sprint towards the prison's perimeter. Makeshift armor of cardboard and duct tape cover their bodies, but they quickly and painfully realize that their cardboard armor and bed mats are no match for the writhing serpentine coils of slashing razor blades. The bleeding convicts are easily apprehended and taken to the hospital for evaluation and repair of their many lacerations. They soon realize that not only did they not escape, nor did the world did come to an end, but that they also each receive an additional five-year sentence for attempted escape because of their misguided beliefs and allegiance to the jailhouse prophet.

Neither I nor Charles, the other inmate I work with here at Springfield, have serious thoughts of escape. We are each only a couple of years or months from going home and perfectly content to do our time before running back to whatever is left of our lives. Charles comes from a completely different social spectrum than me. Charles, aka "Charles, the crazy Cajun," is a squat, stocky all-American white dude and military prisoner like Rick. He has a noticeable scar across his forehead and will talk your ears off while chewing a pinch of tobacco. He delights in telling anyone who is willing to listen about the variety of Cajun dishes he has mastered, along with his pronounced longings to return to military service. Charles is a good guy who has a serious drinking problem that resulted in his incarceration here.

Charles was labeled with his "crazy" nickname for two reasons. For one, before joining the military, he worked as the head chef at his parents' Cajun restaurant and catering company. To hear him tell it, he was the sole reason it was a huge success. Secondly, after joining the military, his increasingly excessive drinking drove him crazy—batshit crazy. His last alcohol binge ended his military career and landed him here. He always carries around the "Big Book" of Alcoholics Anonymous. Charles told me in his thick New Orleans accent that he remembers drinking whiskey with his buddies in the middle of the afternoon but specifically remembers nothing else. He, obviously, deeply regrets his actions but is also deeply reluctant to share what he later learned had transpired that day.

One night while eating dinner with Rick and a newly arrived military inmate named Stan, I bring up the topic of "Charles, the crazy Cajun." Rick's friend, Stan, perks up immediately. "The crazy Cajun" is here?" Rick nods affirmatively, to which Stan whistles lowly. "I'll be damned. That crazy fucker almost killed me and put on a helluva fireworks show."

Rick cuts into his mystery meat, stabs it onto his fork, and waves it in my direction. "Tell Mark what happened; he'll get a kick out of it."

Stan nods. "I'd just got back after a fucked-up tour in the Middle-East and was trying to relax by getting a haircut and shave at the PX when machine-gun fire erupts that shatters the windows and rips the walls to shreds. Everyone went from enjoying a peaceful, mundane day to diving to the floor to save their lives." He mimics pulling a gun from his side. "Being an MP, I pull my gun out of my holster and inch towards the blown-out window, believing we are under some sort of attack. Looking out the window, I see that shit-faced, drunk, crazy fuck on the back of a jeep. In one hand he has a 50-caliber machine gun and in the other a bottle of Jack Daniels, and he is hollering at the top of his lungs—I shit you not—'Ayieee!' Stan's scream causes a guard to glance in our direction before grinning and putting his finger to his lips to notify us to hold it down.

Stan raises his hand in compliance, then continues, "As I crawl out the bullet-riddled front door, I see everyone else in the area is pinned down, too, including my fellow MP's who are slowly moving their way to his position."

"Wow!" I exclaim. "I'm surprised he didn't get shot."

Stan waves off my observation. "We could have taken him out like they do in civilian life, but he wasn't really aiming at anyone. He was just swaying back and forth, pulling the trigger in a drunken haze, and fucking shit up. And remember, some of these guys that come back after the war are fucked-up in the head, and we take care of our own."

Rick holds his fist out with conviction. "Semper Fi."

Stan fist-bumps Rick's scarred knuckles. "Semper Fi."

Stan chortles. "And it's a good thing he wasn't a civilian that day because right after I take cover behind a Humvee, the "crazy Cajun" releases one last volley of machine-gun fire that shatters windows into the street around me. Then, everything goes into slow motion as I watch the last shell casing eject from the 50 and its bullet slam into the wall 10 inches from my head."

Stan again blows a low whistle. "Missed me again, bitch." We all laugh at his dumb luck and the ridiculousness of the situation. Stan chuckles. "Seeing our opportunity, we all rush his dumb ass as he lets loose one last crazy Cajun yell, takes a final swig of Jack Daniels, and flips backwards, right out of the jeep bed. As I put him into handcuffs, the crazy fucker is barely conscious with a nasty gash across his forehead, but he asks me with the seriousness of a heart attack, 'Did I get them all, sir?'" We all belly laugh—including the guard who has been eavesdropping.

When I see Charles the next day, he is sitting with a few men in the TV room. The volume of his voice rises with excitement as he tells them of his special recipe for Cajun gumbo. Looking at him, I couldn't help but smile and feel a bit sorry for him as I realize that my fellow orderly is, for the most part, a relatively decent person. He just made a stupid mistake and has now found himself in this place, being a lackey for the man. Being an orderly in federal prison isn't that hard. It primarily consists of being a gopher for a guard, waxing floors, housekeeping, handing out food trays during meals, cleaning up, and dealing with the occasional crazy. My first experience of dealing with the occasional crazy occurred during the first month into my stint when Mike dispatched me to the forensic unit to retrieve a bottle of cleaning solution.

The forensic unit is set apart from the other units at Springfield and is strictly off-limits without proper credentials. Its sole function is to house inmates who are not mentally competent to stand trial. The goal of this unit is to medicate the accused back to competency so he may stand trial or at least to sedate him enough to give the illusion of competency while facing justice. I was an inmate housed in the forensic unit twenty-eight years earlier when my competency required evaluation. Now, in a strange twist of fate, I'm back on my old unit—this time as a sane person who is greeted by the blank stares of the overmedicated while childlike pleadings for cigarettes seem to come from every direction.

"Got a cigarette? Hey, buddy. Can I get a square from ya?"

Empathizing with their plight, I reach for a cigarette, but my concentration is broken by two guards anxiously running towards me barking orders: "Hey, you! Come with us. We may need your help!!!"

I can see a nurse running towards them while screaming, "Get the fuck down here and help us! Hurry!!"

The guards and I sprint down the hall and follow the nurse through a doorway. We are met by a sadomasochist's nightmare. A large black man with tears running down his face stands naked in the room, howling at two male nurses. Through tears of confusion, he sobs, "Don't come closer, or I'll cut off my dick!"

I look down and stare in disbelief. In one hand, he is holding a toothbrush with thin shaving razors protruding from the bristles, their bases securely fixed to the underlying plastic via melting. In the other hand, he is holding his large penis, which is painfully stretched out, with the end tied with a shoestring to a stark, white metal bedpost.

One of the guards puts his hands up and attempts to build rapport. "Now come on, Clarence. You don't want to do that."

"I wanna go home," Clarence whines.

The older of the two guards sympathetically chimes in, "That's what we're doing here, Clarence. We're trying to get you better so you can go home."

Clarence's demeanor immediately relaxes. "Really?"

"Really." As the smiling guard issues reassurances, he simultaneously inches closer to the trembling, 300 pound, mentally-ill inmate.

Seemingly out of nowhere, an out-of-breath female nurse nervously scurries up behind me. Her latex-gloved hand holds a syringe, ready to sedate Clarence into a better place—oblivion. Her hot breath on my neck is unexpectedly titillating given the circumstances, but that sensation dissipates as the smiling guard closes the gap to stand within a couple of feet of the crazed inmate.

He appeals to Clarence's inner child, "So, why don't you hand me that toothbrush, so you can go home, and we can all get outta here tonight?"

Clarence nods, "Tonight?"

"That's right. Tonight." The guard coos.

A calm yet still maniacal grin creeps across Clarence's face as he senses, in some crazy sort of way, that everything is going to be okay. He hands the guard his homemade knife and relaxes his grip on his swollen member. Suddenly, with the speed of a rattlesnake, the previously smiling guard flips Clarence's wrist, sending the knife to the corner of the room; at the same time, he latches onto Clarence's arm and pulls him toward all of us. Clarence shrieks as another guard appears from behind him with scissors and cuts the shoestring, releasing Clarence's bloated dick from the bedpost. The nurse with the syringe leans forward as the two guards restrain the terrified inmate.

A guard barks a command at me: "You!!! Help hold him down!" In response, I rush over and help hold Clarence's thrashing body to the floor as the nurse jockeys for the proper position to place her money shot. Holding down the 300 lb. mentally ill inmate feels like wrestling a demonically possessed grizzly bear. It's an unforgettable ride.

The nurse's needle finds its mark, and Clarence howls with betrayal. "You motherfuckers tricked me! You tricked me...you..." His voice trails off as his massive body relaxes and drifts to the floor.

As I loosen my grip, I can't help but look at this poor soul and think, once again...

That could have been me.

CHAPTER 5

One of my inmate orderly duties is taking care of patients. Greg DePalma is one of the patients who has a particular medical issue—bad lungs. If I was having breathing problems, I'd probably quit smoking. Not Greg. He is a life-long smoker who continues to smoke in prison at least two to three times a day. But a problem exists for all prisoners who smoke because cigarettes are slowly being phased out of the prison system, especially on hospital units. Prison officials promised to make examples out of prisoners caught smoking on this unit. One caught smoking should expect to lose his canteen privileges, visits, and be burdened with a variety of other restrictions designed to make life a living hell.

Even if Greg was inclined to follow the smoking rules, he has a serious logistics predicament. He must wheel himself almost 1/8 of a mile through a labyrinth of basement tunnels and elevators to reach the main yard. With his breathing problem, this presents a considerable hardship, especially if he just wants to take a quick smoke. On the other hand, if he decides to forego the rules and smoke on his unit, then he has an intelligence problem because he must know where the guard is at all times—that's where I come in.

Being a prison orderly and working for the guards has several perks, one of which is knowing the guards' schedules. I like Mike, the guard on Greg's unit. He is educated, doesn't bust my balls, and even lets me have an extra food tray when one is available. Despite some demonstration of goodwill, however, the prisoner/guard relationship remains clearly delineated—the guards have their rules, and we inmates have ours. My rule is that I don't run the gauntlet for a smoke. Since I've started working here, I've been sneaking smokes in the bathroom, an activity timed perfectly to coincide with Mike's shift changes or other moments of preoccupation. Realistically, unless you're stuck with someone like "Black Bart," most guards don't give a rat's ass what's going on unless someone gets stabbed, caught smoking on the unit, or their daily routine is disrupted by a knuckleheaded inmate who makes them look bad in front of their superiors.

Ever observant, Greg notices my clandestine operation and catches me alone watching TV in the communal room to make me an offer.

"Hey, Mark. You got a minute?"

"Sure, Greg. What's up?"

In a hushed voice, Greg makes me a proposition: "I've noticed you have the screw's schedule down pretty fuckin good. How about letting me ride in the car with ya when you go take a smoke, and I'll do you a favor later, like letting you put your merchandise in my room after canteen, so you don't have to make the long trek back to your unit to lock it up."

It is no doubt a hassle to stand in the canteen line for an hour to buy supplies and perhaps an ice cream, then rush back to my unit with a melting ice cream in my hand, put these items into my locker, then rush back to work. Greg's right. This arrangement would save me a lot of time every week, but in prison, there are plenty of cell thieves.

I state the obvious, "Sorry, but I can't risk my shit being taken by some cell thief."

Greg looks offended, then huffs, "Nobody's taking shit outta my room. Guaran—fuckin—tee. I leave my cigarettes out on my bed, and I don't worry about it. Nobody's touchin' shit that belongs to me." He points his big finger at me for emphasis. "You hear me!"

Clearing my throat, I jest, "Yes, sir. My belongings are always safe in the House of DePalma."

Greg squints his eyes to tell me he's not bullshitting and grunts, "Fuckin-A it is!"

His seriousness was sobering. I knew that only a handful of inmates in prison were powerful enough to leave their property lying on their beds unattended, daring anyone to cross a line of no return. *Was this balding, overweight, old man one of those guys?*

"Ok, ok..." I concede. Not wanting any of Greg's Mafia wannabes increasing our chances of getting busted by tagging along on our smoke runs, I demand one condition—as long as it's just you and me, buddy."

Greg nods his understanding and agreement. "See ya when you take a break, Mark. Thanks."

An hour later, Mike tells me he's taking a break and another guard will be taking over his shift.

I acknowledge with a thumbs-up. "I got you covered."

His replacement is a blonde kid with a buzzcut who looks like he is straight out of high school. I knock on Mike's office door and ask the kid if he needs anything. He leans back in Mike's chair like he owns the place, puts his feet on the desk, lights a cigarette, and tells me through a smoky haze. "Yeah, to be left the fuck alone unless there's an emergency. And close that door behind you."

I salute in compliance. "You got it."

As I close the door, I mutter, "What an asshole. I then walk straight to Greg's room and find him sitting on the bed reading the *New York Times*."

"You ready old man?"

Greg comes off the bed with his fists up. "Who ya callin' an old man?"

We both chuckle and rib each other all the way to the bathroom until we're interrupted by two self-proclaimed Italians who come out of nowhere like paparazzies.

These two individuals at Springfield are known as Luigi and Mario, and you never see one without the other. Like life preservers, they cling to each other in this uncaring sea of misery. Mario is the tall, older, skinny one with graying long hair and thick black eyeglasses. He is the more intelligent of the two and speaks first. "Hey, Greg. Where you going? You gonna smoke a cig in the head?"

Before Greg can answer, Luigi, who is a short, squatty, dim-witted man with beady eyes, chirps their intentions, "Can we bum a cigarette and go with ya?"

I feel my eyes about to roll inside my head when Greg cuts in, "Hey, Paisan. We only have room in the car for the two of us. But here's a few cigarettes for you to smoke later."

Luigi's and Mario's eyes light up as Greg hands a few cigarettes into their grateful hands.

They thank Greg profusely and promise to pay him back whenever their money hits the commissary. Greg waves off their promises with, "Forget about it."

Greg has a big heart. Both of us know Luigi and Mario will receive no help outside these prison walls. They are one of society's many throw-a-ways, left to rot in prison with only Greg to lend a helping hand on this day. Turning towards our destination, Greg leans into my ear. "Gotta take care of the Paisans."

I give Greg an unsure look and a half-smile as I open the door to the bathroom. We head to our right, past a yellow-tiled shower area where the sunlight flitters harshly through opaque windows. Walking past a row of toilet stalls on the left, we make a visual check at each stall for any unwelcome guests before finally arriving at our destination, a small area in the back with a row of urinals on one side and a bench on the opposite. Greg pulls a cigarette butt from his shirt pocket and chuckles. "Fucking got a half a lung and still smoking these goddamn things—damn, it's hard to quit."

Lighting our cigarettes, I agree, "I've been trying to quit for years."

Greg takes a short puff and holds up the smoldering butt. "And just think the Feds jailed more than half these men for drugs that are way less addictive than this shit."

I reply, "It's the irony of life, my friend."

After a brief but soul-quenching smoke, Greg and I take our last drags and flip our butts into a urinal.

"Well, buddy, it's time for me to run errands for the guard. See you later, unless one of us dies."

As we walk to the door, Greg pats me on the shoulder. "Wouldn't miss it for the world."

Leaving to run errands, I step into the elevator as Greg wishes me a nice evening while talking to someone on the telephone. The elevator door shuts between us as I throw up my hand to wave goodbye. From that day forward, until I complete my sentence, we sneak into the bathroom to smoke cigarettes like delinquent kids in high school.

CHAPTER 6

When the elevator door opens, I reflect on the fact that I've logged another day here and, therefore, am another day closer to going home without getting stabbed. As I walk into the communal lounge, I notice a black guy named Curtis, who suffers from kidney disease, sitting and watching TV. Curtis is known to have his ear to the ground on everything happening on this floor. He also knows many of these inmates, including Greg, from his days on the streets.

Curtis flips his head towards an old chess set sitting on the bookshelf. "You play chess?"

"Yeah, I do."

"Well, you're looking at one of the best players on the unit. Let's play a game and see what you've got," he says with a voice edged with a competitive tone as he brings the board back to the cardboard table.

Despite being "one of the best players on the unit," Curtis rarely wins a game, but it really doesn't matter. This is a perfect way to kill time and, in here, time is all we have. During one of our games, he discloses exactly how he landed in prison.

"Back in the 80s and 90s, I was the man. I had my hands in everything, including slinging crack and pussy from New York all the way down south to Florida. Goddamn, those were the days. Then the DEA figured out they, too, could make big money off the drug trade by busting us and ripping us off to line their pockets and coffers."

I nod my head in agreement. "Yeah, I was snitched out by a meth head for ¼ pound of marijuana, then charged for the guns the informant left at my house after I helped him off the streets."

Curtis shakes his head and starts setting the chess pieces up on the board for another game. "That's some cold shit, my brother. No good deed goes unpunished when you help a drug addict."

"You got that right," I concur. "So, you were a pimp out in the world. Any pretty girls?"

Curtis smirks. "Pretty? Shit, those bitches were beautiful."

In the distance, the guard abruptly yells, "Count!"

Curtis stands like the Manchurian Candidate. "Gotta go, but the board is set up and ready. Wanna play after count?"

"I'm here all day," I smile.

After count clears, verifying to all concerned that no inmates escaped, Curtis returns with several binders and places them on the card table. Taking a seat, he picks up a thick white binder and flips through page after page of pictures of him dressed in expensive suits and wearing fur coats. In one, he is smiling with his arm wrapped around a high-class call girl as they stand next to a sleek black Rolls Royce. He smiles broadly with pride at his former life, which was straight out of a Hollywood rag.

"See? What did I tell you? Beautiful!"

"Damn!" I exclaim, blown away by the bevy of beauties who worked for him.

Tapping the page with a well-manicured fingernail, Curtis reveals, "Not only do these little bitches make me money slinging pussy on the street, but they're my little spies too."

"Really? How so?" I ask, still transfixed by the fact these gorgeous girls are hookers.

Curtis grins. "I learned a long time ago sex is a powerful tool for eavesdropping on your enemies and competition. That's because crooked cops, big drug dealers, and the Mafia guys are always wanting to fuck the hottest girls. And when they're banging my smokin' hot bitches, they would always blab about all kinds of stuff related to their business and personal lives. And on the street, information is key, baby!"

"Unbelievable!"

Still fixated on the incredible beauty of the binder girls, I sit stunned as Curtis flips the page to show me a gorgeous blonde wrapped in a black evening gown.

"Wow, that girl could have been a movie star," I exclaim.

Still dumbstruck, I ask, "How'd you get those beautiful girls to fuck other guys and then give you the money?"

Curtis leans back in his chair and smiles broadly. "Sell 'em the dream, like any good politician or preacher, and they'll give you their money and follow you into hell."

I move a pawn to begin the game. Curtis counters with his pawn, then remarks nonchalantly, "I see you hanging out with Mr. DePalma. Watch yourself. That guy is dangerous."

I move my knight as I'm taken off guard by his all-knowing eye.

"Greg? He's a pussycat."

Curtis becomes animated. "No! I'm serious, my man. He runs with the Gambino crew and takes his orders from John. Remember that guy that hit Gotti's kid, Frank?"

I had no idea what he was talking about. "No, I don't."

Leaning over the card table, Curtis brings his voice to a whisper, "The guy's name was John Favara. He hit and killed John's son with his car by accident, and it wasn't his fault."

"What a tragedy," I sigh.

"Yeah, bad shit all the way around. Poor bastard was threatened multiple times by friends and associates of Gotti's and told to leave the neighborhood. He didn't get the hint. Then, he was kidnapped from a furniture store and never heard from again.

Word on the street is that Greg's crew was responsible for that disappearance and then dissolving the poor bastard in acid. Not sure if it's true though."

Curtis's words are troublesome for sure, but still...Greg? He didn't look like he was capable of that type of violence upon another human being, and stories from the street are always overblown, like fishing tales.

I wave off his comment, "Come on, man. That's gotta be street gossip. You can't believe everything you hear. Besides, Greg's just an old man."

"With all due respect, that guy is a fuckin' psychopath. And while I'm not 100% on John Favara, one of my girls was banging a guy from Greg's crew and got told another story. I verified this one, and it's some maniacal shit."

"Really? One of his guys would just open up about the Mafia to a prostitute?"

"Shit. When a beauty is riding your dick, and you're high as fuck, a guy will say anything in the moment to impress these chicks. Hell, I've seen guys fall in love with these girls—when it's just the little head talkin' for the big head, if you get my drift."

I chuckle, "I do, and I don't doubt that at all. Well, what'd he spill?"

As Curtis moves his bishop across the board, he paints a nightmarish picture straight out of a gangster movie.

He begins his story in the middle of a harsh winter, with snow swirling around a dilapidated warehouse. At its front entrance, two Mafiosos dressed in heavy overcoats act as sentries while huddled around a barrel fire to keep warm. A black sedan pulls up, the driver's door swings open, and a middle-aged Greg DePalma climbs out dressed in an expensive suit and a heavy overcoat. He walks back to the trunk of the car and retrieves a sledgehammer, which he slings over his shoulder. Closing the trunk, he saunters past the two Mafiosos who give him a heads up.

Seemingly without a care in the world, Greg struts through the front door while whistling Bobby Darin's "Beyond the Sea," and he walks straight towards the sound of fists striking flesh, which is emanating from behind a rusted-out caboose. Behind the caboose, a man named Johnny is tied to a chair that is sitting in a puddle of water between two sets of railroad tracks that lead to nowhere.

Johnny squeals in pain as a powerfully built Mafioso mercilessly pummels him in the face. The punches, coming from every angle, cause the victim's blood to fly through the air and his head to rock violently back and forth before finally coming to rest with his chin on his chest. A second burly man nonchalantly stands to the side of the victim, warming his hands over a barrel fire. As he sees Greg walking towards them, he gives notice, "Hey! Here comes the boss."

The Mafioso beating Johnny pauses his assault. "Hey, boss! I don't think he knows nothing else. All he does is squeal like the little bitch."

Greg drinks in the atmosphere of violence and growls, "We'll see, Tony."

Greg walks up to the victim and poses a question, "You wanna know why I'm wearing gloves, Johnny?"

Johnny raises his bloody face towards Greg. "B-b-b-because it's cold?"

As Greg responds, "Nah, I just don't like gettin' blood under my fingernails," the man standing by the barrel fire points out that Johnny is urinating on himself. Urine dribbles over the chair and splatters into the pool of bloody water at his feet. Greg guffaws, "You don't have to be scared. Just tell me the truth, because if you lie to me, I'm going to think we're not friends."

"Please, Greg! I swear on my muddah, I don't know nuttin'. I don't even know why I'm here."

With a flash of brutality, Greg brings the sledgehammer down on Johnny's foot. Johnny's shrill screams reverberate through the old warehouse before fading and being replaced by the gang's uncontrollable laughter.

Greg leans the sledgehammer against the rusted caboose and moves his face inches from Johnny's bloody mug. Through clenched teeth, Greg lays out Johnny's charges. "You're here because somebody thinks you fuckin' snitched to the Feds. You're in my crew, and somebody has to clean this shit up. And that somebody is fucking me."

Johnny's bottom lip begins to tremble uncontrollably as he sobs, pleading for mercy, "Please, Greg. Please! I don't know what you're talkin' about."

Greg explodes at Johnny. "Listen, you fat fuck! I'm not standing out here all night to make you talk! You're talkin' fuckin' now!"

Greg then nods towards the man standing by the barrel fire and barks an order, "Angelo, stuff that fucking rat's mouth with a rag soaked in gasoline."

Without hesitation, Angelo grabs a rag and douses it with gasoline before forcefully cramming the foul-smelling rag into Johnny's mouth. Johnny convulses, shaking violently in his chair. He tries unsuccessfully to spit the rag out, prompting Tony to hold him down.

Greg pulls a Zippo lighter out of his pocket with one hand, flips it open, and lights it. Tony violently grabs Johnny's hair, jerking his head back so he is looking directly at Greg's enraged face. Leaning towards Johnny's frightened, swollen, bloodied face, Greg begins to wave the flame in front of Johnny's terrified eyes. He then leans in closer. "Did I ever tell you I like to hurt people? Especially those who are motherfucking snitches? You're gonna tell me what I want to know, right the fuck now, or I'm going to bring your little brother in here, set him on fire, and let you watch him burn. Then it's your turn."

Greg glances over to Angelo, who is warming his hands on the barrel fire. "Angelo, where's Joey?"

Angelo doesn't miss a beat. "He's in the trunk of Tony's car, boss. Want me to get 'em?"

Greg nods. "Yeah. Since his brother won't talk, maybe Joey will. Grab his skinny ass so we can make him into a tiki torch."

Angelo chuckles and starts towards the door. Johnny's muffled shrieks reach a whiney crescendo as he shakes violently against his restraints.

"Noooo! Nooo!"

Greg signals to Tony, who pulls the rag from Johnny's mouth. "I'll talk... I'll talk!"

Greg hisses, "This better be fucking good."

Johnny looks down at his battered reflection in the blood and urine-stained water and reveals the truth. "It's just me! I swear to God! It's just me!"

Looking up, he pleads with his former gang members, "Leave Joey out of it. Desiree gave me up to the Feds to get out of a dope charge, and they had me dead to rights on a couple of kilos of cocaine. I knew if I told you guys, you'd kill her, and she told me she's pregnant."

Greg's eyes widen. "Desiree??? Who the hell is that?"

Angelo supplies the answer, "That's the little blonde at the club with the tight ass, boss. And she ain't pregnant."

Greg's jaw clenches, and his fists tighten. "You little piece of shit. I trusted you!"

Tears run down Johnny's blood-streaked face as he pleads, "Please don't hurt Joey, he didn't..."

Greg's contemptuous laughter interrupts Johnny's desperate pleas. "I never had Joey, you dumb cocksucker. He's a good kid—unlike your fed-snitchin', rat motherfuckin' ass!"

A look of shock and confusion spreads across Johnny's face as he looks at his former friends. He stutters in confusion and pain, "Wait. Wha...whaa...what?"

Greg laments his weakness as Tony and Angelo shake their heads side to side with sinister smiles. "It's my big heart that's gonna be the downfall of me."

Tony chimes in from his place behind Johnny, "You do have a big heart, boss."

Greg's anger intensifies yet again. "Shut the fuck up! And fuck this guy!"

Shaking with fear, Johnny attempts to save himself by elaborating more information, "Boss, I swear. I didn't give up you or our guys... only the teamsters down on the docks."

Disdain and hatred seethe through Greg's final response. "I don't wanna goddamn hear it, you fucking idiot! You're working for the fucking Feds! How long do you think it's gonna take before the teamsters give us up? You stupid fuck! You're fuckin' dead to me!"

Greg's anger boils over, and he grabs a piece of 2-foot rebar off a concrete platform. The sound of metal scraping against concrete echoes through the old warehouse as he picks it up. The rebar arcs through the air before striking Johnny's kneecap with a sickening "Thwack!" His head whips back as he screams in pain. Greg bellows another order, "Hold his mouth open, Tony."

Tony wraps his arm around Johnny's throat, then uses his other hand to force Johnny's mouth open into a bloody "O." Then, with unbridled ferocity, Greg rams the rebar down Johnny's throat, forcing his eyes skyward. Johnny thrashes against Tony's grip, with gurgling sounds and blood oozing from his throat as his eyes grow wide with pain and horror.

Nodding to the rebar, Greg snarls another order, "Angelo! Hold that!"

Angelo hurries to help his compatriots and relieve the rebar from Greg's hand. Filled with rage, Greg grabs the sledgehammer from against the wall and turns toward Johnny. "Hold him steady.'"

Angelo earnestly implores Greg, "Don't hit my fucking hand."

Greg's eyes go wild. "Don't worry about it. It's like playin' golf!"

The sledgehammer sweeps through the air and strikes the rebar, impaling Johnny with a loud "Clink!"

Sounds of pain and terror reverberate throughout the warehouse as Greg's sledgehammer strikes the rebar again. The force of this blow drives the rebar out of Johnny's side, putting an end to his tortured screams. A low gurgle momentarily emanates from his throat and the hole in the side of his chest before everything falls silent.

Greg leans the sledgehammer against Johnny's motionless body. He pulls a cigar out of his overcoat's inside front pocket and briefly smells its aromatic flavor before putting it into his mouth. He looks around at the chaos. "Let's get outta here. It stinks like shit in here. Angelo, stuff that rag in the rat's mouth and douse that bitch."

Angelo stuffs the rag around the rebar and empties a can of charcoal fluid over Johnny's broken body. Flipping open his lighter, Greg lights his cigar, then sets the rag on fire. It bursts into flames, engulfing Johnny's body in a conflagration that causes all of Greg's crew to take a step back. Taking a long drag from his cigar, Greg blows out a bluish smoke of satisfaction. He spits on Johnny's flaming body as he walks by.

"Fuckin' rat."

His associates walk after him as he struts towards the front of the warehouse. Tony tries to lighten the mood, "Where'd you learn to swing like that, Mr. DePalma?"

Greg proudly grins from ear to ear. "Golfing with Dean Martin."

The crew laughs as Angelo opens the front door for Greg, who pauses. "One last thing. Pick that rat's whore up and tell her Johnny wants to meet with her."

Both men respond in unison, "Will do, boss."

As the story ends, I'm left in stunned silence. Curtis makes another move on the chessboard and smiles as he studies my silence.

"I told you it was some maniacal shit. Still think DePalma is a harmless old man?"

CHAPTER 7

Every time I see Greg's jovial face during the next week, I envision flashes of the warehouse scene and still can't believe this man is in the Mafia, let alone capable of such violence. But then, again, none of these guys are here for good behavior. Lately, my mind wanders elsewhere, however, as word quickly spreads of my unbeatable chess skills. A growing audience and list of competitors come to the commons room to watch or to try to push me off the proverbial mountain.

After a month, the chessboard becomes a symbolic campfire where, to help escape reality, we exchange stories about prison and our former lives. The campfire sessions become such a regular occurrence that the chessboard is already set up and waiting before I even step foot on Greg's unit. When I walk in today, Curtis is studying the board.

I give Curtis a little shit, "You do know that's not going to help you."

He chuckles. "Well, look at the head on that boy."

As our laughter fades, he asks the obvious question, "How the hell did you get so damn good at chess?"

As I move my pawn to king 4, I answer his question, "I've played since I was a kid. My best friend, Steve Hoel, was pretty awesome in his own right but, while incarcerated at El Reno's federal prison, I met the Bobby Fischer of the federal prison system. My first encounter with him was a scene right out of a gladiator pit in ancient Rome."

Curtis counters my move and twirls his hand to continue my story. "Please continue, my man."

"I'd just been transferred from one of Oklahoma's state prison hellholes named James Crabtree, where they housed me in an overpopulated airplane hangar with hardly any sunlight and where temperatures would climb to 120 during the summer. I was transferred to the federal prison in El Reno, Oklahoma. I was awe-struck. I had never seen a prison that big before or one that modern, with central heat and air. Its living units reminded me of a huge, two-story rectangular coliseum that encircled an area the size of two football fields. After I received my bedding, I was taken to F unit, where a laid-back guard told me that I'd be housed on the 2nd floor. I climbed the metal staircase while marveling at the massive skylights lining the roof and allowing the sun's precious light to stream to the bottom floor, where large plants flourished in containers.

For a moment, I forgot that I was even in a prison, and I thanked my lucky stars for my new surroundings after being incarcerated in one of Oklahoma's inhumane, dark, cramped, and unventilated state prisons. But in any prison, as in a war zone, feelings of peace and serenity rapidly evaporate. Upon reaching my cell, I was greeted by chaotic screams ascending from the ground floor.

Standing on the second floor with a bird's eye view, I watched a gang called the "Dirty White Boys" swarm an accused snitch in the downstairs T.V. room. All the inmates were aroused from their surrounding cells by the ensuing chaos and anticipated watching a bloodbath. The snitch was violently pulled into the middle of the bottom floor, and his T-shirt was pulled over his head while he was beaten mercilessly by fists protected by leather work gloves. Cheers erupted from the crowd as each blow spattered blood through the air and across the floor, quickly turning the white T-Shirt crimson red.

Looking down on the bloody carnage, it seemed surreal—as if I'd been transported to a Roman coliseum, circa 400 A.D. On the top floor's run, spectators leaned over the metal railing like vultures, cackling for the snitch's demise. The onslaught of cheers intensified for the gladiators as the ground-floor inmates surrounding the action tightened their circle to keep the snitch from escaping his fate.

One Dirty White Boy grabbed the snitch's shirt and tried to throw him to the ground. Realizing the noose was tightening, the snitch jerked away from his attackers, violently ripping his T-shirt off over his head. His face was a bloody mess, with one eye completely shut from a massive cut across his brow. A groan of despair escaped his lips as he swung wildly at his attackers, but it was all in vain. The gang pummeled him again and again, splattering his blood on the frenzied audience.

In state prison, I saw so much violence that I was nearly completely desensitized. Standing there completely detached, I watched the Dirty White Boys finally knock their victim to the ground. He curled up in a ball in an attempt to protect his head as he was ruthlessly kicked until someone yelled, "The guards are coming!"

Everyone scattered except for the snitch, who slowly started crawling away, leaving a bloody trail. I thought that it was over, but then a short, stocky gang member with a day-old beard suddenly broke from the group. He ran back to the snitch and savagely kicked him in the head, like a football player kicking a field goal. This vicious blow finally knocked the snitch unconscious and onto his back. Raising his arms in triumph, the victor roared, 'Dirty White Boys!' In response, cheers and chants of 'D.W.B!' 'D.W.B!' 'D.W.B!' resonated through the rowdy crowd while one of his brothers in anarchy pulled the placekicker away, yelling, 'Let's go! Let's GO!' Before leaving the makeshift arena, he paused long enough to spit on the disfigured face of his vanquished foe in a final act of disrespect, defiance, and total dominance.

The DWBs melted into the crowd giving them thunderous applause for ridding the prison of another snitch, but the sounds of accolades quickly turn to boos as five guards pile into the area screaming, 'Everyone get in your fucking rooms!'

Familiar with this drill, I turned toward my open cell door as a siren blared across the complex, signaling that the entire prison was going into lockdown. Moments later, the short, stocky DWB ran past my cell door, then stopped and glared straight at me, hissing, "Hey FNG! You'd better keep your fuckin' lip zipped." I knew the drill on this one, too. I nodded my head and gave him the universal zip-my-lip gesture. He returned a satisfied grin and calmly walked over beside me. "The guards are coming. They're going to lock us down in our rooms, make us strip, and inspect each of us for bruising or cuts to indicate involvement in this incident. If the guards find even a tiny scratch, it's to the hole until they figure out what happened. Keep cool. Keep your mouth shut. I'll talk to you again when they open the doors."

Lockdown was lifted the next day. True to his word, he came to visit me, sporting a completely different demeanor. Sticking out his hand, he introduced himself, "The name's Paul. Welcome to El Reno penitentiary, where snitches get stitches."

Curtis smiles. "That's a pretty good one."

"After Paul and I had a good laugh, we became pretty good friends, and he invited me to join his chess club. It didn't take me long to realize that Paul was a freakin' chess genius—one of the best chess players I ever met. He could anticipate 15 to 20 moves ahead, and I never saw him lose a match. Under Paul's mentoring, I learned everything I know."

From out of nowhere, Greg's booming voice interrupts our conversation, "That's a pretty good story. You should write a fuckin' book."

Curtis looks up with admiration. "Good evening, Mr. DePalma."

Greg is standing in the doorway with a wide grin on his face. "Good evening, Curtis. How's it dangling?" He then turns to look at me with a thoughtful expression. "I'm serious about the book. Hey, you about ready to hit the head for a smoke? I'm fuckin' dyin' here. Plus, I want to talk with ya."

Before I can answer, in walks Lex Luthor.

CHAPTER 8

Lex Luthor is, of course, a comic book villain—the fictional arch-nemesis of Superman. But in here, "Lex Luthor" is a moniker for anyone who is super-intelligent with a diabolical twist, often with a predilection for scheming against the government. Lex's doppelgangers are incarcerated throughout the prison and jail systems of America. All they want to do after being incarcerated is burn the world down around them by teaching fellow inmates their particular expertise of mayhem and how to avoid the associated pitfalls for detection.

Peter is today's particular "Lex," and he has sporadically popped into our chess campfires, not to play chess, but to advocate for his personal form of anarchy to all present. Peter, a 5'9", 300-pounder, who is legally blind, wears thick pop bottle reading glasses that advertise that fact. He always carries a folder of documents beneath his arms. His severe nearsightedness causes him almost to walk into Greg, whose demeanor suddenly sours. "Hey, watch where you're going, four-eyes! You almost stepped on my new house shoes."

Peter backs up before leaning closer, trying to focus on Greg's face. "Oh, I'm sorry, Mr. DePalma. I didn't see you standing there. I..."

Greg is not amused. "Back the fuck off and quit breathin' on me. What are ya, fuckin gay?"

Peter looks down at the ground and shuffles past Greg to take a seat.

"No sir, Mr. DePalma."

Peter generally sits in a gray metal folding chair with his back against the wall. Most guys, like me, who have done serious time, sit with their backs against a wall. It's an unconscious defense mechanism that allows one to see any threat approaching from the front while not getting stabbed from the back. It's a fucked-up way to live, but it is what it is; with Peter being almost completely blind, it's more than understandable.

Charles, the "crazy Cajun," suddenly walks closely past Greg without an "excuse me" and plops down in a chair between Curtis and me.

"How's it hanging, fellas?"

Greg shakes his head, then thumbs at Peter. "You should listen to this one's story, Mark. He's in here for identity theft and is doing more time than any of us in this room. And get this, he didn't even kill anybody."

Charles pipes in, "I heard Pete's doin' three life sentences. Ain't that right, Petey?"

Peter fumbles through the papers in his folder without looking up. "Something like that, Charles."

Greg sneers. "Only the feds could come up with some crazy shit like that. Whatever happened to an eye for an eye, for Christ's sake?" Raising his eyebrow, he emphasizes the point, "And that's why we don't fuck with Feds like Peter did. Those Feds are some vindictive motherfuckers."

Focusing back on me, Greg feigns hurt feelings. "You're not gonna forget about me, are ya?"

I smile and return a feigned look of empathy. "How could I forget about you? I think we're good to go in about 15 minutes. Sound good?"

Greg grins and gives me a thumbs-up before sauntering back down the hallway. I look at Peter's roly-poly stature, thinking that he didn't look like much of a national threat. But when he opens his mouth, his story comes right out of a supervillain's handbook. It all starts with losing his health insurance.

Peter fidgets in his chair. "Mr. DePalma is right. I didn't kill anyone. When I first started doing this, I wasn't a criminal—I was desperate. I was going blind from diabetes and just needed to make some money because my insurance company raised its rates for pre-existing conditions..." He scowls. "...making dialysis completely unaffordable. At first, I tried to pay for the medical expenses myself, but with a new wife and newborn baby, I quickly became overwhelmed by the financial pressure. When she left me, I thought about killing myself as well as the insurance salesman who sold me the policy. I spiraled into dark thoughts of no return and no longer gave a flying fuck what happened next."

I completely sympathized with him. Before prison, I also contemplated killing, but now that I am here and only months from going home, I desperately want to live, love, and forgive. Peter doesn't have this option. He has the state of mind that, if he's suffering and is going to die in this shithole, then he's going to create havoc and make everyone else suffer too.

Peter continues, "I was a dead man walking, but before I went completely blind, I had two objectives. I was going to try to keep my sight and destroy the insurance agent who sold me that worthless insurance policy. I needed to make as much money as possible to accomplish my goals. I chose identification theft as the means, but I immediately found two problems with historical methods of operation.

A young black kid who came in to browse the books in the massive bookcase turns towards Peter and repeats, "Identification theft?"

Peter warmly smiles at the kid and continues, "The first problem is how the old-timers obtain people's personal information—usually from cemeteries, mailboxes, etc., which is very time-consuming, and which leads to problem number two—stealing only identities that will be lucrative. The only identities you want to steal are from people with excellent credit, ensuring approval for anything from credit cards to car loans. A guy with less than outstanding credit is of no use to you and a huge waste of your time. But there's really no way of knowing if their data is relevant until you test the waters."

The black kid inquires, "Why do you have to date a relative to test the waters?"

Without losing his cool, Peter exhales under his breath. And with the patience of Job, gives a 4th-grade explanation of "data" and "relevant." Charles gives a big, animated yawn in Peter's direction, then shuts his eyes for a siesta. In walk two more potential students—an older white guy and a known gang member. The black gang member looks at Peter. "Hey, old-timer, is this the place they're teaching a class on identification theft?"

Peter doesn't miss a beat. "You've come to the right place, gentlemen. Please, take a seat."

After giving a quick recap, Peter leans forward. "Returning to our previous problem and lesson number one... you don't go out and find those with good credit. No sirs! You make them come to you by using one of mankind's greatest weaknesses—greed." Rubbing his hands like a materialistic miser, Peter continues, "The first time I tried my own method, I started by creating a fake international security firm, tailored to entice high-income earners and elicit information from responsible individuals. This solves the old-timers' problem of trying to figure out who has good credit versus bad. And the ruse of an expanding, high-powered, international security firm remedied reluctance in divulging sensitive information, as applicants expect to answer personal information as part of the vetting process. To further add to an air of lofty status, I chose the most prestigious building in town, the Williams Center in downtown Tulsa. He grabs a document from a thick binder, holds it inches from his face, then turns to his audience. "Yes! Here it is."

Peter passes the document around, which was marked "Government's Exhibit D." As the gangbanger passes it to me, I see it clearly shows a photograph of the Williams Center skyscraper in Tulsa, Oklahoma. Peter folds his hands in front of his chest before further elaborating on his diabolical plan.

"First, I broke into the insurance agent's house who I'd sworn vengeance on. He never even knew I was there, as I didn't disturb anything while copying down his and his wife's personal information. Using all their pertinent information, I ordered new credit cards under their names and had them sent to a P. O. Box. As I waited for the credit cards to arrive, I broke into a small town's DMV office and stole all the necessary items to make a driver's license."

Peter hands out several photocopies marked "Government's Exhibit H-N," which were photographs of all the machines and accouterments required to make a fake driver's license. Clearing his throat, Peter imparts a tip from the past, "It's always better to break into small-town DMV. There are usually only one or two cops who can easily be distracted by a bogus emergency call or a fire on the outskirts of town."

Peter momentarily loses his train of thought. "Where was I? Oh yes, from there, I opened a few bank accounts and was issued checks. By Thursday, I leased an office suite for one year at the Williams Center, including rented office equipment and a new nameplate for the door that read 'Spector International Security Firm,' with all these expenses paid by post-dated checks from our friendly insurance salesman. Then, for the crème de la crème, I put a real hook line and sinker of an advertisement in the local paper guaranteed to pull in only the most respected, triple-A rated individuals in the area."

Peter held his audience's full attention. He chuckled to himself as he relished the memory of exacting revenge on the man and the system that had taken away everything he loved. Frankly, while I have zero interest in partaking in any further criminal activities, Greg was right—this was a hell of a story. Peter gushes with pride and continues, "The advertisement read like a dream job. 'International security firm is looking to hire three individuals. Starting pay $250,000 a year, plus bonuses, a $5,000.00 retainer upon hiring, life insurance, health insurance, retirement package, car, expense account, and use of a new house for those willing to relocate.' I set interview dates for Friday and Saturday from 9 a.m. to 2 p.m. to allow me to scam the banks also."

This raises the eyebrows of all the "students." The white guy asks, "How?"

Peter eyes the room quickly. "If you write a check on Friday, Saturday, or Sunday, the check won't register in your bank account until Monday; therefore, I can write checks worth thousands of dollars on the weekend, and the banks are unaware until Monday at the earliest..." Peter smirks, "...but I never intended to stay until Monday. By Sunday night, I'd be packed and was on Route 66 getting my kicks with a completely new identity."

Charles, who has been sitting in his chair, opens one eye. "What about the actual job application, genius? How'd you pull that one off?"

Peter ignores his insulting tone. "Excellent question, Charles. For my security firm's application, I just went to a local home improvement store and picked up one of their job applications. I used good old whiteout to cover their company's logo and typed my company's name in its place. Afterward, with my newly purchased office copier, I made hundreds of copies for my applicants to complete when they arrived on Friday. Then, like the proverbial spider, I waited behind my rented desk."

Peter fumbles through his folder before handing out several more documents and pictures detailing some of the information gathered by the Justice Department that allow him to relive his glory days. "I think visual aids always improve the teacher/student interaction."

I'm actually shocked at the amount of material the courts allowed Peter to acquire, which he uses for his fiendish lessons on how to screw society. He had photo documentation of everything from driver license machines stolen across America to a variety of machines used to produce credit cards and rewrite existing magnetic strips. Peter had every piece of evidence ever used against him at his disposal to show and teach his students. He snickers as he pushes his heavy pop bottle glasses further up the bridge of his nose. Several more potential protégés arrive to hear his madness. Soon, it's standing room only.

Charles comes out of his coma and grabs one of the photocopies from Curtis's hand. "How the fuck did you get this shit in here?"

With a serious look, Peter tries to focus on the crazy Cajun. "Please, Charles. Do not mishandle my material."

The fastest way to get stabbed in prison is to disrespect someone who is doing a life sentence. Even the Cajun wasn't that crazy. Charles realized he'd cross the line, and he stepped back. "Sorry, Peter. But this is ..." Charles frowns, "...some communist shit."

Peter waves Charles off and continues to school him and the others in the room. "On the contrary, Charles. The Constitution requires that the prosecution discloses to the defense all exculpatory evidence within its possession or control. It's Brady v. Maryland, my dear Charles, and, if they refuse, it's a violation of my due process rights. I'm appealing my case, and all these photocopies and transcripts are evidence the federal government used to prosecute me. Now I'm using it against them, teaching my students how to create the perfect forgery. Isn't that ironic?"

CHAPTER 9

Peter grins with satisfaction as he inspects himself in the mirror before he makes society pay for its transgressions. Standing tall, he straightens out his hundred and fifty-dollar tie, brushes off his $1,000.00 suit, and...

"...It's a gorgeous Friday morning as I arrive in a limousine at the Williams Center's underground parking lot. By 8:30, I'm walking towards my office door, and there's already a line of over 100 hundred applicants waiting to be fleeced. As I stride past the line of well-dressed and clean-shaven hopefuls, several FBI agents and police officers flash their badges in my direction, either trying to get to the head of the line or to emphasize their resumes. I curtly smile and nod. It really is like taking candy from a baby – even I was a little surprised that the FBI agents, in their zeal to land this job, didn't catch on to the possibility that this was a ruse."

Peter laughs maliciously and proudly exclaims, "By the end of Saturday, I'd collected over a thousand applications and made photocopies of their driver's licenses. For good measure, I also made photocopies of the FBI and police officer's ID cards with their badge numbers."

By this time, everyone in the room is mesmerized by Peter's story, while he is ecstatically pleased that his genius is no longer lost on this audience. He further expands his brilliance as he leans back into his chair. "To elicit even more information from this interview, I told a few of the higher wage earner applicants that it usually takes at least two weeks to vet an applicant before a decision is made but that I was so impressed with their resumes and characters that I was going to hire them that day, on the spot. You wouldn't believe their excitement and how easily they gave up their banking account information so that I could wire their bogus $5,000 retainer fee the following week."

Peter chuckles to himself, "And just so I could scam every single one of them in the same manner, I casually requested that they please do not let anyone else know you've been hired as they exit. I claimed we didn't want any hurt feelings. Now that I have their banking information, social security numbers, and basically everything I need to assume their identity, it's time to cash in and head out of T-town. No one suspected a thing until they checked their bank accounts to ensure they were $5,000 richer and, instead, found that they were entirely wiped out.

Peter grins a big Cheshire Cat smile as stunned silence filled the room.

"On Monday, I'm a busy bee flushed with more money than I'd ever seen in my life and with a new identity. I paid cash for a cargo van and a large enclosed trailer. Then things really got fun! With over a thousand new identities and associated bank accounts to choose from, I use a copy machine to create a checkbook, using the routing numbers and personal account number from an FBI agent to go on a no-holds-barred shopping spree—buying everything from TV's to a German Shepherd guard dog."

Peter hands out a photograph of the copy machine with documents from FBI experts detailing exactly how he pulled off his forgeries. Stifling a laugh, he relishes in his own particular type of meticulous mayhem, "This is so funny when I think about it. At Utica Square in Tulsa, I hit all the high-end stores, buying several $1,000 suits with a variety of shirts, belts, colognes, shoes, wallets, and even throw-in hats for good measure. As I'm paying these bills with a postdated check exceeding $5,000 dollars, I make sure they see the scammed FBI agent's identification. They don't even blink an eye as they approve the purchase with a smile and admiration after taking one look at the credentials. One of the sales associates even asked, 'So, how do you like being an FBI agent?'"

Peter gestures to his body habitus, causing us all to laugh hysterically at the thought that someone could mistake him for an FBI agent.

Before leaving town on Monday, I clean out another 50 applicants' savings accounts, write another $20,000 in checks for a shitload of merchandise throughout the city, load it all in the cargo van and trailer, and burn outta town on Route 66."

"Shit, man..." a black kid hoots, "That sounds perfect. How'd you get caught?"

Peter frowns. "By not watching TV, reading the local newspaper, or having a crystal ball. Mind you, I didn't get busted for almost two years after I'd left Tulsa and by that time had swindled thousands of people in hundreds of other towns across the US. The FBI was on my tracks, but I was able to stay one step ahead of them until I bought a brand-new GTO with a guy's identity who, little did I know, had just robbed a bank. Unbeknownst to me, he was all over the news and had an APB out on him, which my friendly car salesman had just seen."

"He casually tells me he's going to the back to get my loan approved. About 15 minutes pass as I sit there, with a secured smile plastered across my happy face, eating and drinking their complimentary donuts and coffee, when in walk two Federal Marshals pointing their guns in my face. At first, the authorities can't even figure out who I am. I had been putting clear fingernail polish on my finger pads whenever I did a job, rendering my fingerprints completely unreadable; however, the FBI took palm prints from various banks where I cashed checks and finally identified me as the man who fleeced their follow law enforcement agents out of thousands of dollars. They were more than a little pissed."

Peter continues his story, but to hear him tell it, the fact that he made the FBI and other Oklahoma law enforcement agencies look like clowns resulted in his life sentence. Now, forever imprisoned, he promises to open the flood gates of hell on the FBI and police by spawning self-replicating students and teachers in this special type of identity theft. By his estimates, it will cost law enforcement agencies and the public billions to combat his clones. If you think people like Peter are a novelty in the penal system, you're wrong. I've met many of them in my time. Inmate-to-inmate schooling is the reason Oklahoma became "The Methamphetamine Capital of the World."

I would be incarcerated in Tulsa County Jail one last time after my release from prison. To increase revenue at the time, the authorities were rounding people up and jailing them for unpaid tickets or child support. I was a target of the latter, even though my mother had given my ex-wife money for my child during my incarceration. My ex took that money without reporting it to DHS. Subsequently, after my release, my child committed suicide because his mother wouldn't let him see me. Wanting revenge, she hired a lawyer who took me to court for the money owed to DHS along with 12% interest, totaling over $20,000. Because I couldn't pay the entire amount at once, I was sentenced to 6 months in the Tulsa County Jail at the taxpayer's expense.

Almost everyone incarcerated was a poor person with a shitty job. They could barely pay their bills, let alone a fine. Now, they found themselves hopelessly imprisoned without a job, in need of fast cash to pay fines, make bond, and pay their family's escalating unpaid bills. Decent people who, normally, would be reluctant to listen to these maniacs were now desperately looking for answers, hope, and maybe revenge of their own on an unfair system. Waiting on these downtrodden souls was my roommate, a pissed-off Aryan Brotherhood gang member, who had been caught up in this dragnet. After a month or so, he did the same thing as Peter. In this case, he taught every white guy on our unit various ways to make meth, including the shake and bake and Nazi methods, while providing the promise of fast money for bond and for their families. When I asked him one night why he did it, he gave the same basic answer as Peter, "To burn those bitches down."

I don't know how much money Tulsa County made from this roundup, but a year later, Oklahoma emerged as the meth capital of the world, creating tighter restrictions on pseudoephedrine, rampant addiction, and an increase in violent crimes and gang activity. If that weren't enough, innocent people were now losing their lives in apartment and house fires where these explosive concoctions are made, leaving Oklahoma taxpayers to foot the bill for costly clean-up procedures in meth-contaminated areas. The state lost millions as "Lex" burned Oklahoma down by using the Tulsa County Jail as his classroom, creating a never-ending drain on Oklahoma's financial and emergency personal resources statewide. After he left, his students continued the use of his destructive production techniques, causing widespread addiction to the poor.

CHAPTER 10

As I stand up and excuse myself to go to Greg's room, Peter calls out, "Hey, Mark! If you want to learn more, come by my bunk, and I'll go over it in more detail."

Looking at Peter's huge eyes through the lens of his thick glasses, I lie, "Sure, maybe later." I never intend to further my identity theft education, nor was I interested in learning how to make meth. I was on another pathway that didn't involve the risks of being shot down in the streets or coming back here to die. Besides, who wants a life of always looking over your shoulder for the FBI or the police? Not me. After spending the last seven years in prison, all I wanted was my freedom and a quiet little place where I could watch the grass grow. But for now, I still had to maneuver my way out of this hellhole alive, avoiding all its pitfalls.

As soon as I walk into Greg's room, he jumps off the bed and grabs his lighter.

"Is the coast clear?"

I give him a thumbs up and, using my best John Wayne impression, I summarize our situation, "Let's go, pilgrim. We're burning daylight." As our laughter and hurried footsteps echo down the deserted hallway, Greg asks what I thought of Peter's story.

"Well, I guess that's one way to get the FBI's attention."

Greg retorts, "No shit. Right?"

As we reach our destination, Greg pulls out a pack of cigarettes, causing a neatly folded letter also to slip from his pocket, fluttering to the floor. Bending down, I pick it up and hand it back to him, and he carefully places it back into his pocket.

"Thanks. It's a letter from the wife."

I nudge his arm and joke.

"Someone married you?"

Greg gives a short laugh. "Can you fucking believe it? She's a hell of a woman, but at the moment, she's bustin' my balls for the life I've brought into our family. They complain when things are bad, but boy do they sure love the money when it's rolling in," he huffs.

He nudges my arm back. "Am I fucking right?"

"You got no argument here, brother."

Pulling his customary half-smoked cigarette out, he returns the pack to his front pocket, puts the cigarette between his thin lips, lights it up, and takes a drag. As he exhales, the blue smoke swirls through refracted sunlight, and his voice becomes agitated. "You know, sometimes I don't think our families can appreciate how hard we work to put food on the table or bring home those expensive gifts they've all become accustomed to."

Placing a cigarette in my mouth, Greg lights it, then pockets the lighter.

"Thanks," I murmur.

Greg waves away my polite gesture. "Forget about it."

"You ever been to New York, Mark?"

"I went to the Van Gogh exhibition with my dad years ago."

With a half-smile, Greg shakes his head approvingly. "Really? I'm an art connoisseur myself. I might have bumped into you." He then rubs his chin and smirks. "You know, Mark. One thing about New York is that, if you know the right people, you can get anything day or night."

Greg becomes animated over his next question. "Guess what I bought off a fucking crackhead for my wife at 3:00 in the morning?"

The first thing that popped into my head was Jean Wilder in Silver Bullet with a boom box held to his head. I snicker at the thought. "A boom box?"

He snorts, "Get the fuck outta here. No! I bought her a mink coat for 25 bucks. Can you fucking believe that? Twenty-five BUCKS! Where the fuck can you get that kinda deal? I fuckin' love New York."

Greg nudges my arm again and takes a small drag from his cigarette. "Tell me a crackhead doesn't come in handy every once in a while. You should have seen her eyes light up when I wrapped it around her shoulders. And do you think she gave two fucks where it came from? Fuck no!"

Even though Greg and I had been routinely sneaking into the bathroom for the last couple of weeks, up to this point, we would typically stand in silence or make small talk. Today, we seemed to step across the line into a more personal venue, at least by prison inmate standards.

With amusement, he reflects, "You know, you're one of the only orderlies I know in here that has any semblance of intelligence or isn't a douche bag."

Taking a drag, I glance back at him. "I don't know. I wouldn't mind being a douche right about now; I haven't been laid in over seven years."

Greg feigns shock. "Well, don't fucking look at me!"

Our raucous laughter echoes off the yellow brick walls, but I get his drift. The term "douche bag" or any other derogatory term used by old-timers in reference to the general population is a way of referring to the typical, low-level inmates who now flood the system. The older inmates constantly complain about this lower class of prisoners and how their presence casts a shadow over the once former glory. They will tell you that, at one time, these walls housed a higher and smarter class of criminal—from organized crime bosses to those on the FBI's most-wanted list.

Now, the federal prison system is flooded with low-level drug peddlers and the mentally ill due to the "war on drugs" and Ronald Regan's edict to shut down mental institutions across America. Prisons now serve as the new asylums for the insane, and they are flooded with mentally ill and drug-addicted inmates, upsetting the status quo for all of those above such nonsense—including Greg DePalma.

Looking at Greg with an amused grin, I jab back, "Well, I'm just glad you don't think I'm a douche. That would definitely turn my mood ring black."

"Get the fuck outta here! You know what I'm talking about. These fucks are ruining this place, just like the airline industry. Did you know that, at one time, on the dome that sits atop a 747, they had a bar with a pianist, and they served drinks to a more refined client? Now, any fat fuck can waddle onto a plane." He pulls a drag off his cigarette butt. "It's the same with this place. Because of the "drug war," anyone who gets busted moving any quantity gets more time than child molesters or murderers—like you.

"Not that I mean you're a child molester or anything," he snorts. "Just someone caught in the 'drug war.'"

I smile at Greg's comment, but he was right—only about 15% of all inmates who land in prison belong here. The rest are here because America's fear-mongers and Justice Department confused the public with respect to who is truly dangerous and with whom they should be angry. As a result, the states and feds now house millions of non-violent Americans at prices comparable to rooms at the Waldorf Astoria. Even people like Greg, who has probably killed someone as described by Curtis, aren't a threat to society in general because of their old school rules.

Greg rolls his cigarette between his fingers. "Fucking drug war. I said it once, and I'll say it again. Shit, look at these goddamn things. Here's the drug they should have outlawed before alcohol or weed. These fuckers are killing me, and I can't quit."

"You got that right. I've been trying to quit for years. And it is really hard to believe so many people are in here for drugs, yet these things are still legal, super-addictive, and super-deadly."

Greg grins. "And that's why the fucking Feds will never win the drug war. Back in my day, they tried doing the same thing during prohibition, turning cops and politicians into criminals and the streets into a bloodbath, as everyone tried to get a piece of the action. They make the Untouchables sound like heroes, but they were thugs—busting people's heads and balls for just wanting to have a drink while boot-stepping like Nazis to whatever bureaucratic bullshit was in place at the time. Exactly what's happening with the drug war today, don't you think?"

I pull a deep drag off my cigarette. "Seems like it's been going on for a while."

Greg reflects, "Longer than you think, my friend, and under the same people that brought you prohibition. When they couldn't bust people for alcohol anymore, they made legal drugs illegal and started crackin' heads under the same banner, just a different name. The DEA is the dirtiest law enforcement agency out there. It's right up there with a few rogue elements in the FBI, who'll break any law or anyone's rights to get a bust or pad their own pockets."

He was right about that, too. The DEA had put marijuana and drug paraphernalia on me twice in order to secure their arrest, strengthen their case against me, and protect a snitch for future busts.

I sigh at the hypocrisy of the drug war as Greg shifts the conversation to prison intrigue and inmate antics. "Hey, you got any connections down in the kitchen? If you do and think you could help me out with a few items, in turn, I could let you in on a real Italian spaghetti dinner."

Living with kitchen orderlies does provide me with numerous connections and opportunities to obtain pretty much anything that flows through the kitchen. And in prison, anything can be bought with either cigarettes or a book of stamps. The main hustle for kitchen inmates is to supply other inmates with whatever they can carry out of the kitchen. I have a kitchen orderly deliver a banana, honey, and a carton of milk every once in a while when I eat oatmeal for breakfast.

For bigger orders, during mealtime, a kitchen inmate will conveniently forget a food tray on the food carrier destined for the hospital units, leaving some poor, hungry inmate without a meal. Predictably, the guards will send an inmate orderly back down to the mess hall to retrieve the missing meal. It's within that package that my fellow orderlies manage to conceal whatever is needed to fill requests and to help our friends. If dinner is crap, and let's face it—we are in prison—I usually make a simple meal with rice and vegetables. So, the prospect of a real Italian spaghetti dinner has my mouth watering.

"Who's going to be the chef extraordinaire on this one?" I ask.

"A personal friend of mine named Sammy. He's an acquaintance from way back, like Tony, and lives right down the hall. I've been wanting you to meet him. He's even heard of ya and wants to play you a game of chess. But, he ain't gonna come outta his room. Let's go meet him after we get outta here. What do ya say?"

I'm intrigued and blurt out, "I'm in! Tell me what you want and when."

Greg pats me on the back. "I knew I could count on you. Do you need any stamps or cigs?

"Nah, I've got your back on the first one."

One of the reasons I didn't have a problem with helping Greg is that I didn't need anything from him, or him from me. We were just two guys making the best out of a shitty situation. Since I really have no idea who he is, I don't treat him any differently than I treat anyone else. I figure if he is respectful to me, I'd return the sentiment. In here, respect is earned rather than a given. After I met Greg, he always had my back and kept his word. In here, just like out in the world, that's all you can expect, even from the best of friends.

Looking at my commissary Timex, I sound the alarm, "Oh, shit, our 15 minutes are up. The guard's break is over." I walk into a stall and flush the handle with my foot. Swoosh!!! I then flick my cigarette in the urinal as I head for the exit. Greg follows my lead without hesitation.

As we are heading out the door, we run right into the guard as he rounds the corner.

Sarcastically amusing himself, Mike asks, "Did you hold the fort down while I was away?"

"Like the Alamo!" I retort as Greg and I walk by, smelling of cigarettes.

The arrangement between guards and inmates is such that, if you're not caught holding a cigarette or blatantly disrespecting a guard, they'll let it slide unless of course, he's a Bart the Blackheart.

"Fuck." I whisper under my breath, "That was a close one."

Greg is in seventh heaven. "Right on the edge. Just how I like it. And we got one over on the screw."

"Screw" is a term old-timer's use for guards. I'm not sure what it means or why, so I ask Greg.

He shrugs. "Hell if I know. Maybe because they're always putting the fucking screws to you or screwing you over..."

Before he can finish, down the hallway come the Mafia wannabes, Luigi and Mario.

Luigi points with his thumb in the direction from which Mike had just walked. "Hey, Paisan. I just saw the guard coming that way."

Greg points in the other direction, "He went that way, Paisan." Confused, Luigi and Mario point in opposite directions.

Greg shrugs off their lack of intelligence as we both look into their needy eyes and know the next word out of their mouths will be to ask for a cigarette. He cuts them off at the pass and doesn't make them beg.

"Hey, forget about it. C'mere. I've got something for you."

Greg hands out a few cigarettes to Mario and Luigi like Halloween candy. They nod appreciatively in unison towards Greg. "Grazie Mille, Pasian!"

After they thank Greg profusely, we watch them scurry down the hallway towards whatever mischief they have planned for the day. We all know that there isn't any respect for a handout in prison—it means you have no hustle. In a place where benevolence is a rarity, I genuinely admire Greg's charity toward less fortunate prisoners. If you met a Luigi or Mario on the street, you'd give them a dollar and wish them the best of luck, but here their luck ran out long ago. Now with no other recourse, they constantly bum cigarettes and Ramen soups off orderlies and other inmates. These types of unfortunate souls are left vulnerable to unpredictability and violence from those to whom they owe money, unsavory lenders called "stores" in prison. I assume Luigi and Mario gravitate towards Greg due to their common Italian heritage and the perception of comradery and protection.

Greg looks back at me as I cock my head. "Yeah, yeah, yeah, I know. They're fuck-sticks, but they're my fuck-sticks, and I try to take care of my own."

I tease him. "St. Gregory."

"That depends on which side of the street you're on. Let's go meet Sammy."

CHAPTER 11

S ammy Cagnina was the most secretive guy on our unit. Curtis told me over a chess game that, like Greg, Sam was Mafia, although associated with a different crime family. He was tied to the Trafficante family, which was supposedly linked to the JFK assassination. Sam is an elderly inmate like Greg, but in contrast to Greg with his outgoing personality, Sam keeps completely to himself, aside from conversing with Greg inside his room. Mr. Cagnina maintains a strict, self-imposed isolation and is one of the few inmates at Springfield who acquired his own room. As long as I worked on this unit, I never saw him come out of his room or dress in anything except huge yellow pajamas that would cover his massive frame, which is what he's wearing today as Greg struts into his room like he owns the place, while I stand in the doorway.

"Hey, Sammy! This is the guy I was tellin' you about—Mark, our official chess champion on the unit."

Sam Cagnina squints his eyes above a huge, red, bulbous nose while determining whether I am worthy of entering his domain.

Greg breaks the tension. "Mark also has a few connections in the kitchen that can help us out with our little dinner dilemma."

Sam cautiously responds, "You don't say?"

"I do say..." Greg takes a step back, puts his arm around me, and pulls me into Sam Cagnina's room. "... and he's a personal friend."

Sam looks at Greg, then at me. "Well, why the fuck didn't you say so in the first place."

Sam sticks a meaty hand that's larger than Greg's prizefighter fist towards me. "Nice to finally meet you. I hear good things about you and that you're a damn good chess player. You know I play myself."

I shake Sam's huge hand. "Don't believe everything you're told except that I'm a damn good chess player, and I think I can help you get some stuff out of the kitchen."

Sam smiles. "I never do, and you'll have to prove yourself on both accounts."

I spout, "I intend to."

Greg then sets the stage, "Well, how about you twos getting acquainted over a game of chess and decide what we need for tomorrow's dinner. You think you can take him, Sammy?"

Sam squints at me in Clint Eastwood fashion and wagers. "How about we play for who pays for the meal?"

I wave my hand through the air and give him the good news. "I told Greg I've already got this one."

Sam guffaws. "Well, hell then, I guess I've already won."

Moving my knight into battle, I kid Sam, "Not yet you haven't."

Sam moves his knight out to challenge the opposition. As we play chess, I find Sam Cagnina's persona not to be the one he projects on the unit of an angry old man who wants to be left the fuck alone. Instead, it is one of lightheartedness admixed with a dash of dark, sarcastic humor. In Sam's small, yellow-painted room that matches his pajamas, we exchange friendly banter over our game. As I move my bishop, I tell him I can place our order during lunch when I see my connection in the kitchen.

Sam grabs a piece of paper and pen, hands them to me, and tells me to write down the list of ingredients needed for tonight's dinner. He then barks the items off like a short-order cook, "I'll be needing some hamburger meat and tomatoes. But, only get the big ripe tomatoes, not the green ones that look like gremlin balls; oh, and some onions, olive oil, garlic—and don't forget the spaghetti."

As I write down the last of Sam's grocery list, I slide my queen in for the kill—"Check mate!"

Sam looks down at the board with a grimace. "Well, fuck me."

Smiling, I jest. "You're going to have to buy me dinner first."

Sam chuckles as we hear the guard bellow, "Chow time. Everyone get in their rooms."

Looking at Sam, I wave the list in his face. "Well, I guess I'm up."

I hear Mike bellow as I hurry down the hall, "Where's my orderly?"

As I round the corner, I raise my hand in Mike's direction to show attendance. "Right here, boss."

Mike gives me my walking orders. "The food cart is ready in the kitchen."

Pressing the elevator's down button, I comply. "I'm on it."

Mike grins back. "That's what I like to hear."

Once at the kitchen, I place my order with a beefy black guy who, in the outside world, was a bodybuilder name Marico. He's in prison for illegally obtaining large amounts of steroids, and I work out with him occasionally. Whenever I need anything from the kitchen, he has always come through, doesn't overcharge, and is discreet. I hand Marico Sam's list and several books of stamps. He quickly grabs the contents from my hand and slips them into his pocket, giving me a thumbs-up while telling me it will be ready when I bring back the lunch food trays.

Once lunch is over, I return the food trays to the kitchen, where Marcio is waiting with a sack of my requested items. Marcio wrote Greg's and Sam's unit name on the sack in thick black magic marker and stapled the top to make it look official, as if I'm transporting a requested item for the guard. So, chances that some random guard will stop me in the hallway are slim to none. During chowtime, orderlies are the only inmates allowed to roam the hallways without a guard escort, and the guards that I may pass are familiar with my face and name.

Once back on the unit, Greg, Sam, and I hide the paper sack in the ceiling until dinnertime. While I work, for the first time, I see Sam out of his room, standing by the microwave in his yellow pajamas. His huge frame envelopes the area as he stirs and heats the ingredients for our meal with the passion of a New York chef. After dinner arrives and I help Mike hand out the food trays, I walk into Sam's room. Greg is already there talking about John Gotti. When Sam notices me, he gives Greg a heads-up that I arrived.

Greg turns my way. "Come on in, Mark; we've been waiting for you."

Waving his hands over three plates of spaghetti dinners with parmesan and French bread, Sam smiles broadly. "Well, what the fuck do you think?"

Looking at this fantastic meal laid before me that is worthy of any 5-star Italian diner, I give my answer, "I think I'm gonna cry."

Pulling a bottle of homemade wine and three plastic cups out of a sack, I place them in front of the two men and split the illegal red liquid evenly. Looking up, I give them back a look of satisfaction. "Well, what do ya think, guys? Are we styling, or what?"

Sam slaps his knee. "Damn, I like this guy."

Greg pats my shoulder. "What did I tell you about Mark; is he the shit or what?"

"Thanks, Greg. Thanks, Mr. Cagnina."

Sam waves a big hand in front of my face. "Please just call me Sam or Sammy."

With this introduction and over dinner, Sammy and I become friends. We play games of chess regularly while planning our next spaghetti dinner, scheduled to take place every Friday night. With only Greg, Sam, and I invited to this little feast, we form a camaraderie that can only be found in prison. Sammy continues to make some of the finest Italian meals to be had at Springfield. He makes our Friday evenings something special that we can anticipate within the restrictive environment of prison. Both old men frequently kid each other about their once illustrious hair, and Greg always surprises me with stories about celebrities like Dean Martin and Willy Mayes, who he considers personal friends. Gotti is mentioned in passing, but for the most part, they avoid talking about the Mafia, and I don't ever ask.

On days when Sammy and I play chess, the games are always played in his room because he will not interact with any other inmates. He tells me that Florida is his home and, before running a crew with the Trafficante family, he was actually a police officer.

"My early days on the force really helped when I started running with a crew. I knew how the cops thought, their tactics, and, for a while, I could stay one step ahead of them. Plus, prohibition had opened up a goldmine for most guys on the force, who had grown up with at least one bootlegger or moonshiner in the family. Despite what you've probably heard, most cops and politicians had an occasional snoot or were downright drunks. If there was booze, drugs, money, or pussy involved, people looked the other way. Hell, Kennedy's old man made a killing on illegal booze and guys like me and Greg. You think anything illegal on that scale didn't run through us? They need us, but then they forget where they come from and get on a fucking high horse, thinking they're better than everyone else. Don't even get me started." Sammy huffs.

I wasn't going to get him started, nor had I asked. But I had noticed that, once a guy who has been subjected to either self-imposed or administrative isolation is with someone they can trust, he will open up more than you'd expect. Other inmates couldn't believe old man Cagnina was talking to an inmate besides Greg, let alone allow one in his room. The same happened with a Nation of Islam inmate who wouldn't speak with any white person—the black inmates said that he hated them too, but, when I was forced to cell with him during a transfer, and we began playing chess, he told me all types of things about his religion and his life.

When Sammy opens up, it's usually about people, places, and names I'd never heard of before—like the "lounge wars" in Tampa, which I gather had something to do with consolidating the lounges in the Tampa area, similar to turf wars between gangs over marijuana and cocaine distribution areas. Sammy makes the lounge wars sound comparable to the streets of Chicago during the Capone era, but the stories may be fish tales meant to entertain his only guest besides Greg. I wouldn't mind, and they were interesting if not entertaining.

In prison, there's a saying: "If you're not doing your own time, time is doing you." In here, where time is all you have, a good story over a good game of chess and a hot cup of joe is one of the best ways to escape the walls. Over the months, I begin to like Sammy's crusty personality, and we slowly become friends—he even allows me to put my personal belongings in his room to ensure no one steals my stuff while I'm out working on the unit. He does that for no one else except Greg.

As we move into the late summer, life is good at Springfield, and I'm seven months from going home. Then, out of nowhere, a monkey wrench is thrown into the system by a guy by the name of José Reyes, aka Jay.

CHAPTER 12

During an intense game of chess with Curtis, a well-dressed inmate in a wheelchair rolls up and parks himself just inside the doorway. Curtis ignores him, consumed by his next move. When I glance his way, I see a paraplegic of South American ethnicity.

I nod. "Hey." I think that he's just here to check out the competition.

He acknowledges me with a tip of his head and belts out, "I want the next game."

I can't help but notice that his tone indicates more of a demand than a request.

As he rolls up to the table, I already don't like him. Who the fuck does this guy think he is?

Curtis moves his bishop and stares at the board in concentration before glancing towards the unexpected guest out of the corner of his eye. With some degree of recognition, Curtis's eyes suddenly widen in dread as the man in the wheelchair stares at our game with the intensity of a predator stalking its prey. Curtis's fear is palpable, and I notice it became impossible for either of us to concentrate on the game.

I decide to break the tension.

I extend my hand. "Hey, my name's Mark..."

"I know who you are. You hang out with Greg and Sam Cagnina."

Without extending his hand, he gives his first name. "I'm Jay."

Curtis looks at me as if he's staring death in the face. "Mark, like I said before I made that move, I gotta go call the wife. Good game. Talk later, bro."

Although I had no idea what Curtis was talking about, I took his lead, assuming it had something to do with Jay. "No problem, buddy. Catch you on the flipside."

Without a word, Curtis stands up and tips his king over on the chessboard in capitulation, then hurries out the door without looking back. Jay completely ignores Curtis's departure and moves into the vacant spot directly across from me. Behind Jay's cold dead blank stare, I can tell there burns an intelligence of pure evil.

Jay makes another demand edged in a monotone voice mixed with malice and confidence. "I want the white chess pieces."

I say nothing and imagine this is probably for some perceived advantage of having the first move. Without any acknowledged agreement, Jay begins to set up the white chess pieces on his side of the board. I don't intend to start an argument over who moves first in a chess game when I'm so close to home. As I pull the black chess pieces towards me, we set up our respective pieces and size up our opponent.

In prison, sizing a man up is a dysfunctional, instinctual survival mechanism caused by years of perceived or imagined violence. Although it may keep you alive in here, unfortunately, it follows you upon your release in the form of PTSD. Today, I'm in prison, and my immediate impression of Jay is that of a well-groomed man of average size who wears wireframe glasses and slicks his black hair back like Italian mobsters in the movies. His neatly pressed khakis project a higher class of inmate with connections on the outside. His attire chisels a powerfully build torso that contrasts with his withering and motionless legs. Although his behavior is a little unnerving, and he no doubt has a violent streak, I still think I could take him with little problem.

This is the first time I have made Jay's acquaintance but, as we set up our chess men with an occasional glance as we size up each other, I do remember seeing him in my peripheral vision, always trying to get in good with Greg. Besides that, he kept to himself except for occasional pleasantries. Now, he's here trying to feel me out, and Curtis is scared—but why?

As he moves his pawn into the middle of the chess board, he casually asks, "So, I see you're hanging out with Greg a lot lately. What the fuck do you guys have in common?"

I counter his move and dodge the question half-kidding, "Why, are you jealous?"

He stares at me with dead eyes and a clenched jaw. "What the fuck did you say? Do you think I'm a faggot?"

Quickly trying to diffuse the situation, I play the joker. "Nah. I'm just kidding, Jay. Greg and I help each other out."

Jay moves his knight. "That seems a stretch. How could you possibly help DePalma out? What, are you the one supplying the goods for Cagnina's and Greg's dinner?

I stare at the board, trying to concentrate.

Jay taps the table with his finger to get my attention. When I look up, he smirks.

"Yes, I know about the dinners. It's the only thing that will get that fat fuck out of his room."

Jay's combines a sneer and a chortle. "Have you seen Cagnina in those big, bright yellow pajamas cooking his dinner and ignoring other inmates? He won't even fucking talk to me. He's like some sort of fucking mental patient. But he'll talk to you, and I don't fucking get it. Why the fuck is that?"

I say nothing and continue to study the board.

Jay waves his well-manicured hands over his neatly pressed khakis then continues his criticism. "And why the hell doesn't he dress up a little, like me? I know he can fucking afford it."

Jay grins a wolfish grin. "You can tell me. You're friends with Cagnina too, aren't you?"

Moving my bishop, I sigh. "Look, Jay. No offense, but I don't know you, and I have a funny habit of not talking about other people's business behind their backs."

Jay becomes reckless with frustration and advances a pawn from its ranks. "Where'd you learn that?"

I quickly move my queen in place for a kill shot. "From my momma."

Throwing another pawn out, Jay snorts a laugh. "Greg's right. You're a funny guy."

One thing you develop in prison is a highly sensitive bullshit detector, and at the moment, mine was going into the red. Studying Jay's chess strategies, I begin to realize he's not an avid player and begin to wonder what game he is playing. Is he a predator, similar to other inmates I'd met before? Is he one of those guys with a harsh personality, pissed off at life, and always wanting to start a fight? Is he just an inmate trying to feel out his environment and project a tough-guy image for self-preservation? After all, he is in a wheelchair. Then again, he could be a rat for the guards. Whatever it is, I get the sneaking suspicion that Jay's true reason for coming into the communal lounge today was to check me out and that the game is secondary.

I move my Queen to f2; Jay has fallen for the classic four-move checkmate.

"Checkmate!" I hoot.

His face contorts with defeat, and, for the first time, he loses his tactical and intellectual balance.

"Wh...wh...what the fuck?"

He grimaces and scours the board for any mistakes or underhanded moves, then blurts out, "Play me another one."

Pushing myself away from the table, I make up a pressing engagement.

"I promised I would meet someone out on the yard in 10 minutes."

Jay pleads, "Ah, come on, man. Just one more!"

I head for the door. "I'm sorry, but I gotta go."

Still studying the board, Jay doesn't even look up or say goodbye.

Taking one last look at my opponent, I can tell Jay doesn't like to lose and looks at everything as a competition. He slams his fist down on his unfeeling legs. "Motherfucker! Fuck!"

I deduce that Jay is overcompensating for some personal deficiencies or physical inferiority by his over-bravado behavior. Obviously, my first guess is his handicap, but what's the deal with Jay dressing like a wise guy? Greg and Sammy obviously do not give a damn about that in here. Curtis's sudden fearful recognition and departure indicated that he knew something that may help unravel a little of this mystery. While walking down the hallway towards Curtis's room, I can still hear Jay cursing at himself in front of the chessboard. "Fuck! Fuck! Fuck!"

CHAPTER 13

Curtis was not in his room. Finally, I tracked him down on the prison's yard, in which a ballfield is centered within the yard's square enclosure. Military inmates and a team full of gangbangers are competing in a highly-spirited softball game, with the bangers occasionally throwing down gang signs declaring solidarity or simply out of habit. Around the ballfield's perimeter, a host of other inmates walk or jog around a well-worn asphalt running track. Placed intermittently along its pathway sit metal picnic tables, either in the sun or under shade trees that allow sunlight to flitter through their leaves onto a mostly grassless ground.

A few yards beyond the picnic tables, encircling the entire yard's enclosure, is an imposing redbrick wall that obstructs any further vertical view. Its steep incline leaves only a gaping aperture of sky, permitting a view of the occasional transient cloud and ephemeral noon day sun that pass over its opening. Jutting out of the wall's ground floor structure are the administrative square detention cells, with their iron bars and rusty grated screens bolted across dirty windows. A few yards beneath one of these windows, I can see Curtis with his back to the wall, smoking a cigarette while sitting alone at a picnic table.

Rick, who is pitching for the military team, yells in my direction as I walk around the track towards Curtis, "Hey, Mark! Pick up a glove and help us kick some ass!"

All the military guys try to juice me into playing by yelling that I'm a traitor to my country if I don't help their cause. Even the "crazy Cajun" shouts that his testicles are bigger than mine unless I join their game. Everyone laughs at my expense; I laugh back but continue on my way to further my investigation of Jay, obviously declining their offer.

Turning back to the game, Sargent Rick Rambo rallies his men from the mound. "Alright, you goddamn degenerates, let's get back to kicking ass! Who the fuck is with me?!"

A resounding "HOOAH!" resonates through the roofless enclosure.

Watching my interaction with my military cohorts, Curtis smiles and waves me over. "Sorry for bouncing out of there, man, but that guy's fucking freaks me out."

I chuckle beneath my breath. "Yes, Jay does come off a bit intense. He was still cussing at the chess board—aka me, when I left him alone in the communal room."

"So, I guess you beat that ass?"

"In four moves."

Curtis high-fives me. "Man!"

Curtis then stares off into some forgotten past while taking a drag off his cigarette,

"Listen, Mark. I know this guy from the street, and he's one crazy cracker. No offense."

I wave off his "cracker" comment with a grin. "None taken."

Curtis flips the ash from his cigarette. "But, for real homes, that guy you just pissed off is a real-life Jekyll and Hyde, and he's a lifer, too. Any misunderstanding or perceived disrespect could turn into a full-blown clusterfuck where you leave in a body bag or worse."

I stand in front of him and nod my head as he continues to school me on the dangers of fucking with inmates doing life, but I already know of these dangers firsthand. I've seen plenty of guys stabbed over the most trivial arguments with lifers or with other inmates who have no release date and not a damn thing to lose.

Most inmates like to think of themselves as stand-up guys who aren't going to take any shit while in prison. But the truth is, unless you're also doing a life sentence or your life is on the line, it's better to just walk away from these guys or they will drag you into an abyss of death and hard time. But, in prison, there is always someone stupid or arrogant enough to poke the bear.

I sit down beside Curtis and light a cigarette. "I hear you, brother, and, unfortunately, I have seen the worst when it comes to these individuals. Hell, while being processed into arriving and receiving in the Oklahoma penitentiary, I saw a young black-gang banger diss one of the lifers. I swear, what followed was one of the most messed-up things I've ever seen in my life."

Curtis's interest is peaked, and he turns towards me as he snaps his fingers. "Well, guess what? I just happen to have some time for a messed-up prison story on this beautiful day here at Springfield."

Flipping the ash off my cigarette, I look at Curtis. Taking a drag, I reflect on one of my most horrific memories while doing time in the Oklahoma system. I see myself sitting on the second floor in A&R Room B, which is a dimly lit, stark white, claustrophobic TV room that has a row of steel folding chairs. Each chair faces a single black and white TV that is bolted onto the ceiling in the center of the room. At the back of the room is a row of four chairs placed against a cinderblock wall with small, square, wired windows embedded at eye-level to let in a semblance of light. Secured into the cinderblock wall at one end of this wall is a steel door, which leads to a unit where fifty inmates live in two-man cells. A guy named Tony is sitting beside the door with his back against the wall. For the same reason, of course, I'm sitting on the opposite side of Tony, with my back against the wall, too.

Me and another inmate named Tony are sitting in the back row. Ahead of us, sitting front and center, is one of the biggest, baddest-looking inmates I'd ever seen in my life. He's tattooed from head to toe and is doing two life sentences on a double homicide rap. He reminds me of a pit bull with steroid rage, powerfully built and huge. This guy is so jacked, he doesn't even have a visible neck. On his muscular body sits a chiseled, shiny, bald head. The back of his head is inked with a large skull with vampire fangs visible through a wide-open mouth and hollow black eyes that stare blankly back at Tony and me.

Before this colossus had his required A&R haircut, he sported a shock of blonde hair fashioned into a Mohawk. He had a German name, which I heard a guard call out during count. "Andreas!"

The monster of a man turned to answer the guard, revealing an even more horrifying image—I could see that his teeth were filed to form fangs, and **"FTW"** (Fuck the World) was tattooed across his forehead in boldly-inked letters. At 6'4" and around 250 pounds of mean, lean, killing machine, Andreas was an imposing figure who would fit seamlessly into any apocalyptic gang of homicidal lunatics found in a Mad Max movie.

Today, Andreas sits in the second row. His girth commands the two center chairs in front of the TV. Under his weight, the chairs creak and strain as he leans back and puts his enormous, muscular, tattooed arms over the backs of both chairs beside him. In his right hand, which is covered in tattoos of swastikas and thunderbolts, he twirls a pencil through his fingers with amazing dexterity. Then, seemingly without a care in the world, Andreas props his feet up in the chair directly in front of him as if he'd just come home after a hard day's work.

I suppose Andreas's size, along with the reputation of having at least two homicides under his belt, gives him the confidence to leave his back completely unprotected from other inmates—in my mind—for this inmate, that is not unreasonable. If his intimidating physique, covered in tattoos of death and destruction, isn't enough to give you pause, then the fact that he hasn't said two words since his arrival should serve anyone who's ever done time with a big, red, flashing "DANGER" sign. Obviously, this is one hombre who should be given a wide berth, just as you would treat any other dangerous animal.

Curtis interrupts as he slowly blows out a whistle along with a puff of smoke. "No shit. Those quiet inmates doing a lot of time are always the ones that have a hair-trigger. And those tattooed, Aryan Brotherhood monsters, are just Vikings on meth, waiting to kill or die with you, so that they can fight forever with their brothers in Valhalla. Nut cases—every single one of them, if you ask me."

Curtis is right about the silent types doing a lot of time. In the bizarre world of prison, where monsters and psychopaths litter the landscape, the quiet, tattooed, brooding inmates doing life sentences are always the ones to leave alone. They have zero fucks to give and come from a place with, figuratively, a nuclear warhead strapped to their backs, ready to unleash hell's pent-up rage on anyone foolish enough to press their buttons.

Lucky for us on that day in A&R, Andreas is mesmerized by a *Twilight Zone* episode named "Nightmare at 20,000 Feet." We all stare at the old black and white TV bolted to the ceiling. Its static image portrays a group of well-dressed passengers boarding a plane, one of whom is a young William Shatner. Andreas continues to twirl the pencil in his hand covered in swastikas and thunderbolts.

He grunts. "That's Captain Kirk." Without needing or wanting a response, Andreas again speaks only to himself. "I fucking love this episode."

In this *Twilight Zone* episode, a man named Mr. Wilson, who is recovering from a nervous breakdown, is flying back home with his wife through a violent storm. A few minutes into the flight, he observes a human-like silhouette walking on the wing. He frantically presses an overhead button, and a pretty, blonde stewardess hurries to his aid.

Tony comments with a Brooklyn accent, "I'd bang that chick in a New York minute even if she ate crackers in bed, if you know what I mean. Hey!"

At some other place or time, that may have been funny, but we are all getting ready to do hard time in a place more chilling than a *Twilight Zone* setting. And I, for one, am not in the best of moods. I nod my head and give an annoyed look. Andreas isn't as kind. Clack! Clack! Clack! Andreas strikes his pencil on the backrest of one of the chairs and hisses a warning in words seared with malevolence and mortality.

"If you don't shut your fucking pie hole, you're never going to leave this room to even bang another goat—if you get my fucking drift."

Tony's terrified facial expression paints a portrait of a man scared right down to the marrow of his bones. He leans forward to say he's sorry to Andreas but thinks better of it when briefly distracted by the emotionless, soulless eyes of the skull on the back of Andreas's head. Instead, he melts back into his chair, tucks his chin into his chest, and folds his arms over his body to make himself look smaller as he stares into the abyss of what may be his last good day on earth.

At some point during the scene, when Mr. Wilson is convinced the human form on the plane's wing is a gremlin, and the stewardess decides to give him a sedative, Tony quietly scurries out the door. Shortly thereafter, in walks Jamal. Jamal is a 19-year-old greenhorn (an inmate sentenced to prison for the first time), a gangbanger who I knew from the Tulsa County Jail but neither respected nor liked.

The reason I don't like Jamal is simple—he's a predator. When I knew him at the Tulsa County Jail, he and his little gang of thugs would prey on older white people, mercilessly beating them down for nothing more than ten dollars' worth of commissary. They took what they wanted and were appreciative of nothing. Personally, I was hoping that I would never see him again, but there he was, bouncing through the door with his earphones dangling out of his ears, slinging gang signs and rapping some bullshit that no one other than himself could understand.

Without acknowledging anyone in the room, Jamal does something he calls "Crip Walking" right up to the front row of chairs. I try to ignore his annoying distractions as Mr. Wilson contemplates whether to open the window curtain to verify whether a gremlin is still up to mischief on the airplane's wing. As Jamal throws a few more gang signs, claiming his turf, Mr. Wilson pulls the curtain back, revealing a leering, rain-soaked gremlin glaring back at him.

Jamal mutters, "I don't wanna watch this old-time, white people bullshit." Without hesitation, he reaches for the channel knob and changes the station to *Soul Train*.

Andreas says nothing. He stares at Jamal with the intensity of a lion sizing up its prey.

Jamal doesn't care about his indiscretions. I shake my head with disgust and feel the tension in the room rise as Don Cornelius introduces a black band to the stage. As he turns to sit down, Jamal notices Andrea's shoes in his newly claimed seat. With irritation, he waves his hand over the chair. "Get those fucking boats outta my seat."

Andreas unexpectedly complies and removes his feet from the chair. He sits upright as Jamal plops himself down into the chair's seat.

Jamal throws another gang sign and hoots as black and white teenagers dance to the latest hip-hop on the TV screen. "Shit! That's what I'm talking about, a little fucking respect!"

Curtis spits on the ground, breaking my train of thought. "Respect? Shit! That punk-ass nigger doesn't know a damn thing about respect." Curtis is, of course, correct. On this day, Jamal will learn about the danger of exhibiting contempt for respect in prison, and his lesson will come via something infinitely worse than any *Twilight Zone* episode; unlike the *Twilight Zone* with its five entertaining dimensions, this abhorrent dimension can be found only in prison's most depraved inmate's psyche and has only one aspect—sadomasochist violence.

Incredibly, Jamal shuts his eyes in arrogance or stupidity, still rapping to a song on his radio and throwing gang signs as Andrea suddenly rips his shirt off, revealing a back covered in swastikas, skulls, thunderbolts, and demons. Jamal is completely oblivious to the hulk growing behind him. Antagonistically, Andreas's powerful shoulders flex towards his opponent. His body seems to broaden and grow into a terrifying monstrosity, every vein engorged with blood and adrenaline. Andreas then swiftly lifts his muscular arms high into the air, revealing two black-winged tattoos with the words "Fallen Angel" inked along his arms and shoulders.

It feels like I'm watching some type of monster rise out of my deepest, darkest nightmares as Andreas's gigantic frame begins to eclipse the skinny gangbanger. From a place where his soul used to exist, Andreas roars while engulfing Jamal's upper body by wrapping his left arm around his neck. He simultaneously drives the sharpened pencil into Jamal's right ear. The radio falls and shatters on the concrete floor as Jamal instinctively tries to jerk free. Andreas prevents any escape by pushing his weight down on Jamal's body, crushing him into the recently claimed seat.

Jamal's strained shrieks reverberate inside the small room as he tries to wriggle free, but Andreas's thick, sinewy arm continues to tighten around his throat like a boa constrictor suffocating its victim. A sickening crunch fills the room as Andreas violently shoves the pencil further into Jamal's ear canal. Then, with an animalistic grunt, Andreas stands, lifting Jamal out of his seat until his shoes dangle just above the floor. Jamal gurgled as he first stiffened, then flailed with a seizure as Andreas sneered, "Time to die, nigger."

Mesmerized by the over-the-top violence, Curtis leans back against the picnic table, takes a long drag, then interjects, "Holy fuck, cuz. My nigger didn't need to go out like that. That's some crazy-ass Aryan bullshit."

I dismiss his premature indignation and continue my thoughts and narration... Jamal then goes limp from hypoxia from strangulation or from having the pencil shoved in his ear and broken off in his brain. As I stare in disbelief, Andreas flings Jamal's flaccid body through the air like a broken doll. It crunched into the corner with a stomach-turning THUD.

I stare at Jamal's broken body lying in the corner of the room with his head and shoulders slumped against the wall. After a few seconds, I notice he begins to twitch, and his eyes flutter as if he's desperately trying to wake up from a bad dream. But his nightmare is far from over. Just as Don Cornelius dances down the *Soul Train* line, Andreas grasps the TV and rips it from its metal bracket like a bad tooth.

With a loud, growling grumble, Andreas jerks the TV side-to-side, ripping all remaining wires free and causing electrical sparks to fly through the air while the overhead lights flicker off and on. I close my eyes and shield my face from the flying mortar and sheetrock raining down on us. Once I open my eyes again, I see Andreas with the TV held high over his head, staring down at Jamal through the flickering light. Then, with a demonic grin that exposed his sharpened teeth, he snarls, "MINDLESS MUSIC OUT!"

Amazingly, Jamal attempts to lift his hand in one last attempt to avoid the oncoming barrage. "Nooooo..."

Andreas's face displays no mercy as he bellows an archaic war cry and hurls the TV down onto Jamal's head with the force of a sledgehammer. The crushing impact of the TV drives Jamal's head into the floor with a loud crunch of bone and glass. Then, everything collapses to the floor in a mixture of glass, plastic, mortar, and an expanding pool of blood.

Curious inmates are now peering through the small windows above the back row of chairs. I figure it is a good time to leave. I open the door just in time to hear a few inmates complain about how this depravity is going to ruin their day.

"Hey! Will you fucking look at that? Andreas fucked Jamal up!"

Another convict sniggers the obvious, "For Christ's sakes! There goes our T.V. privileges."

A greenhorn stupidly yells into a crowd of inmates milling around on the bottom floor. "Tell the guards they're tearing up the TV room!"

A couple of inmates from the bottom floor immediately yell back at the greenhorn, "Fucking snitch!"

Another shaggy-bearded inmate, standing near the door, sighs in defeat, "This is bullshit. We are going to get locked down."

Somewhere on the unit, a guard bellows a command that fulfills the last inmate's prophecy. "Inmates, get in your fucking rooms!"

The sighing inmate frowns and throws up his hands. "See? What did I fucking tell you? Now we're locked down for the night. Shit."

Just before leaving Room B, I take one last look at the horrific chaos and stare in disbelief at an image that will haunt me for the rest of my life. In the corner, the two blood-covered adversaries are locked in a horrific display of depravity and brutality. Jamal is dead with a vicious gash etched across his head and is face down in a pool of his own blood and drool. Andreas knelt into the sticky blood, brutally jerked Jamal's pants down, exposing his buttocks, and began sadistically fucking Jamal's dead body in the ass."

With flickering lights above and a hot wire from the ceiling still spitting sparks, Andreas then leans over his victim and takes a bite out of his back. As I close the door, he looks right at me with a piece of Jamal's flesh visible around bloodied, sharpened teeth and laughs hysterically, babbling some crazy shit about using Jamal's blood for lubrication and Jamal being his bitch in Valhalla.

Curtis gasps. "Jesus Fucking Christ! That's some crazy, psycho, white-boy, bullshit." He then collects himself with a drag from his cigarette and stares me right in the eye. "Listen up, my nigger, you think that guy is nuts? Shitttt. He is no worse than that methodical psychopathic killer you just left cussing at the chessboard."

Taken back, I stare quizzically at Curtis.

"No fucking way."

Curtis snorts. "Fucking way! That cracker is your worst nightmare, and he's down for seven murders. Can you dig what I'm saying, Mark? That boy has no way outta here besides leaving here in a pine box, which means he has less to lose than that psychopathic Aryan. And for your information, brother, his name isn't even Jay."

CHAPTER 14

Curtis flips the ash from his cigarette, and we both watch it fall to the ground as we give our minds a rest from the images of Andreas and Jamal. After a couple of minutes, I refocus on the present and ask Curtis to expound on the inmate I know as Jay.

"He's from Puerto Rico, and his real name is José Reyes. I've known of him since the 80s after Reagan pulled the plug on most of the social services, thinking this would get young blacks and immigrant families off their asses and into the workforce. But in the ghetto, there are no jobs. I was pimpin', but everyone gravitated to where the big money was—slinging drugs, and that included me and my homies."

We are momentarily distracted by whoops and hollers from the baseball game each of us had completely forgotten. The military team cheers as Rick pumps his fist in the air after striking out another gang member.

"You see, Mark. Back in the 80s, the Cartel flooded New York with a shitload of cocaine. We were all young and hungry and started slingin' cocaine, heroin, and crack. José was only in his teens when he started doing the same under a guy named Chocolate."

I interrupt, "I thought the CIA invented crack to destroy the black community?"

Curtis frowns, visibly upset. "Where the hell did you hear that shit from, the Enquirer? Mark, since I've been in here, I've had a lot of time to think about what I've... we've done to our neighborhoods. Let me break it down for you, homes. As far as I can tell, the black community has done a pretty good job fucking itself up. We shit where we live, glorify the very thugs that prey on our own people and, if a nigger makes it out of the hood, they hardly ever give back to the community. It's always about "getting mine" and fucking everyone else, of which José is a master."

Curtis rubs his chin and reflects, "And when the po-po puts one of us in prison, someone is waiting in the hood to take over their position. It was the same for José. When the feds threw his boss in prison, it didn't stop the drugs or violence from coming into the community. It never does. On the contrary, José just took over the operation and ramped up his operation by surrounding himself with a small army of dealers and hit men that would kill for him on a whim. He was a meaner, leaner, Chocolate and, when crack was king, José made millions a day and became one of the most ruthless dealers on the street. Shit... that honkey would cap a nigger's ass just for looking at him wrong. He's in here for seven murders, but everyone on the street knows that's only the tip of the iceberg of his real kill count. José and his crew are straight-up psychopaths. Do you know what his main enforcer's name was on the street?"

I shake my head. "No idea."

"His real name is Francisco Medina, but he was known on the streets as Freddy Kruger, and I heard José paid him over $10,000 a day to be his hitman and light-up a motherfucker on his orders. This guy was a straight-up OG, Mark. He has at least a 30-body count, loves the AK and 9-millimeter, and will empty the entire clip into your face just to make a point. He took down one of my niggers whose mom had to have a closed casket at his funeral."

My mind conjures an image of Freddy Kruger from the *Nightmare on Elm Street* as the maniac behind the trigger of an

AK-47, making nightmares into reality, one riddled corpse at a time. Curtis's next words are loaded with a peculiar mixture of respect and loathing.

"Once José took things over, he was determined to be the most ruthless drug lord of Washington Heights. Everyone was scared shitless of him, and for good reason. His murderous rampage was so out of control, bodies began to turn up everywhere uptown, and all in a three-year period. Medina is such a psycho that he even iced a mark on a bridge in bumper-to-bumper traffic."

Curtis paints a picture of a complete psychopathic person, devoid of empathy or compassion, standing on a car's hood during gridlock traffic atop a New York bridge. His AK-47 sways back and forth through the air as he sprays bullets into the cars of innocent bystanders and a taxicab, where a rival drug dealer and his girlfriend sit in the back seat. The automatic weapon jumps in his hand with an explosive RAT-A-TAT-TAT, as armor-piercing bullets rip his intended target to shreds, ending with a spent clip, riddled bodies slumped over a cab's bloody back seat, and Freddy Kruger's maniacal laughter booming in the background.

Taking a drag, Curtis sneers with disgust. "Shitttt. José and his crew were out of control, mad-dog killers that racked up so many kills from rivals as well as the innocent. Everyone got tired of their shit. The Feds, the cops, and even other NYC gangs, including me, wanted José and his crew taken off the street. And, where there is chaos, there is opportunity for information to become a powerful weapon that can form allies and be used to take revenge on rivals."

Curtis's lips form a mischievous grin. "Hmph, José was just 22 when one of my niggers saw him walk into a corner deli for the last time. He was going to a birthday party and was on his own turf, but when you have that many enemies, no place is safe. Homes said he was holding a stuffed animal when someone came out of the shadows and shot him twice as he stood in the doorway—once in the stomach and the other in the spine, putting him in that wheelchair forever."

"You make him appear like a very disagreeable fellow. Did being shot and wheelchair-bound bring on an epiphany to change his obstinate ways?"

Curtis takes a long drag off his cigarette, taking on a serious tone. "Not a lick. You think being in a wheelchair slows someone like José down? Only in your dreams. He just kept killing. I'm fucking serious, Mark. You need to watch yourself with José. This guy is dangerous, especially if you get in his way."

I try to make amends for my flippant attitude. "I'm sorry, Curtis, I do believe you, and I appreciate the heads-up. I was trying to bring some levity to a serious conversation. So, you knew José on the streets?"

"Who didn't I know back in the day? If my girls weren't getting information from fucking gang and Mafia high ballers, my niggers on the streets knew everyone that was slinging coke and heroin in the New York area. That includes Gotti's crew, and even the guy I mentioned earlier named Chocolate, aka Rogelio Perez Almodovar. Back when everyone dealt heroin and crack, I knew him personally, and Chocolate was the guy who took José under his wings when he was just a kid. When Chocolate went to prison in 1987, he left the entire operation to José to handle until his release. He was a quick learner who read Machiavelli, Mario Puzo, and Sun Tzu. Within a year, through these ruthless principles, he was able to bring in a couple of million dollars a day and leave a slew of bodies in his wake. Later, when Chocolate came back, José arranged to have the old man shuffled down to South America for retirement. Rumors have it, José then had him whacked so Chocolate couldn't threaten his empire."

"Unbelievable. But why would José have his mentor and friend assassinated?"

"Look, Mark, when I say empire, that's what these guys believe they are building, and everyone else are just pawns shifting in the wind to whoever has the power at any given moment. And, every single one of these guys follows a philosophy that fosters an attitude of the ends justifying the means to eliminate any threat to their reign."

As I listened to Curtis, it became apparent that, although he probably never had a formal education, he was well-versed in a variety of philosophies and philosophical caveats, including "know thy enemy," that aided his survival on the streets.

"It really warms my heart to learn you are so well-read, as I find it most problematic to discuss even the most basic concepts of philosophy with the majority of inmates within this fine establishment."

Amused, Curtis gazes upon me fondly and smiles. "I feel the same, and it's the reason I hang with ya. I love my niggers in the hood, but they make you dumb-down everything you say until you're stuck on stupid. And for the moment, you seem to be the only breath of intelligence in this place, and it's probably why Mr. DePalma also enjoys your company."

Taking a drag, Curtis taps the ash from his cigarette and glances my way. "You certainly don't look or act like you came from the mean streets, but I did, and so did José. Everyone, including Mr. DePalma and Gotti, had to climb a rope through blood, bullets, and deceit to make it to the next level. But, once they claimed their thrones, they only found more blood, bullets, and people they thought were their friends, waiting to slit their throats to lay claim to their turf—or, eventually, make a deal with the feds to escape prison time and bury their asses in here."

"It's no doubt an environment that perpetuates a strong propensity towards a Machiavellian philosophy, although it hardly seems worth the end game. So why do it?"

Curtis replies, "Besides the money, women, respect, and a chance to crawl out of the ghetto to live like a normal person? I never knew anything else besides this life and did okay for myself, but I never wanted to build an empire like José and Gotti—too much heat. I preferred to stay in the shadows and under the radar after realizing early on that I could take out my enemies or advance my position by whispering in the ears of the right people."

"Whose ears are you whispering in now?"

"Yours, of course. And, now that José has made an unexpected appearance, I predict a storm is brewing with you in its crosshairs, and I'd like to know why. Any ideas?"

I shrug my shoulders. "Not a one, besides knowing Greg."

Curtis taps his lips with his finger. "That's what I'm thinking, too. José's obsessed with the Mafia. But, why bother with you? I know how José thinks, and everything he does is calculated to benefit himself. My guess is he's trying to understand where you lie in his equation and size you up to either use you or take you out, if required. Until I can figure out what that equation is, I say again, be careful. Right now, since he can't gain your respect, he's going to roll the dice with fear."

Taking a drag off my cigarette, I continue our Machiavelli discourse with a paraphrase, "It's better to be feared than loved or respected. The latter is maintained by obligation, the former by punishment. José is not indebted to me, nor I to him. How in the world is José going to punish me from a wheelchair if he thinks I've wronged him?'

Curtis pauses a moment. "Any way he can, brother."

I frown. "Well, that doesn't sound very encouraging."

While the baseball game rages on, the inmates enjoy the last rays of the autumn sunlight before being locked down for the night. Curtis nudges and waves towards the field. "Well, at least your military friends have your back, and they're the scariest people in here."

"I know. Their friendship is appreciated, but I don't know if they could make it in time if something jumps off on Greg's unit. They're not omnipresent. Do you think they could have helped me in time if Andreas would have turned on me?"

With a worried look, Curtis takes a drag from his cigarette and blows the smoke skyward. "Probably not."

Talking to Curtis about the drug trade triggers memories about how much cocaine was flooding into Tulsa in the 80s, I make an educated guess. "I assume that José was dealing coke when it hit in the 80s and made a killing until busted."

"True that, my friend, and that's not even the half of it. Oh, Man! When that shit exploded on the streets during the 80s and 90s, it made Washington Heights the crack and cocaine capital of New York. Even Gotti's crew started slinging drugs under a guy named Dellacroce, who was Gotti's mentor. Dellacroce was old school and, although he was one tough son-of-bitch, he was a fair man who inducted John into the Costa Nostra. Gotti's crew weren't supposed to be dealing drugs according to family rules, but do you think any organization that rewards its biggest earners can stay out of the drug trade with that type of jack to be made? Hell, the cops and guards can't even keep their hands out of it."

Based on my own experience, I agree with Curtis. "You're right on that account, brother. Everywhere I've been incarcerated, guards are selling drugs. Before I left El Reno, a guard was caught with pounds of weed, heroin, pills, and a bunch of other shit."

Curtis looks at his fingernails. "Same shit is going on here. You need anything?"

"Nah, I'm good. I'm a few months from going home and don't need anything to screw it up."

"Excellent choice, M'man." Curtis smiles with a know-it-all look. "Here's a little tidbit for you. One of my girls who was banging one of Gotti's crew saw José personally deliver a package when they were under Dellacroce. And, this is at a time when the five families were opposed to dealing drugs of any kind."

"So, you think that's how José knows Greg?"

"I wouldn't doubt it," Curtis remarks nonchalantly. "My sources told me that when Dellacroce was over Gotti's crew, they were dealing drugs under the table with Dellacroce protecting them by turning a blind eye. But, when old man Gambino died, Dellacroce was passed over to lead the Gambino family in favor of Big Pauli, and Gotti and his boys took it personally for three reasons."

Curtis extends one finger. "The first was that everyone on the street knew Big Pauli was more of a businessman who hadn't got his hands dirty or paid his dues by running the streets or climbing the rope through the bullets, blood, and deceit as Dellacroce had or Gotti. He was picked solely because he was a brother of old man Gambino."

Curtis extends a second finger. "Two, once Dellacroce died of cancer and no longer had Gotti's back, word had it that Big Pauli was going to have Gotti and his crew whacked to send a message that no drugs were going to be dealt under his reign."

The third finger extends. "And third, Big Pauli disrespected Dellacroce and his crew by not attending Dellacroce's funeral, which Gotti took personally. So Gotti and his crew struck first, killing Big Pauli and his bodyguard in front of Sparks Steakhouse in Manhattan, without the other families' blessings."

I give a low whistle. "Sounds like a helluva hit and a bold move by Gotti."

Curtis smiles. "It was! Some say Gotti didn't need to kill big Pauli because he was going to prison anyway, but we both know sending someone to prison doesn't stop anyone from running their empire. Besides that, Big Pauli had passed over Dellacroce when alive and made a guy named Bilotti the underboss. Bilotti would have followed Big Pauli's orders to make the hit on Gotti and his crew, even from prison."

"What happened to Bilotti?"

"Hahaha. Bilotti got whacked with Big Pauli as they stepped out of their black Lincoln sedan by three handpicked goombahs wearing identical Russian hats and trench coats. Personally, I was glad when Gotti took over. He was from the streets and old school like Mr. DePalma with all those old Mafia codes. Some say Gotti broke all the Mafia's rules, but that's bullshit. He never became a snitch like everyone else, and, like Mr. DePalma, he has rules—unlike José, who knows no rules except those that favor himself. Now that the Feds are taking out these old-school mafiosos, guess what's left?

Watching Rick pitch a fast ball into the catcher's mitt, I shake my head without a clue.

"Just a bunch of cold-blooded cowboys like José, slinging crack, heroin, and cocaine with no rules and no qualms about killing for either personal or business reasons. Hell, his crew would even open up on rivals with innocent families and children in the crossfire. You think DePalma would ever do that?

I shake my head no. "Never."

"Goddamn right he wouldn't. The Mafia even banned killing their rivals by explosives so no innocent bystanders would be killed—old school." Curtis punctuates his words by grinding his cigarette into the side of the picnic table, then letting it drop to the ground.

Striking out his opponent, Rick does a victory dance on the mound as the crowd and his men chant, "Rick Rambo! Rick Rambo! Rick Rambo!"

Rick looks at me and pumps his fist in the air. I smile and return the gesture as everyone on the yard takes notice that I am Rick Rambo's civilian friend and, by extension, I am under his wing.

Curtis looks at Rick, then at me. "You're damn lucky to have that guy on your side. You're virtually untouchable in here. Those guys, like the Mafia, don't have to wear colors or throw gang signs for other convicts to know they're dealing with man-eating lions."

Watching Rick lead his team to victory, I point at my friend. "He's a good guy..."

Curtis cuts me off with a sneer. "That guy is a killer, just like Greg. They're both cut from the same fabric that made them soldiers through and through. Granted, they both follow a code of conduct and a line they won't cross, which is admirable, but they're stone-cold killers nonetheless who will blindly follow orders to the detriment of their enemies. Speaking of man-eating lions and stoned-cold killers, before you got here, the Crips got into a beef with one of those special forces dudes and tried to stab him right over there."

Curtis points to a concrete enclosure off to the side of the main yard where men are playing racket ball.

"Thinking it would be to their advantage, my niggers tried to sneak up on him in a closed area to prevent escape. They didn't have a fucking chance, and that enclosure turned into a killing field. That military cracker disarmed, stabbed, and sliced the shit out of my homies with their own knives after breaking their arms and legs. When the other military inmates on the yard ran to join their brother-in-arms, it was game over. They left five Crips on the ground bleedin' out and one hurt and limping away, screaming bloody murder like a little girl. You think Greg or Rick's friends would ever abandon their brother like my niggers in the hood?"

"Never," I say in admiration.

"Old-School." Curtis and I bump fists.

Curtis reflects. "You gotta admire that type of loyalty when more time is on the line. That's why I respect Mr. DePalma, Gotti, and even Cagnina. No matter what they throw at those guys, they are never going to snitch out the Cosa Nostra."

"No shit!" I exclaim, "Everyone's your friend when the money flows, but when the road darkens, only the loyal will remain."

Curtis looks over at the racket ball court again and expands on the day Achilles came to town. "Because most of the guards also came out of the military, they looked past their brother-in-arms overkill and figured the Crips got what they deserved."

Curtis nudges my arm. "Hell, you know what happened after lock down was over, and they let us out of our cells?"

As I shake my head no, Curtis continues, "The military guys went straight after the Crip's lieutenant who ordered the hit on the special forces guy. When they were through with him, his face was unrecognizable, and they broke almost every bone in his body. We were locked down for another two days over that shit. And again, the guards looked the other way with not one military guy going to the hole, only Crips. Then they shipped their asses off the yard to God knows where. Some of my niggers claimed it was a white and black thing, but it wasn't. It was a loyalty thing that few of them will ever understand."

As I watch Rick high-five his brother-in-arms, I have a whole new respect for that type of shared honor and loyalty that very few will experience in their lifetime.

Taking my last drag, I flip my cigarette into a butt can a few feet away. "I never even considered the guard factor with the military guys, but it explains their favoritism towards Rick and his men. And, I do see your comparison with Greg. I think he does see himself as a soldier for his Mafia friends."

Curtis punctuates. "Damn right he does. He'll follow Gotti into hell and back, just like Rick will do for his men without ever blinking an eye."

"So, if the Mafia has so many rules, then why have the streets of America turned into killing fields with people like José at the helm?"

"Well, it's hard to keep the wolves in check when the Feds are clawing at the warden's door. Look, Mark, the Feds have had a hard-on for the Italian Mafia for a long time. And they are doing everything humanly possible to dismantle all the crime families. In their place are the upstart drug lords, who will kill anyone to make a buck. With the families in disarray, they swoop in to pick up the pieces like vultures. As bad as the Mafia was and is, as I said, they have a code, whereas José and his like have none. They talk the talk, but only Greg and his kind walk the talk. Now they're a dying breed thanks to the Feds, and they have been replaced by guys like José. I'll take a Greg DePalma over a José any day, wouldn't you?"

I nod my head as Rick hits a home run. The crowd cheers as he rounds third, smiles, and gives me the finger.

Curtis laughs, "Well, that's uncivilized."

CHAPTER 15

Curtis glances in my direction then lights another cigarette. "Just watch yourself with José. Ya hear me, my brother?"

"I definitely will, Curtis. Thanks."

As I looked around at the inmates in the prison yard, I knew 80% percent of them were here for drug charges. Most guys involved in the drug business were not like José, determined to build an empire at any cost. They represented a spectrum of people, from those like Curtis, who needed money to survive, to recreational users like me. Then, there were the true outliers like Frank—an upstanding citizen who went to church and worked hard to pay his bills but, in the end, got screwed by the very system he invested in. Ultimately, he felt he had no other choice but to dance with the devil. I chuckled to myself, thinking about some of his crazy antics, when Curtis broke my train of thought with a bump to my arm.

"What's so funny?"

"Oh, I was just thinking about this totally strait-laced guy who got caught up in the drug trade. Man, did he have a wild story."

"You can't leave me hanging like that, brother."

I smile at Curtis as my mind again drifts back to 1999 and El Reno's federal penitentiary. "Well, it all starts with a tragedy..."

Frank has a hint of sadness in his eyes as we play a game of chess in the recreation room. "If she hadn't contracted cancer, I would never have gotten into the drug business."

His words come out of nowhere. Nothing I did or said prompted Frank's confession. At first, I think maybe he's trying to throw me off my game. But, then again, maybe he just needs an ear to bend from a friendly face.

I soften my tone and issue my condolences, "I'm sorry to hear that, Frank. That's really gotta suck."

"Yep. Before the cancer, everything was fantastic. Had a good job as a crop-duster, owned my own plane... but, Jesus man... the damn medical bills—they just kept coming."

"I can't even imagine losing someone loving another person like that."

"Childhood sweethearts, Karen and I. And you don't know the half of it, Mark. We weren't rich, but we weren't poor either. We went to church, and our faith was strong that God would come through in the end. We gave thousands to Oral Roberts Ministries in hope for a miracle, but that miracle never came. When I went to their offices in Tulsa for financial or medical help, they turned me away like I was a leper and said they would pray for me. I sat in my car for an hour, staring at the pair of gigantic praying hands that graces the City of Faith's entrance and cried. I have never felt so hopeless and was at a loss about what to do. Karen's treatments were bankrupting us, and she wasn't getting any better. All I could do was my best, as the love of my life slipped away from me."

Frank moves a knight to counter my pawn as his eyes water. I think he's going to start crying.

"But my best wasn't good enough, and holding everything inside with no one to talk to lead me down to the local crop duster's pub. As I sat at the bar drinking a beer and trying to figure out what I was going to do, a guy—let's call him Jim, sits down beside me, and we start talking about planes. Not even five minutes into the conversation, I break down and just spilled my heart out to the guy. With concerned eyes, he tells me, 'If you don't mind doing something illegal, I know how you can make that money fast.' All I heard was 'money fast,' and two days later, I was flying my plane to Columbia to pick up a payload."

"Jesus. How'd you sell that to the wife?"

"It wasn't hard. I just told her I had a new job opportunity and would be away from home for a few days. Then, I put a full-time nurse on the credit card to take care of her while I was away. I figured if what Jim told me was true, I could pay my debt and, if not, and I didn't make it back..." Frank's voice falters, "...it wouldn't make any difference at that point, anyway. She was on death's door, and I was losing it."

Moving a bishop, I inquire, "So, how'd it work out?"

"Like a motherfucker. After only ten trips, I was sitting on a little over $300,000.00 dollars and had made enough to pay for my wife's treatments and to pay off most the bills we had, including the house."

Frank's face reflects duty and loss as he continues his story.

"My regular routine would be to fly to Columbia, pack the plane full of cocaine and a little weed, then fly back to Florida. After those first ten fights, I was a trusted asset and was making fistfuls of money with the potential for more. Karen even started getting a little better because I was able to pay for the best doctors and treatment money could buy. It gave us hope. Then, our hope ran out as the cancer won and finally killed her. But, I gotta tell you, Mark. I was not ashamed of what I did. I was proud that I was able to give her everything she needed to the end, but once she died, I was totally lost and empty inside. I threw myself into my work and started partying on product inflight."

Frank moves his queen and cracks a big smile. "Do you know why drug-smugglers love crop-dusters?"

With no clue, I shake my head.

"We know how to evade radar. They can't see you if you fly low, and that's where my crop-dusting skills came in handy. When I was about 30 miles out from Florida, I'd drop below 1,500 feet, then gradually lower myself until I was almost skimming the water at about 35 feet. Once I passed the coast, I'd raise her back up to about 1,500 feet and continue along as normal. Usually, we came in over unpopulated areas, but one time I'd partied on the product so hard, I got lost in a storm, and it blew me right over the Clearwater coastline—and right over a crowd of people celebrating college spring break. Just before I reach the shore, I take a big slug of Jack, slit open one of those bags of cocaine, and take a big snort. Then, I bring the plane from 1,500 feet to 30 feet, skimming the ocean. I could see the waves trying to lick the bottom of the plane. So here I come, low on fuel, balls to the wall, and looking like a powdered donut with cocaine all over my face. When I come upon the beach, I could see thousands of young college kids partying on the sand. Several kids raise their beers to the sky, and one young girl even flashes me her tits as I pull my plane skyward. It was fucking amazing that I didn't kill anyone, including myself!"

Frank moves his knight out onto the field of play, lights a cigarette, and muses through a haze of blue smoke. "Then it was over as fast as it started. Everyone got busted and started snitching everyone else out for a lighter sentence. I was pretty low on the totem pole and among the first to go. On my next trip out, they were waiting for me."

Although I know the answer, I ask anyway, "The Feds?"

Frank scoffs, "Do you know anyone else that can fuck-up a good time like they can?"

We both laugh. "So, I'm assuming you would you do it all over again?"

"I've had a chance to think about it, and the answer is that I would in a heartbeat. My wife was dying, she needed my help, and I wasn't going to let my baby down. I think that under similar circumstances, most men that love their wives or kids would have done the same thing."

Leaning back, Frank takes a deep drag off his cigarette. The smoke billowing into the air expands, as do his thoughts. "Let me ask you a question that a psychiatrist threw at me, to better understand my situation and unresolved guilt. A man's wife is dying from a rare form of cancer. The only medication that can save her is excessively expensive and out of reach. Desperate, the man breaks into the pharmacy and steals the drug to save his dying wife. Should he have done it?"

He waits for my answer.

I nod my head and smile. "In a heartbeat."

Frank and I, along with 25% of the other inmates in prison, will never fit society's stereotypical criminal image. In many instances, we were just trying to survive environments and situations that we didn't choose or deserve. We never wanted to be in any type of criminal enterprise or gang and never contemplated or planned to find ourselves in a situation where we would have to murder someone, especially an innocent person. As Curtis pointed out, however, psychopathic killers like José do exist, and they are so dangerous and unpredictable that even hardened criminals, who are usually not opposed to violence, want them taken off the streets for good.

Most inmates I've met wholeheartedly agree that there are certain individuals who belong behind bars forever. It's simply because a small percentage of the criminal population will unblinkingly use wanton, unpredictable violence, and never play by the rules regardless of where they reside. They are a threat to any society they populate, whether in prison or on the streets. They are often not the guy with the face tattoos who appears visibly disturbed. Instead, they're normal-looking people like José, but who possess psychopathic tendencies with a remorseless capacity to murder guilty or innocent people as needed to climb incrementally ahead. Interestingly enough, when describing his own arrest one night while playing cards in El Reno, a guy name Steve Harston made an astute observation with respect to identifying who is a true psychopathic criminal and who is not. I call his one basic tenet "Steve's Rule."

"Yeah, I was a great safecracker," Steve laminated. "Had all the tools and schematics. Then, the Feds started tracking me after I unwittingly heisted some hot ivory they were tracking via Interpol. I thought I was a real gangster and had a drum-fed 12-gauge shotgun to prove it. I also thought I'd fight myself outta any situation until the shells ran out. But all of those fantasies went up in smoke when the Feds moved in on me as I sat in my car, in an underground parking lot."

Steve sighs. "I glance in my rearview mirror and see a guy coming up from behind me, so I pull up my shotgun to fire. And you know what I did? I see the letters "FBI" emblazed on his bulletproof vest, and I hesitate. He probably has intel that I'm armed and dangerous and sees the barrel of the shotgun sticking over the car seat, so he takes his shot."

Looking at our faces, Steve grimaces. "Did I mention I hesitated?

"I hear an earsplitting boom as his bullet rips through the back window, making a big fucking hole and a bigger fucking hole in the front window after it whizzed by, inches from my head. It was at that moment that all that tough gangster shit went straight out the window, and I decided two things. First, I didn't want to go out in a blaze of glory and die. And two, even though I could have blown that agent out of his shoes with my next shot, I know in my heart of hearts I couldn't kill anyone that was wearing a badge. I'm a safecracker, not a killer."

I nod my head in agreement.

A Spanish guy doing time for being a drug mule for the cartel agrees, "Same experience here. I wasn't anybody, but just an ese trying to make a buck for my family when I was pulled over in Chino Valley, Arizona, by Barney Fife. The cartel gave me a machine pistol with instructions to kill anybody that tried to stop their shipment, and I could have wasted the cop, no problem—but I couldn't do it."

A guy in the Mexican Mafia put his two cents on the table. "You should have smoked that po-po, homes! You got thirty-seven years and might have gotten away with it if you did. And, even if you got caught, it's basically the same time. Am I right?"

A black kid agrees. "True that. I'm wasting the motherfucker next time. I got twenty-eight years on a drug-and-gun charge and didn't even kill anybody."

Unfortunately, my observation during my extended incarceration is that this seems to be a growing sentiment among the younger crowd in prison who received mega time for drug charges without committing any murders. They now talk of killing police or witnesses if drugs, guns, or the "three-strikes-and-you're-out" law is implicated. Non-child molester convicts passionately endorse the three-strikes-and-you're-out law as it was originally designed, which was promulgated to stop child molesters. If a pervert molests three times, he receives a life sentence. The problem is that lawmakers, in their infinite wisdom, eventually thought it a good idea to apply this law to all felonies. Now, stealing a carton of cigarettes, breaking and entering, or any other non-violent crime may result in a life sentence. That often leaves a poor, uneducated young adult involved in non-violent crimes with a dilemma—whether to take his chances with the mandate of a life sentence despite the absence of violence or kill to eliminate any witnesses. Listening to most of these urban youths talk, my guess is that the odds you and your families will die if caught in such a scenario are 50/50 or higher.

Greg also mentioned how the prisons and justice system are turning out a more vicious criminal. "Not only do they want to rob ya now, they want to hurt you and your family, too. What a bunch of fucking animals."

That's a lot coming from Greg, but that's what prison or the threat of prison does to some people—it turns them into violent animals. Misguided or misinterpreted legislation such as the three-strikes-and-you're-out law counterintuitively endangers the society it is designed to protect. Unfortunately for me, José is not among those who require a personal dilemma to resort to violence. He fits squarely into that small percentage who require no prodding and use violence as a first-line response to any situation where it may be marginally beneficial.

I need to get back to Greg's unit, so I leave Curtis. While walking off the yard, I playfully give Rick the finger, but Curtis's warning is still playing in my ear. "Just watch yourself with José. Ya hear me, my brother?"

CHAPTER 16

As the weeks pass, I notice José talking to Greg more frequently. He occasionally makes small talk with me but always interjects Greg's or Sammy's name into the conversation when he does. I try to keep my distance, but it's difficult when I'm working on his unit every day.

One evening, as I'm getting ready to hand out food trays to the inmates, Greg shouts from down the hallway, "Hey, Mark! Look what my wife sent me!"

Moving quickly towards me dressed in his pajamas with his house shoes flopping and robe flowing behind him, Greg waves a newspaper over his head like a paperboy on a New York street corner.

A big smile spreads across his face. "Look, Mark! I got a picture of me when I had freakin' hair."

Taking the paper from Greg's hand, I see it's a tabloid rag with a huge picture plastered on its front page that flaunts a smiling Frank Sinatra, who is surrounded by a group of jovial, well-dressed men. Beneath the photo, in big, bold letters, the caption reads: "Sinatra and the Mafia!"

Greg points to a guy wearing a big grin and a well-tailored suit, whose arm is around Frank Sinatra. "Can you believe that, Mark? It's me when I had hair! Not too fucking bad, huh?"

"Lookin' good, Greg. Wow, I can't believe you hung out with Frank Sinatra or had hair."

"Very funny, my friend. And I was playing golf with Frank on a regular basis until he passed away. Besides that, I knew everybody back in the day due to the fucking fact we ran all the big nightclubs. The Westchester was my baby—I built it from a fucking dump into one of the classiest joints in New York, worth millions of dollars. You couldn't get a gig at the Westchester without knowing somebody that knew somebody, if you know what I mean. You know who performed on opening night?"

"Led Zeppelin?"

"Get the fuck outta here. I'm talkin' about real music. Diana Ross performed to a sellout crowd on opening night, followed by Frank, Dean Martin, Johnny Carson, Liza, and Tom Jones—who, by the way, had women throwing their underwear on stage. Now that's some classy music that puts your club on the fucking map, letting the good times and money roll in on a regular basis."

Pointing to an older gentleman that could be my grandfather, I ask, "That old man is in the Mafia?"

Greg looks around to make sure nobody is listening then blurts out. "You better fucking believe he is. That's old man Gambino, who helped finance the Westchester." Greg points to himself and Frank Sinatra on the tabloid. "For whom, as a token of our appreciation, Frank and I personally put this gig together."

Greg begins to reminisce. "To my left is his brother, Big Pauli, who got whacked, leaving John in charge. Greg waves his big finger around the picture naming people from his distant past. "Then you got Tommy." Greg then sneers under his breath as his finger wavers over two other men in the photo. "Then you have these two cocksuckers, Jimmy and Sal—two fucking rats who weaseled their way into the photo. The guys at the bottom are

Joe and Richie "Nerves," my partner and a hell of a consigliere. Both were stand-up guys, in my opinion.

"Looks like good times were had by all."

Greg gloats, "The fucking best! Not only was our club a gold-mine with all the top acts, I bled that bitch dry for the family, and within a year after me and Richie opened the Westchester, I was a made man," He exclaims as he gives a hearty laugh.

I try to give Greg the reaction he's looking for, but I really have no idea who any of the people in the photo are or what they represent. And, even though I'd heard of Frank Sinatra, Dean Martin, and the other entertainers mentioned, they were more in line with my dad's era. Mike suddenly sticks his head out of his office and smiles at Greg as if to indicate he heard all these stories before.

"Hey, DePalma! Leave my orderly alone. I need him getting the food trays ready for dinner."

Greg takes the paper from my hand and shows Mike the picture. "Look at that, will ya? That's me when I had a full head of hair and was on top of the world."

Mike laughs softly. "You were a regular Gorgeous George, but it doesn't look like you're on top of the world at this moment. Now get back to your room so we can start dinner."

Mike returns to his office as Greg lowers his voice and growls. "What a fuckin' screw. Let's catch a smoke after dinner. I need to talk to you in private."

I give Greg a thumbs-up, and he turns and saunters back down the hall, continuing to wave the paper above his head. "Best fucking time of my life, Mark! The best fucking time!"

After dinner is over, Greg and I sneak back to the bathroom to catch a smoke. He catches me off guard with a loaded question. "You know that I trust you, right?"

"Sure, Greg. Why wouldn't you?"

"Exactly. Why wouldn't I? And I hope you know by me trusting you, I consider us friends. So, you can count on me if you ever need my help and, I'm hoping I can count on you for a favor, too."

"Well, I'm honored as long as that favor doesn't jeopardize my departure from this place.

Greg places a gentle hand on my shoulder. "Mark, I would never jeopardize your going home." He points his big finger at me for emphasis, and his voice takes on a serious tone. "You got that?"

I nod my head. "I got it. I just don't want any misunderstandings regarding which road I'm headed down because, at the moment, I'm trying to follow a Buddhist teaching which states: 'There are only two mistakes one can make along the road to truth—not going all the way, and not starting.' And I, my friend, fully intend to follow this truth so that I can walk out of these prison doors forever."

Greg lights and takes a drag off his cigarette, blowing the nicotine-laced smoke into the stale bathroom air. "You and José really should hang out sometime. He's always pulling that same philosophical bullshit too, but with a gangster's twist. However, the idea of following your truth to the end does make a lot of fucking sense if you don't want to look back with any regrets or become a fucking rat. Right hand to God, Mark. I never wanted to be anything else besides the guy in that picture standing with my paisans."

I stand quietly as I listen to Greg's interpretation of the Buddha's message.

"Even with all the bullshit I've had to fucking endure, I wouldn't change who I've been for nothing. It's the only life I've known. I know you don't give two fucks about who I am, but back in the day, not only did I know Johnny and Liza and played golf with Frank, Dean, and Willie Mays, me and the people in that picture ran New York like we were fucking kings. We could get or get away with anything in a New York minute. You know anybody else who can fucking say that?"

"Not at the moment."

Greg takes a drag off his cigarette. "It was a helluva life."

He nudges my arm. "Hey, here's some philosophy for ya. You know what they call guys that don't follow their truth?

I shrug.

"Pussies!"

Our loud laugher reverberates through the bathroom.

"That's pretty good, Greg. I'll have to write that one down as Greg DePalma's Philosophy 101."

With a smile, Greg flicks his cigarette into the urinal. "Get the fuck outta here."

As we exit the bathroom, Greg turns to me and whispers, "Hey. I might have a friend coming to Springfield. Can I count on you to help me take care of him once he's here? It would mean a lot, and I'll return the favor someday. You have my word."

"Who's that?"

Greg winks. "John Gotti. But don't say anything to anybody. Ok?"

"Sure, Greg. It's just between you and me."

When Greg divulges this sensitive information, I immediately think of two things. One is that he's full of shit, and the other is that he's testing me to see whether I can be trusted not to blab this sensational news to another inmate. If revealed, this news would no doubt return to Greg through the prison grapevine and expose me as a gossipmonger who could not be trusted with confidential information.

This type of suspicious thinking occurred because I had the same technique used on me before while incarcerated at a minimum-security state prison by a 28-year-old man named Rocky, who was planning to escape from the Jim E. Hamilton Correctional Center (JEHCC), which was on the northern edge of the Ouachita National Forest in Oklahoma. Late one night, and out of the blue, Rocky's 18-year-old boyfriend came into my room and told me that Rocky had cancer, but not to tell anyone. I didn't and, after a week, Rocky explained it was all a ruse to see if I could keep my mouth shut. As far as gossip is concerned, prison is worse than a small town where everyone knows your business. Once Rocky knew that I could keep my trap shut, he told me he was planning an escape in association with a hit on an inmate. A drug dealer named Jeff planned the hit on another inmate named Kirk, both of whom I knew from Tulsa.

Rocky also explained that he was incarcerated as the result of a botched jewelry store robbery in some small Oklahoma town. "Nobody was supposed to get hurt, my right hand to God. We came in posed as customers and looked around for any problems. Then, as planned, my partner pulled a gun and forced the owner and his assistant to lie on the ground. I had my head in the vault emptying the shelves and saw a huge diamond—just as I'm reaching for it—BOOM!"

The explosive sound startled Rocky, who forcefully banged his head on the top of the vault leaving blood and hair, which the D.A. later used as positive identification. Dazed, he pulled his head out of the vault and saw the assistant manager lying on the floor with his head blown off, his hand on a gun he attempted to pull from an ankle holster. Rocky vomited uncontrollably, either from the concussion or from seeing the man's brains blown across the jewelry store's floor. At this point, his unglued partner screamed at Rocky and the dead man, "I didn't mean to kill him. He was getting ready to shoot us! You stupid fuck! I didn't mean to kill you!"

Rocky sighs with regret. "The owner is now on his knees, hysterically pleading for us not to kill him because he had a family—we didn't but should have. He promises to wait fifteen minutes before calling the cops, but as soon as we leave the store, he calls them. As we run through the forest behind the store with the cops chasing us, I stuffed loose diamonds and jewelry into knot holes and under tree roots. We temporarily escaped and stayed on the run for a couple of days, but we never made it back to retrieve the loot before we were arrested, and it was never found."

Rocky dismisses his misfortune with a tidbit of information and a proposition. "Probably still there and, if you help me, I'll tell you where you can find it."

The short end of this account is that, after I talked to Kirk, he pulled a picture of a beautiful girl and a baby from his wallet before telling me his side of the story, which only involved money and dumb luck. At that moment, I decided I didn't want to be any part of an assassination plot and pulled the plug on the drug dealer's hit on Kirk. I didn't care whether Rocky escaped or not, but I was doing time for a DUI and wasn't a murderer. Years later, I was again certain that I made the right decision after both Kirk and Jeff turned their lives around.

Rocky was, of course, disappointed but told me the show must go on. Two weeks later, he and his boyfriend drove straight out of JEHCC's front gate, wearing stolen guard uniforms from the prison laundry and driving a correctional van that other inmates had been working on in the prison garage. They even exchanged cordial waves to the prison guards before they forever disappeared into the Ouachita Mountains of Oklahoma.

Was Greg playing a game to see if I had loose lips like Rocky had? Or, should I just take everything Greg said with a grain of salt? Three days later, I had my answer and learned that Greg DePalma does not play games or mince words with a person he trusts or considers a friend.

CHAPTER 17

As forecast by Greg DePalma, John Gotti made his appearance at Springfield, with certain sections of the prison on full alert for his arrival, which was not unexpected given his notoriety. All medical prisoners on Greg's unit were confined to their rooms as they escorted Gotti to a restricted area. I was mopping the floor in front of an elevator when a guard walked out of his office and, with the intensity of a drill sergeant, barked an order:

"Face the wall and do not make eye contact with the prisoner!"

Although somewhat surprised as this particular request is a first for me, I comply. A few moments later, I hear the elevator door slide open, then hear the sounds of a prisoner in chains being led off towards solitary confinement, escorted by the footsteps of several guards. Just before they go out of earshot, I hear the prisoner laugh and jokingly say, "So, this is my new fucking home."

Once the prisoner and guards are out of sight, Mike hollers down the hallway, "You may carry on as before!"

Five minutes later, Curtis walks up. "Psst! Come over here for a minute. I got something to tell you."

I push my mop bucket around the corner and ask, "What's up?"

Curtis is beside himself. "You know who they just brought in?'

I play dumb. "I have no idea. The guard told me to face the wall like he was a hall monitor."

"John Gotti, that's who! He was just transferred back here from Marion because his cancer returned, and I hear he only has months to live."

"No shit! Why did they take him to the hole?"

"My guess is officials are worried someone might try to kill him to make a name for themselves. Word through the grapevine is he called one of my brothers at Marion a nigger, and my nigger gave him a black eye. Then, shit hit the fan when John hired the ABs to kill him. My nigger didn't end up dead but was dragged off to the hole and then to some undisclosed prison."

The acronym "AB" stands for the Aryan Brotherhood, one of the deadlier gangs in prison. Their motto is "Blood in, Blood out," which means that you must kill to get in the brotherhood, and the only way out is to die. Some white guys claim to be in the AB and even have "AB" tattooed on their abdomen in an attempt to prove it, but once the imprisoned impersonators are identified by the real Brotherhood, they wish they never heard of them.

Paul, a chess mentor at El Reno and a member of the Dirty White Boys gang, had affiliations with the AB. He told me one of the AB wanna-be's came to El Reno sporting an AB abdomen tattoo he'd gotten out on the street. When he met the real ABs, they gave him a choice—kill a black guy or remove the tattoo. Unfortunately for him, he couldn't pass Steve's Rule and wasn't a killer in his heart-of-hearts. As a result, his heroes held him down and used sandpaper and razor blades to remove the tattoo and resolve the dilemma.

Looking at Curtis, I muse, "The AB are some serious business, but do you think the blacks will try to retaliate, and with Gotti in the hole and unavailable, maybe go after Greg?"

In prison, the blacks, the whites, the South Americans, and many other gangs often work together to make everyone's time easier and to make money. The reason is simple. No individual or gang can supply one's every need in prison—needs that range from alcohol and drugs to steak and pizza. Conflicts inevitably arise. When a member of one group disrespects another group's member, those in charge usually let the subordinates in conflict fight it out mano e mano in a secluded area. This practice cuts down on wanton violence, the inconvenience of everyone being locked down for days and disrupting each groups' ability to profit or carry on day-to-day business. But, when a dispute spills over into a racially-charged hit, the dispute turns into a black versus white thing, and gangs whose members are normally in conflict suddenly unify under the concept of "the enemy of my enemy is my friend."

Curtis shoots back, "You can bet your lily-white ass there's some badass homie just waiting to tag Gotti if they get a chance, but it will be tough with him in the hole. Mr. DePalma should be safe, but hell, who knows what a crack head will do? Hey, speaking of the Gambinos, Mr. DePalma wants to see you ASAP. No doubt about Gotti."

"No doubt."

As I walk to Greg's room, I ponder Gotti's dilemma. Unfortunately, being in the hole doesn't completely protect one from a hit ordered by a gang superior. Case in point: In El Reno, there was a tough-talking guard who constantly bragged he could kick any inmate's ass, whether or not the inmate had a knife. One day, as he led a shackled prisoner from segregation to the medical unit, two Mexican mafia gang members ran up on them with knives and began stabbing the fettered inmate. The tough-talking guard bolted from the scene, screaming like a little girl and leaving the inmate, who had no way of protecting himself, to be brutally stabbed to death. There is still a possibility that someone could still take out Gotti in a similar scenario.

When I find Greg, he's as happy as a clam.

"Hey buddy, did you want to see me?"

"Yes, I do. Did Curtis tell you John was here?

"John who? Gotti?" I sarcastically grin.

"Get the fuck outta here! Fuckin' A John Gotti! I was hoping you could help me out with communicating with him. If you could help me out here, Mark, we would forever be in your debt."

Greg's obvious sincerity and loyalty to Gotti were admirable. Plus, Gotti could use all the help he could get while in the hole. Some people say there are things far worse than being placed in solitary confinement, but I've seen guys go crazy while in the hole. Being locked in a 12 x 9 all day without contact from other prisoners and with their own unchecked thoughts eventually makes them insane. Gotti is dying of cancer and rumored to have only months to live, making his situation even more mentally taxing. The quality of his life during his final months will depend directly on Greg's undying friendship. Greg's loyalty and willingness to do everything within his power to help his friend during his dying days will earn my lasting respect for Greg DePalma.

"Sure, Greg. What can I do to help?"

Greg rubs his hands together. "Well, you're the main orderly up here, so the guard is going to ask you to clean up John's area and bring him his lunch and evening food trays. If you wouldn't mind, I'd like you to slip him a kite."

A kite is an inmate-to-inmate messaging system accomplished by a folded piece of paper with a message on it being passed between prisoners. This is most often a necessary form of communication when one of the inmates is in a restricted area that can only be accessed by an inmate orderly. It's the only way for the isolated inmate to communicate secretly and safely.

Greg hands me three folded pieces of paper. "Please give these to John."

I take the kites from Greg and stick them in my pocket just as the guard bellows, "Food carriers are on the unit. Everyone in their room. Chow time!"

"Gotta go, buddy. I'm expecting a package for our dinner tonight."

Greg pats my shoulder. "I told Sammy we could count on ya. Just keep this between us. Ok?"

I give Greg the thumbs-up as I head down the hall to get ready for mealtime. I anticipate receiving a package hidden in the food carrier as a result of a new arrangement I made with an inmate who works in the kitchen. My previous method was questionably reliable, and I required a more dependable technique to bypass the guards and have more of Sammy's ingredients delivered directly to this floor. Today is the trial run.

Our daily routine commences with me pushing the food carrier down the hall and handing Mike food trays, which he then passes on to the inmates, who are standing in their cells. Most of the inmates know me by now and say hi. Sammy similarly acknowledges me and asks if I'm free later for a game of chess. As I'm handing Mike the last of the food trays, I notice a rather large package at the back of the food carrier. Keeping my composure, I move the package closer toward the front of the carrier with every tray I give Mike until it's easily within reach.

Mike turns to me. "Ok, that's it. Let's head back to my office so I can pick up a few things, and then we'll feed our guest in the SHU." SHU is the acronym guards use for Secured Housing Unit or the hole."

I follow Mike down the hall. As we pass Sammy's room, I grab the package and fling it into his room. Sammy's eyes grow wide, and he flinches as the unexpected package hurls in his direction before landing squarely on the bed next to where he sits eating. Without slowing down, I pass his room and continue to push the food cart down the hall until we arrive at Mike's office. I then ask Mike if I may take a five-minute bathroom break, and, once approved, I run back down to Sammy's room.

When I arrive, the old man is smiling from ear to ear. "You almost gave me a fucking heart attack."

"What's in the package?" I ask.

Sammy retrieves the unwrapped package from under his bed. "Hell if I know. I was waiting for you to get here to open her up."

Sammy's eyes light up like a kid at Christmas when he opens the package. Inside is a pound of choice hamburger meat, chopped onions, peppers, olives, tomatoes, a can of tomato paste, spaghetti, and baggies containing all kinds of spices and herbs.

Sammy stares at me. "Oh, you did good, Mr. Black."

"Gotta jet, Sammy. We're feeding John in the hole."

Sammy becomes animated. "You're seeing John! Let... let me send him a quick kite."

The fat man moves more nimbly than expected as he grabs a pencil and paper, scribbles something down, quickly folds it, and sticks it in my face.

"Thanks, Mark. I really appreciate it."

I pluck it from his hand, and I turn towards Mike's shouts, which are coming down the hallway.

"Where's my orderly?!"

Mike is waiting for me when I turn the corner.

"Grab a food tray and follow me."

Mike jangles a big set of keys in his hand as we walk past the line of no return that leads into solitary confinement, over which inmates are prohibited from crossing without a guard chaperoning them. We walk towards the end of the hallway, where a set of drab yellow prison bars completely cover the hallway from floor to ceiling. A single light hanging from above creates a chiaroscuro effect on Mike and me. Mike turns the key and releases the heavy iron door. Clank!

Past these bars is a small enclosure painted the same stark yellow with two opposing cell doors embedded into the concrete. Each door is fitted with a small window and a slot below known as a "bean hole" through which food trays may be passed.

A set of quizzical blue eyes flash the anger of a caged lion through the door's window to the immediate right. In a rough, unfettered voice, Gotti cracks a joke, "Not fucking filet mignon again."

Both Mike and I stifle a laugh as he opens the door. Mike signals for me to hand the tray to Gotti.

I expected a more imposing figure. When I stepped into his room, rather than the "Dapper Don," I found an older, balding, gray-haired man with a slender build and a tight jaw, which was disfigured from surgery. His commanding personality, however, has not waned as he continues to make jokes.

"Welcome to my fuckin' home."

John's home is a 6' x 12' x 9' cell, which was painted in the same drab yellow hue. In his room, a bed is bolted to the floor, and an aluminum combination sink and toilet stand near the door. Above the sink is a metal mirror with pictures taped to its side, which I assume are of John's family. A very small desk sits below a dingy 4'x4' barred and steel-meshed window, through which I can see inmates on the yard engaging in various activities. Looking back at John, I see lines of stress etched onto his face. I sense an air of sadness, realization, and acceptance of his grim destiny. It must be to keep a stiff upper lip under these conditions, but he pulls it off. Sitting on the bed, he pats the mattress, indicating that I should place the meal tray there.

As I place the tray on his bed, I glance over my shoulder and see Mike walking over to the adjacent cell.

Still leaning in, I grab the kites out of my pocket and toss them to Gotti's side. Without hesitation, he pushes them behind his bed, just as Mike returns. It feels like my heart is going to beat out of my chest as Gotti looks back up, now with the cocky grin and confidence I'd seen in the newspapers.

He sticks out his hand. "The name is John Gotti. It's a pleasure to meet youse."

His grip is firm. "My name is Mark Black. And I wish it were under better circumstances."

Before John can return the banter, Mike chirps in, "Listen, Mr. Gotti. After you're through eating, have your trash ready, so we can pick it up with your food tray."

John grins. "Will do."

After Mike locks the SHU down, we walk back to his office.

"Take 30 minutes for chow and then meet me at my office. Oh, and by the way, that's John Gotti in there."

I wave my hand in the air as I walk away. "That's what everybody keeps telling me."

Mike's astonished voice trails from behind. "Goddamn, word travels fast in here."

CHAPTER 18

While I'm on break eating lunch in the common area, Greg finds me to ask about John's welfare.

"So, how's John look?"

"Well, he isn't the guy I remember from the papers, but he's still cracking jokes."

Greg frowns. "Hey, I don't look like the guy in the paper anymore either."

"You were in the paper?"

"Fucking right I was, and I had a full head of hair, too, if you remember."

"Yes, I do. And you were a regular Gorgeous George."

"Get the fuck outta here. You know, back in the day, I was a real lady's man."

"Really? Who's the hottest woman you've ever dated?"

Sporting a wry grin, Greg doesn't hesitate. "How does Elizabeth Taylor sound? Ever heard of her?"

I look at Greg with amusement and disbelief. "Get the fuck outta here."

He laughs, then flips the script, "Before I forget why I came in here, Sammy is making spaghetti tonight while everything's fresh and wants us there around 4:30."

I give Greg a thumbs up as he turns and walks away, leaving me to finish my lunch. He walks down the hallway while giving a trailing admonition, "Don't be late!"

After Greg leaves and I've eaten lunch, I pick up the inmates' food trays and head back to the SHU with Mike. As soon as Gotti's door opens, he winks and puns, "Long time, no see. What's happening, my friend?"

"You see it."

"No shit." John sneers, eyeing the trash can.

Pulling a small trash bag from my pocket, I bend down to empty John's wastepaper basket. As I remove the trash bag from the can, I notice two kites on the bottom—one with Greg's name written on the front and the other with mine. I take the kites and slip them into my sock while placing a new bag inside the can. Then, I pick up his tray from the desk and walk past Mike to place it on the carrier.

Despite our developing friendship, I never outwardly appear overly familiar with John in order to avoid arousing suspicion, which would result in increased scrutiny of our interactions. John and I purposely keep the conversation light and unassuming. In prison, you don't have any rights to privacy. If a guard suspects any dubious activity, he can shake you down on a whim, anywhere or at any time and without notice. Over the years, I found the best way to stay off the guards' radar is to appear to be a good inmate and let them think they are running the show.

After delivering the food carrier to the kitchen, I find Greg and tell him I'm heading to the bathroom to take a smoke. Once Greg and I meet in the bathroom, away from any prying eyes, I pull out the kites. I hand Greg his and open mine. After quickly reading the kite, I show it to Greg:

Thanks for lookin' out.
John Gotti

I know John's kite would be considered serious contraband if discovered. If caught with it, I would earn a write-up resulting in my privileges being stripped for at least a month, and it could cost me my upcoming release to a halfway house. I tear it into tiny pieces and flush it down the toilet.

"I'm getting too close to home to get caught with this shit."

Greg chuckles. "You should wrap that in saran wrap and stick it in a jar of peanut butter. It's probably going to be worth money one day."

In a place where a fanatical guard can tear your room to pieces and have you stripped naked to search for contraband, I give a half-grin. "One day may never come if I get busted."

Greg chuckles again. "You may have that right."

Greg opens his kite before letting out a "Hmmph?" He then tears it up without letting me look at it.

"I guess Sammy told John we were having spaghetti tonight. You up for trying to get one of these dinners to him?"

"I don't know, Greg. I..."

Greg cuts me off. "Look, I know you don't know who I am or, apparently, Sammy either, which is one reason we like and trust you. But, me and John have this thing..." Greg stumbles with his words, "...and we go way back and, well, fuck. We've been through a bunch of shit together, and John is my friend no matter where the chips fall. Now, I don't want to ask you to do anything you don't wanna do, because I know you're going home soon. But, if you could help me out here, I can help you later when you get out..."

I cut in, recognizing the loyalty of a friend when I see it, and I respect it. "Nah, that's okay. If I can help you out—hopefully without getting busted—I will."

Greg mimics biting down on his fist in a show of heartfelt gratitude.

"I really appreciate this, Mark. Let's go talk to Sammy."

Once we are all together, I come up with a plan to get Sammy's spaghetti dinner into John's room. It's a simple plan, primarily based on the prison rule that all meals served on hospital units must have a metal plate cover or a cloche, with the intent of encouraging sanitary conditions but which also hides the contents of the meal. Through my connections in the kitchen, I plan to obtain a clean plate and cloche and have it delivered to Sammy's room. Sammy will then fill the plate with spaghetti, which I will then deliver to John's room, right under the nose of the guard. Over the next several months, the plan works like a charm and provides John with sorely missed Italian food. John repeatedly expresses his gratitude to Greg and me via new kites.

Life is pretty good at Springfield as I count down my days to going home. On the weekends, Greg and I attend mass, with him still sitting in the back talking to his friend, Tony "Ducks." Greg confides that "Ducks" wanted John whacked at one time, but now all is good between them. And Greg, John, and I always look forward to Sammy's spaghetti dinners. But there is always a monkey wrench lurking in the system. For me, this wrench comes in the form of José Reyes.

Over the next few months, José becomes a permanent fixture on our floor, watching our chess games and demanding to butt in when he wants to play. I suspect that his true motive is to feel me out and try to learn more about Greg's business. Ever since his arrival on Greg's unit, he is obviously very eager with attempts to gain Greg's attention and develop a friendship. His actions are difficult to understand because he doesn't need Greg's money or reputation to survive in prison—José appears to have plenty of help from the outside, and his reputation is far scarier than Greg's.

Today, during a chess match, José again relies on his Machiavelli fixation to tell me why he's enamored with the game, "This is why I love playing chess, my friend. 'To know how to recognize an opportunity in war, and take it, benefits you more than anything else.'"

José cocks an eyebrow. "You know who said that?"

I don't miss a beat. "Machiavelli."

I smile and take his pawn with my knight.

José's eyebrows furrowed. "See, that's what I like about you. You're smart and know when to take advantage."

He scratches his neck. "So, do you agree with Machiavelli's premise?"

"Not really. My battles are within, and I think Machiavelli was commenting on what to avoid in government leaders rather than how to use it against your enemies. As for chess, it's mostly proactive moves building towards a calculated result, right?"

José stares at me like I'm something from the *Twilight Zone.* "What are ya? Some kind of fucking Buddhist Monk? That's some real bullshit. Machiavelli was a genius on how to defeat your enemies."

With a sneer, José knocks my knight over with his bishop. "Take that Kwai Chang Caine."

He grins. "Ever watch *Kung Fu,* the TV series?"

Amused, I smile. "Yes, I did and especially enjoyed the parables and quotes, as in, 'Expect the unexpected.'"

The bishop José just moved had been protecting his king's pawn, which I now take with my queen, preventing any escape by his king.

"'Yippee-ki-yay, motherfucker,' checkmate!" I sit back in my chair, undoubtedly with a smug smile of satisfaction. "That's from *Die Hard."*

José's jaw clenches. "I know where it's from motherfuc..."

Just then, Greg sticks his head in the room. "Hey, Mark. You wanna take a walk?"

José glares at me, then looks at Greg with confusion. Greg thumbs my way. "I told you he was better than you. Did he beat you again?"

José gives his excuse. "He confused me with his Buddhist bullshit!"

Greg cracks a smile. "Never heard that one before. So that shit works pretty good, does it?"

I laugh as I push my chair back to join Greg.

José looks at Greg and nearly begs, "Can I ride in the car, too?"

"Nah, I wanna talk to Mark alone for a minute."

José's face relays hurt feelings, but he nods. "I understand, Mr. DePalma."

Greg and I walk down the hallway leaving José to fume at the chessboard.

"Greg, I don't mind if he comes and smokes with us this one time. Maybe it would give us a chance to be on better terms."

Greg huffs. "He doesn't even smoke. He just wants to hang out with me. Besides, it's better to leave what's said between you and me just between us."

"Hmmm, so... why does José maintain such a disagreeable persona with me?"

As I hold the bathroom door open for Greg, he answers my question, "Well, José is doing a couple of life sentences for murder because people ratted him out. That's gotta piss you off, right? Didn't it piss you off when you were ratted out, and you only got seven years? Multiply that by forever, then put yourself in a wheelchair, and you'll start to get a picture of why he's not the most agreeable person to be around."

After lighting our cigarettes, I ask the obvious, "So, you think you can trust him not to turn on you?"

"He has a short fuse, but don't we all? The main thing is that he's not a rat and, at the moment, that's all I give a shit about."

Greg nudges my arm. "Why, Mark? You don't think you can take a guy in a wheelchair?" He laughs through the smoke. "You fucking worry too much, Mark. He's not a problem."

I force a laugh, but José's explosive temper is a problem in my eyes, and I personally don't trust anyone I don't know without a full body frisk. Since I'm getting out soon, I definitely don't need some hothead jeopardizing my release.

Greg grinds his cigarette out in a homemade aluminum ash tray, then pockets the other half to save for later tonight. He then sighs. "Listen. I got José, so don't worry. Ok?"

I toss my cigarette into a toilet, flush it, and watch it swirl into the abyss. "Thanks, buddy. I appreciate it." But the truth of the matter is, I didn't trust José, especially after listening to Curtis's stories about his instability. Unfortunately, as I walk out of the bathroom after Greg's assurance, unbeknownst to us, José is planning a confrontation in the communal area.

I find Curtis already waiting with the chess board set up when I arrive back at the communal lounge; Charles is quietly reading his *Alcoholic Anonymous* Big Book in one corner of the room. Before I can take a seat, José wheels in behind me, demanding satisfaction.

"I want a rematch."

Before Curtis can answer or capitulate the game out of fear, I respond to the blatant disrespect. "Dude, you're going to have to wait your turn."

In a flash and without further provocation, José pulls off a handle of his wheelchair, the ends of which he has altered into sharpened, makeshift knives. He bellows, "I'LL FUCK YOU UP, PUTA! YOU CAN'T DISRESPECT ME LIKE THAT, YOU SON-OF-A-BITCH!"

His roar echoes down the hall for all to hear. As I take a step back toward the bookshelves, I see Curtis recoil in fear while staring at José.

José points the sharpen handle at Curtis. "WHAT THE FUCK ARE YOU LOOKIN' AT, YOU MOTHERFUCKIN' NIGGER?!"

Charlie doesn't even flinch as he calmly looks over his glasses to survey the situation. My assessment is that José is purposefully blocking the door to prevent any escape from his maniacal assault. I'd been in prison long enough to know that when the shit hits the fan, you don't think—you just act and go into combat mode. Without hesitation, I use my foot to push the card table toward José's wheelchair, blocking his mobility. Chess pieces tumble all over the floor as I back towards the large, heavy bookshelf and ready myself to knock it over onto José if he makes any movement towards me.

Suddenly, Slim sticks his head through the door to analyze the situation. Like a box turtle sensing danger, he quickly withdraws to a safer environment. Curtis remains frozen in place as I see Charles calmly put his book down in the chair beside him, stand, and give José an order, "You better holster that shit right now, cowboy, or I'll..."

José cuts him off in midsentence and screams, "SUCK MY DICK, CRAYFISH BOY! COME AND GET SOME YOU PUNK-ASS BITCH!"

The crazy Cajun, caught off guard, stares wildly at José for a second. Then all hell breaks loose. Charles picks up a chair and advances towards José like a lion tamer, screaming, "I'LL TIP YOU OVER AND STOMP YOUR FUCKING BRAINS OUT ALL OVER THE CONCRETE FLOOR! YOU FUCKING PIECE OF SHIT!"

José lifts his makeshift knives higher in the air to fend off the oncoming blows, just as Slim sticks his head back into the room to warn in a hurried voice, "The guard's coming! The guard's coming!"

Just before the guard enters, José holsters his weapon, and Charles puts down the chair.

Mike glances around at a room in disarray, then abruptly stares at José and demands, "What the hell is going on in here? I could hear you yelling all the way down in my office."

I observe a complete transformation of José's demeanor as it switches into one of a delightful, decent human being. He calmly tells the guard, "Nothing going on here, sir, just a little misunderstanding."

The tension in the room is as thick as cordite over a battlefield. Mike studies José's composed face in comparison to Charles's enraged, reddened face. He then flips his gaze to Curtis's fearful eyes, followed by studying my "what-the-fuck-just-happened" expression.

"Sure doesn't look like it to me."

Curtis interjects, "It's okay now. We're okay."

"I don't really give a flying fuck what's okay. Clean this shit up! As for you..." Mike points at José, "...get back to your room."

Mike leaves in a huff with José in his wake. But just before he exits, José turns back to give all three of us a sharp, menacing glare. Charles glares back and mouths, "You're fucking dead, bitch!"

Once José leaves the room, Charlie scowls. "I'm not waitin' for that crazy fucker to sneak up behind me. I'm gonna crack his head open and make it look like an accident."

Curtis interjects, "I wouldn't do that, man. José's crazy."

Charles looks at Curtis and beats his chest. "Fuck that punk. I'm crazy!"

Curtis interrupts, "But you don't know who he is..."

Charles interrupts Curtis with words that drip vindictiveness and hate. "I don't give two fat fucks who that guy is. My brothers and I are going to beat that asshole down with his own wheelchair handle. And then, I'm going to personally rip out his catheter and pour his own urine on his face.

Charles storms out the door muttering below his breath, "Crayfish boy. Fuck that motherfucker!"

As much as Curtis may not want to believe it, the crazy Cajun was right. As a military prisoner, Charles was part of an elite brotherhood of trained killers out of Leavenworth. All he had to do was tell them José threatened him, and they'd make José pay in spades and blood.

Later that night, back on my own unit, Rick grabs my arm and pulls me into a two-man cell where six men have come for business.

"Get in here, Mark. You need to hear this."

With a twinkle in his eye, Rick unveils their plans. "We'll make masks out of t-shirts and, when Mark gives us the word, we'll catch that fucker in the shower. Blake, you're in charge of wrapping a wet towel around his head to muffle his screams. Then we flip him out of his wheelchair and stomp on his arms and hands until they're no longer useable."

"Fuck yeah!" Charlie gloats. "I'm busting his teeth out with that fucking wheelchair handle!" Everyone bursts out laughing but me.

Most people don't realize that prison fights are hardly ever man-on-man. Your enemy comes out of the shadows to exact revenge, just like the Special Forces. This shower attack thing is nothing new. In El Reno, the Mexican gangs began stabbing rivals in the shower while they had shampoo in their eyes. It was like the movie, *Psycho,* on steroids. And while I'd become desensitized to this type of horrific violence over the years in prison, I didn't laugh because, somewhere deep inside, I was still hanging onto a shred of humanity.

Curtis's brothers had their guns locked and loaded for tomorrow. I have no illusions and know the score—it's time to stand aside and let prison justice be served. One of the special forces guys states their motto, "Remember, everyone. Speed, surprise, and violence of action are how we are going to make this fucker pay."

Blake, the big-muscled black guy, bumps his chest against Charles's while chanting, "Heartbreakers and lifetakers, my nigga!" It's like they're planning a mission in Afghanistan. No amount of money, notoriety, street creed, or other influence will save José Reyes now.

CHAPTER 19

I walk into the yard the next day before work and sit on a picnic bench. I close my eyes and enjoy the sun's warmth upon my face, think, and mutter softly, "Well, this is going to be a fucked-up day..." When, out of nowhere, THUNK! Startled, I open my eyes to see that Greg has rammed his wheelchair into the picnic table.

He smiles a toothy grin. "Excuse me, sir. Do you have any Grey Poupon?" Despite the seriousness of the day, I can't help but laugh. But Greg's expression quickly deviates to one of concern. "Hey, I heard what happened earlier. You okay?"

"Yeah, but it's not over. I think José is through with money."

Greg cocks his head. "What are you talkin' about, Mark?"

"José threatened all of us in the lounge, including Charles. If the guard hadn't come in when he did, one of them would be dead right now, and I'm betting it would have been José. Then, as José was leaving, he glared back at us like there was more to come. As you know, no one is going to wait to be stabbed in the back."

"Yeah, no one in their right mind is going to wait to get whacked. Just ask John. And he threatened the crazy Cajun, huh?" Greg snickers.

"Yep, called him crayfish boy and told Charles to suck his dick..."

Greg finds this absolutely hilarious and laughs so hard he starts coughing.

"...and you know Charles and his brothers in arms aren't going to let that stand. José crossed a red line, and they are going after him today to make him pay."

Lighting half of a cigarette, Greg takes a drag. "God, you gotta love those guys. Are you involved?"

"I'm giving them logistics on Mike and intel on José, but Rick told me to stay out of the fight because I'm going home soon."

Greg snorts. "A true friend indeed. Can you give me a few more details?'

Greg listens intently as I describe the plan in more detail. Inmate rules dictate, of course—if Charles and I don't stand up for ourselves, we're punks while snitching on José is totally out of the question. And nobody is willing to spend the rest of their time looking over his shoulder, waiting for José to exact revenge. For all intents and purposes, José brought the wrath of the military inmates down on himself.

Greg appears impressed as he listens to our plans before giving his opinion, "Forget about it, will ya? And let me see what I can do to smooth this shit over between everyone."

"Forget? How can I..."

"Listen. I can talk to José and get him to calm down. I know him from the street. Nothing's going to fucking happen."

I wasn't so sure Greg realized that these military guys were not going to back down from a fight due to the fact that they strictly adhere to both military and inmate codes—if someone threatens you and you don't retaliate, you're a punk. Even though these military guys are not a gang, per se, fighting for respect and money, they do fight for honor. Most of them know much more about killing than the other inmates here. Hell, everyone knew that if you fucked with one of the military's own, you could expect hell to come to dinner—today, José was the entrée.

"What about the military guys?" I quip.

"I know a few of these guys, and most are reasonable men. The crazy Cajun is fucking crazy as advertised, but he's going home soon, too. So, he has an incentive to cut the crap before more time is doled out or shit gets outta hand. However, I do need you to talk to your friend, Rick, and his special forces buddies. They're the wild card, and I know Rick doesn't like guys like me."

"Because you're in the Mafia?" I jest.

"Something like that. Look, if you will talk to your friend, I would consider it a personal favor."

I laugh as I tease him, "You're going to owe me a million bucks before it's all said and done."

Greg rubs his chin. "Like I said. I know that you don't know who I am, but a guy like me can help out a guy like you once you're released. Let's head for the door to leave this shit hole, Mark, and put this crap behind us."

At the moment, it seemed like I was doing all the favors, and I did find it a little strange that Greg already knew who the key players in José's planned attack were, but this is prison. And, Greg was right. I've seen the best-laid plans in prison spin off into clusterfucks, where all involved end up either dead or doing more time.

"May I ask why you want to save José?"

Sporting a confused look, Greg lifts his hand up in the air. "What? I can't be a nice guy?" Then he chuckles. "Nah, I have my reasons. Just trust me on this one, and I'll tell you later. Ok?"

"I'll see what I can do. I suppose a diplomatic solution is always better than violence."

Greg guffaws. "Hey, I wouldn't go that far."

Laughing again, I high-five Greg's raised hand.

"Hey, Mark. You think you can push an old man back to his unit? I wheeled myself all the fucking way out here on my own, so we could talk in private. See how much I fuckin' care?"

While I push Greg through the corridors back to his unit, we talk about Rick and the other military guys on my unit. Suddenly,

Greg blurts out, "I know your friend doesn't appreciate the business I'm in, but I've always been a good soldier, too. And, even though I have regrets pertaining to my personal family, especially my son, I've had a helluva life, Mark. I've always kept my word, and that's why you can count on me. How the fuck do you think I made it this long without getting whacked? I don't fuck over my friends. Remember me telling you about Elizabeth Taylor?"

"Yes, I do. I was in love with her at one time, and, quite frankly, I thought you were bullshitting me."

Greg grins. "Who wasn't? And I wasn't bullshitting you, either."

"Remember when I told you I dated her? I wasn't joking around. I knew her and Richard Burton personally."

I didn't see that coming. "Wow! Really?"

"Yeah, back in the day when I ran that club in New York, I told you about where all the A-listers performed. Hell, like I said, at one time, we ran all the entertainment joints. Because of that, I've hung out with or dated more celebrities than most."

As I wheel Greg to his unit, he brags, "You probably won't believe this, but I've known Elizabeth Taylor for a very long time."

I'm again surprised. "I thought she was in love with Richard Burton."

"No doubt about that. But Burton was a fuckin' drunk, off-set, on-set, wherever, and a womanizer. Liz looks like she can take on the world, but even the toughest broad can only take so much, and then they need real friends like me..." Greg sneers, "...instead of those two-faced, plastic, exploiting, Hollywood cocksuckers who use you then set you aside like yesterday's trash. I was a true friend. You think anyone fucked with Liz when I had her back? Not on your fucking life. Too bad Marilyn didn't have somebody like me protecting her back. We had some good times, her and me, and she's a helluva woman."

"Well, there's one memory to hold on to."

"You better fucking believe it is. I loved Liz."

Greg changes gears. "Speakin' of friends, don't forget to talk to your military buddy today."

I push him into his room while reassuring him, "Yeah, yeah, I won't forget. I really don't want to be involved in something like this before I leave."

"My sentiments exactly."

Greg stands up and changes his shirt. "Well, I got people to see and people to do." Laughing at his own joke, he bids me farewell. "I'll talk to you later, Mark."

Mere hours before José takes his daily shower and is scheduled to receive the beating of his life, I take my lunch break and make my way back to my unit where Rick is waiting for me.

"Hey, Rick, I need to talk with you."

Rick lowers his voice. "Take a walk with me."

Rick delivers the latest breaking news as we walk down the hall. "Guess what? Your friend, DePalma, headed us off at the pass and said you were having second thoughts about José Reyes. Is that true?"

I mused to myself, Wow, that old man really gets around.

"Well, that's not exactly what I said, but yeah, if we can end this diplomatically, I'd prefer that route instead of the alternative."

Rick scoffs, "I'm not much of a diplomat, but it seems that's what Charles wants, too. He's ready to go home and put all this bullshit behind him."

With a grimace, Rick points his finger at my chest. "But you tell DePalma that if José touches you or one of my brothers, there will be no further negotiations. I'll personally be coming for José with my claws sharpened. You tell DePalma that, word for word."

"I will, Rick. Thanks, buddy. It's really appreciated."

He holds out his fist. "Semper Fi, Motherfucker."

CHAPTER 20

O ver the next couple of weeks, without any further apologies or threats from anyone involved, all animosities seemed to melt away like nothing ever happened. Although José is no longer confrontational, he is always watching in the background and moving ever closer to Greg. Greg, Sammy, and I keep the spaghetti dinners and kites flowing to John. During one visit to John's cell, while emptying his trash bucket, I remarked about what a nice-looking family he had, which set off an unexpected tirade.

"I'm proud of my son, John Jr. You'd like him. He has what it takes and is his own man."

Looking at John Jr.'s picture, you could tell he wasn't a bullshitter, and he had the same cocky good looks as his Dad.

"Looks like a good guy who would give you a hand or a fist depending on which side of the fence you're on."

"Fucking right he would! I know you ain't supposed to have favorites, but I love that kid and am goddamn proud of the man he's become."

Rubbing his face, John gazes out the dusty steel grate and barred windows and waves his hand through the air. "The others are acting like a bunch of fucking niggers."

Shocked, I ask, "How's that?"

John begins to raise his voice, "Oh, you know—that fucking nigger shit where you don't have rules and don't live by a code of honor. It's always about 'I'm going to get mines' without even a fucking thought of loyalty. That's why I respect your military friends' motto, 'Death before Dishonor.' And, it's the reason I'll never snitch on my family no matter what they do to me. Right hand to God, Mark. I've come to realize that, except for my son and a few others, blood can't be counted on when the fucking wheels fall off. Did you know some of these people I helped in the world act like it's too much of a fucking annoyance either to write or come see me, and if they do, they act like it's a fucking inconvenience. That's nigger shit!"

John had a way of going from 0 to 120 in a millisecond, prompting the guard standing outside the gate to ask, "Is everything okay in there?"

I empty his trash, then grab a broom and begin to sweep his cell. John has a look of disgust not directed at me, but rather caused by reflection regarding the whole situation he described. He pulls at his shirt to compose himself. Then just as quickly as his outburst began, he falls back into his usual calm persona and, with a forced grin, tells the guard, "We're just talkin' amongst ourselves, and I got a little excited getting this stuff off my chest with Mark."

Fortunately or not, depending on how you look at it, I have the type of personality that seems to make people feel comfortable discussing their problems with me. I have considerable empathy with John's situation and his not having anyone else to talk to on a regular basis.

John rubs his head. "It's this goddamn place. Gives you time to think and see that blood's not always family or vice fucking versa. You're supposed to be able to count on family."

Sadly, I learned this same lesson during my first year in prison years ago, when family and friends started to fade, and it became obvious what they'd always been—people whom you could never really count on.

"Boy, isn't that the truth?" I retort.

John stares out his single barred window, replying, "Fucking sad but true. Wish I would've fucking known this shit when I was on the streets. I would've whacked and smacked a lot more ass out there." He laughs at his own joke.

Raising my eyebrow with an upward nod, I voice my agreement, "Don't we all?"

Outside the cell, the guard gives his best shot at levity and expediency, "Hey, you guys aren't planning on taking a long hot shower together, are you? Hurry up. I got other shit to do!"

John and I both give each other a WTF look and, as I turn to go, John grabs me by the shoulder and whispers. "Tell Greg to be outside my window after chow." I acknowledge with a nod.

On several occasions, prison officials warned Greg DePalma to stay clear of Gotti's window, but the old man's loyalty to his friend never wavers. To ensure John is not without human contact, most days, Greg sits outside his window in his wheelchair, talking until the guards run him off. John is dying of cancer and only has months to live. For him, this is it. And the quality of his life in the coming months will depend solely on Greg's undying friendship. To Greg's credit, I see him doing everything possible to help his friend in his dying days, a loyalty that solidifies my respect for Greg DePalma.

John frowns. "I love that old fuck. Greg's made a lot of mistakes, but haven't we all?" Then, with a smile of pride and satisfaction, John gives an assessment of his old friend. "But you know what? He's always stuck to the fucking rules and never tried to be something he wasn't, unlike a lot of the cocksucking rats that stab you in the back. Loyalty! It's what we used to have back in the day, and Greg has always been loyal and... well, you gotta respect that. Am I right?"

"Absolutely."

I gather my cleaning supplies, and the guard escorts me away from the SHU. Looking back towards John's area, I see his bespectacled face staring through the small window on the door, making him look smaller, older, and isolated.

As the guard and I leave the restricted area, he remarks. "I heard you and John talking in there about finding out who your friends are when you are in prison. Same shit happens when you go to war, too. Friends say they will write but never do. Girlfriends say they will wait forever but end up fucking their ex-boyfriends six months into your deployment, and your country basically abandons your ass if you make it home. I know this shit all too well."

Looking down at the ground, I shake my head as my voice trails off, "My girlfriend made it two years..."

As we walk down the hallway, I remember sitting in a windowless 20x20 room with 30 other inmates waiting to be processed into the state penitentiary, when an old black inmate delivered an anecdotal warning to a black gangbanger who was new to prison life. I can hear a guard inform us that we'll be led out in threes to have our heads shaved, and then they'll issue us our toiletry items and an orange jumpsuit. An older Native American prisoner with long hair tells the guard that he has never cut his hair and refuses to have it cut based on religious convictions. Sneering, the guard lays down Oklahoma's justice system policy on religious tolerance, "I don't give two shits about your religious beliefs! You're either going to get your haircut, or you'll sit right here eating sack lunches of baloney sandwiches for the rest of your sentence." Glaring at the other thirty men, his voice drips with malice. "Any more demands, numb-nuts?"

No one says a word.

"That's what I thought, maggots!" Then he turns and slams a heavy steel door behind him. KaBam! Once the room stops reverberating, the young gangbanger begins throwing gang signs, telling everybody how he's not afraid of the po-po. The older black man who was sitting in the back asked the kid why he didn't say anything when the guard was in the room. The youth ignores the old man's questions and continues bragging about how his homies are going to take care of him in prison and raving about how his loyal gang members are going to send him money while his girlfriends will be visiting every week to supply him with sex and drugs.

The older man rubs his head as if nursing an excruciating migraine before he explodes. "Shut up! Shut the fuck up!" The youth stops his rhetoric and stares at the old man, who has tears in his eyes and is seething in anger.

The old man speaks sternly and with an eerie calm. "You don't even know what the fuck you're talking about. Let me tell you what's really going to happen. Your fucking homies are going to abandon you in here to rot. They're not going to send you one fucking red cent. As a matter of fact, they're probably banging your girlfriend right now as we speak. And the only person that's going to come see you, if you're lucky, is the person you treated like crap all your life—your mother." His eyes then hazed over as he lapsed into a thirty-year-old reminiscence of when he once walked in the kid's shoes. But the gang member waved off the old man's nuggets of truth.

"Shut up, old man! You don't know what you're talking about." But the old man did know exactly what he was talking about. In the following days and weeks, the young gang member's buddies will abandon him, and his girlfriends will never write. Left without financial resources, he will slip into debt to predatory inmates who pimp him out for cigarettes like a common prostitute. But for now, he just keeps bragging, unaware of his future.

Prison is a tough place where you learn who are your true friends. But, inevitably, the rug will be pulled out from beneath everyone's life and force each to confront the true meaning of loyalty and friendship—including the notorious, streetwise John Gotti.

CHAPTER 21

As Christmas and the new year approach, Greg, Sammy, and I begin to secure items for the holidays. First on the list are steaks, which are only served to prisoners at Christmas, although the guards take the best cuts of meat for themselves. My connection with an inmate who cooks for the guards and Greg's access to a little cash dramatically increased the likelihood of checking this item off the list. We were able to arrange a purchase of large quantities of quality steaks from the guard's cook. Additionally, for this year's festivities, Greg bought four ounces of Crown Royal to toast in the New Year at $150 an ounce, which is hidden inside one of the large deliveries of meat.

It is to our good fortune that it snowed almost every day leading up to Christmas and New Year's Eve. I am able to take full advantage of the winter flurries by obtaining the large quantities of steak and then refrigerate them on a window ledge behind my bunk, camouflaged with snow. Without fail, we make sure John receives his fair share. Now when John says his usual, "Ahh, for Christ's sakes, not filet mignon, again," it always elicits a laugh from the guard; there actually is filet mignon his plate.

The holidays are also a time when inmates expect a visit from their loved ones. It's a pretty big deal, and most everyone has a special set of pressed khakis they wear for the occasion. The day my parents are scheduled to come, I'm waiting at work in my best khakis, handing out food trays with Mike. I grab John's food tray, and the guard and I head to the SHU. When John's iron door opens, I see he's wearing his best-pressed khakis, too.

"You're looking sharp today, Mark. You getting a visit?"

"Thanks, John. You're looking pretty sharp yourself."

"They don't call me the Dapper Don for nothing." We all have a hearty laugh at the irony of the contrast between John's khaki attire and his tailored Brioni suits from his Dapper Don days.

"And, yes, I am expecting company. Thanks for asking. My folks are coming in from Oklahoma. Are you getting a visit, too?"

"Your parents sound like good people. Yeah, my favorite boy came down from New York today to see me. So how do I fucking look?"

The pride in John's face is unmistakable.

"As dapper as ever."

John gives me a belly laugh. "Get the fuck outta here."

I place his food tray on his bed and toss his daily kites behind it as he gives me a wink and asks, "Do you think you can empty my trash?"

Pulling a small plastic bag from my pocket, I bend down to change the trash liner and pick up the outgoing kites. There are quite a few.

John's face brightens, and with a big smile, he states, "It's days like these that you really appreciate the people who actually give a shit about us. I wish my son and I were visiting in the general population room. I'd come over and say hi and let you meet him. But, what the fuck, huh? Maybe another time. Don't forget to tell your parents that John Gotti sends his regards. I really hope youse has a good visit."

"Thanks, John. I will. I hope you have a good visit with your son, too."

Later, when I meet my parents in the prison's visiting room, I tell them John Gotti said hello and that his son, John Jr., is coming to see him today. As my dad immediately begins talking about *The Godfather* movie and his fascination with the Cosa Nostra, in struts an imposing John Jr., dressed in black, hair slicked back, and with a gold chain around his neck. He looks every bit the mafia tough guy. A guard greets him at the visitors' desk and then leads him back into a restricted visiting area for inmates doing time in the SHU.

John Jr. follows the guard and swaggers out of view, but when he exits the restricted area a short time later, the tough guy persona has vanished; instead, a visibly shaken man emerges. Tears streak uncontrollably down John Jr.'s cheeks as he tries to hide his face and wipe them away. His distress is, undoubtedly, caused by seeing his father in the inescapable clutches of cancer as well as the Federal Bureau of Prison's draconian solitary confinement. Devastated, John Jr. brings his hand up to massage his eyebrows as his massive chest heaves a sigh before walking out the front door.

My mother states the obvious. "You sure can tell he loves his father."

I tell my parents about John's favoritism towards his son. Although theirs is probably not a normal father and son relationship, it is obviously marked by a profound love and respect that any father or son would be proud to experience.

As I serve John his dinner later that evening, I can tell he had been crying, too, and he seems quite depressed.

I try to cheer him up by blurting out, "Fuck the feds!"

John smiles. "Yeah, fuck the feds."

Mike sticks his head into John's small room. "Hey, hey, hey, come on guys, I'm standing right here."

Grinning at Mike and John, I explain my "fuck the feds" outburst. "Nothing against you, Mike. I just remembered when I was in the SHU at the Oklahoma City transfer center and saw "Fuck the feds" written inside a big penis that was drawn on a wall."

145

A broad smile grows across John's face. "You were there? That was fucking me! I drew that!"

"I know!" I exclaim. "I saw your name under the big dick."

John laughs. "That's a fucking John Gotti original, and I even had to use one of those shitty little golf pencils."

As John and I share a laugh, Mike throws in his two cents, "You do know that it's a federal offense to destroy or deface any federal building with a sentence that carries up to $250,000 dollars in fines and up to 10 years in jail."

John interrupts, "Hmmph! Get the fuck outta here!"

For a moment, there is silence as we stand there with stupid looks on our faces. Then everyone erupts in laughter so hard we have tears rolling down our cheeks. That leaves John in better spirits than I found him—mission accomplished!

Later that night, when we take our bathroom smoke, Greg asks if I saw John Jr.

"Yes, I did, and it was damn sad. He left with tears in his eyes. You could really tell he loves his father and that John loves him, too."

"Yeah, you got that right. He's a good kid, and John is incredibly proud of him. Hell, I'd fuck Phillis Diller to have a son like that."

Reflexively, I punch Greg in the arm. "Well, at least she has enough money to buy you dinner first."

Greg starts wheezing in between guffaws.

I hand John's kites to Greg, and he opens one that is filled full of betting slips.

Greg fumbles the betting slips through his fingers and laughs. "Just between you and me, John will bet on a fucking cockroach race and, nine times outta ten, he'll lose that bet. But he loves to gamble and ain't gonna stop just cause he's in that federal shithole. Plus, it's gotta help with the fucking boredom of the hole. Am I right?"

I am aware that bookmakers and betting are prevalent in prison, with many inmates undoubtedly participating out of the extreme monotony of penitentiary life. I give Greg an affirmative nod.

After a few more puffs, we leave the bathroom. As we walk down the hallway, I inform Greg that I acquired the Crown Royal for our New Year's Eve's festivities. Greg grabs me by the arm and looks me in the eyes with the sincerity of a good friend. "I just want you to know that I really appreciate what you've been doin' for us lately."

Patting him on the back, I return the sentiment, "What are friends for?"

"Exactly! Hey, by the way, what do you do when you're not behind bars?"

I think Greg was expecting me to say something criminal, but I tell him the truth. "I like to paint and draw."

"Are you any good?"

"Well, I probably need further study, but I'd like to think there's something there."

"How would you like it if I put you under the wing of a famous artist as his apprentice and get your paintings in a couple of high-class galleries in New York?"

"No shit?"

"No shit. I know a few people. Before you leave, we'll exchange numbers, and I'll make it happen. It's the least we can do. I do, of course, require a 15% managerial fee from every painting you sell. But I swear I'll personally handle any problems you run into while you're in New York. We'll both make some money, and you'll become famous. How's that sound, my friend?"

Again, I don't know whether to believe Greg's grandiose plans for my future or not, but I do sense his sincerity and thank him for the offer.

"Sounds great, Greg. I appreciate you looking out."

"After everything you've done? Fucking forget about it. And I mean that. This comes with John's blessings."

Once Greg walks me to the elevator door so that I can leave for the evening, I stand in the elevator's doorway where Greg conveys that Sammy is going to cook us a meal fit for a king on New Year's Day. Giving Greg the thumbs-up, I press the elevator's down button. Just as the elevator door begins to close, I notice José sitting in the shadows, watching, listening, and taking mental notes on our every move. I'm not sure what he's up to, but it seems like he's trying to collect intel for some hidden agenda, which, I'm hoping, doesn't involve any of the business between Greg and me with me so close to going home.

As New Year's Eve rolls in, José is still in my peripheral, and Mike takes a two-week vacation. Mike's absence leaves an older guard to fill his position temporarily, whose every conversation revolves entirely around his upcoming retirement. When the guards are away, the inmates will play, and my motley crew intends on taking full advantage of this new guard's lackadaisical attitude.

Greg and I start by bringing our New Year's supplies straight through the elevator in wheelchairs and right past the guard's door. For his part, Sammy makes an over-the-top spaghetti dinner with French bread, and I secure us a bottle of wine. Greg's holiday benevolence even includes Luigi and Mario, who receive a taste of Sammy's masterpiece and wine. But Sammy doesn't share Greg's holiday attitude, and he does not allow the misfits to sit in his room while we are eating.

Even John seems in good spirits when I deliver his special food tray filled with Sammy's spaghetti dinner, a glass of wine hidden in a juice box, and one ounce of Crown Royal concealed within a carton of milk. As I place John's food tray on his bed, I take Greg's kites out of my pocket and toss them to the side of the bed, and we wish each other a Happy New Year. I then quickly turn to replace the trash liner and see only one kite, which is addressed to Greg, Sammy, and me. As I slip the kite into my sock, I hear the guard shuffle up behind me.

"So, you're John Gotti?"

"In the fucking flesh. Would you like to see my dick? It's way bigger than people say it is."

I start to laugh when the guard sneers with disgust. "Well, that's just plain rude. Orderly, grab that trash. I think we're through here."

I look back at John, and he gives me a heads-up and a cocky grin. For an instant, he becomes the young, tough, defiant John Gotti who ruled the streets of New York.

The guard mumbles to himself as he walks out of the SHU, "One more week of this shit is all I have to take, and then I'm out of this clusterfuck."

When we get back to his office, he tells me not to bother him again for the rest of the night. I give him a thumbs-up and put my cleaning supplies away before heading straight to Sammy's room, where we are to meet and toast in the New Year. Sammy and Greg are already sitting on the edge of the bed waiting for me with our meals on a bed tray.

I pull up a chair and take out John's kite as Sammy begins to pour the Crown Royal into our coffee mugs.

Greg gestures at me to hand him the kite, then opens it and reads it out loud.

Happy New year, my Pasians!
Saluti, to this thing of ours!
Fuck the feds!
—John Gotti

Greg grabs his coffee mug and raises it towards Sammy. "To John and this thing of ours."

He then raises his cup to me. "And, to the friends we meet in places like these."

In unison, we all click our plastic coffee mugs together as I mimic their gestures of friendship.

"Saluti!"

149

Closing my eyes, I enjoy the sensation of the golden amber liquid burning slowly down my throat. When I open them, Sammy is looking at his empty cup.

"I think I'm going to cry."

Greg takes the kite, sets it inside an empty tuna can, and sets it on fire. Then he fills our coffee mugs with the last of the Crown Royal. We all watch John's kite ignite quickly into flames, then reduce to ashes. Its embers glow as Greg puts a lid on the can to reduce the smoke. Sammy gazes at the tuna can and reflects, "I suppose everyone dies, but until then..."

In unison, we finish the last of the Crown Royal and bring in the New Year with three words, "Fuck the feds!"

CHAPTER 22

January passes with the monotony you'd expect of prison life. Charles left on parole without announcing his departure to anyone on Greg's unit. Things are quiet until the middle of February when Curtis brings me the latest news.

"Watch out! Greg DePalma is on the warpath."

I ask for details, but Curtis has no idea what set Greg off, except that it seemed to stem from a visit earlier in the afternoon. When I walk by Greg's room to inform him that I'm going for a smoke, he's writing furiously on a kite.

"Hey buddy, if interested, I'm headed to the bathroom to take a smoke break."

An obviously irritated Greg dismisses me with a wave of his hand without even looking up.

Getting the hint, I continue to the bathroom alone. As I begin to enjoy a cigarette near the back by a urinal, a very incensed Greg DePalma storms through the bathroom door without saying a word. He walks to the back of the bathroom, lights a cigarette, and stares at the urinals like he wants to smash them to pieces.

"That fuckin' cocksucker is gonna pay! Who the fuck does he think he is?"

I learned a long time ago that, in prison, guys will abruptly explode for a variety of reasons that are well beyond their control—from girlfriends who are now banging their best friends to not being able to attend a loved one's funeral. I also learned that during these ticking scenarios, it's better to just listen and let them blow off steam.

"Shouldn't fuckin' matter if I'm in here or not! If that motherfucker thinks he can fuck me or my family over just because I'm in prison, he's got another think coming. I'll have that motherfucking cocksucker whacked before I let that piece of shit disrespect me like this."

Greg takes a deep drag from his cigarette as he tries to regain control. I freeze and remain silent as smoke billows out of Greg's mouth like smoke from that of an aging dragon with one last kill in him. Looking into Greg's steely, unflinching eyes, I suddenly realize that I am looking into the soul of a man that can, has, and if allowed, will kill again. He takes another drag off his cigarette. "There are still people who fucking respect me in here and out on the streets that will take that mother fucking cocksucker out. Nicky's gonna pay."

Greg raises his voice, "I swear to fucking God, Mark. Nicky is going to pay, or he's fuckin' dead!!!"

Taking a drag from my cigarette, I try a little levity. "Bad day at the office?"

Greg smirks, flips his cigarette into the urinal, then slams his fist into his open palm. "Nothing I haven't dealt with before."

Suddenly Greg grabs my shoulder and barks, "I gotta get John a kite ASAP. Can you help me out here?"

"I'll do what I can, Greg. Do you have it with you?"

"Nah. I was so fucking frustrated I didn't finish it. I'm not even sure what to fucking say, but I'll get something to you later."

"Ok. Just let me know."

Greg slaps his big hand on my back as we leave the bathroom. "Thanks, Mark. I know I blow my top every once in a while, but it ain't got nothin' to do with you, so never take it personal. Capiche?"

I understand that this place can bring out the worst in people. I give a heartfelt, "Same here, my friend. Same here."

As we walk down the hall, I suddenly remember that I left my lighter in the bathroom. I bid Greg farewell. As I stride through the bathroom door, I am faced with José sitting in his wheelchair, waving my lighter in his hand.

With a stupid grin, he stares at me in amusement. "Did we forget this?"

The fight or flight response kicks in as I feel adrenalin coursing through my veins. Although I decide to stand my ground, I'll be damned if I'm going to get within stabbing distance.

"Looks like." I hold out my hand. "Toss it here."

José waves the lighter through the air. "Not so fast, Brok. You know I couldn't help but hear DePalma's little dilemma.

"How'd you hear that?"

"I was outside the door, and DePalma is rather loud when he's angry."

"Why didn't you come in?"

"DePalma seemed a little upset, and I lost the urge."

"How convenient. Toss me the lighter."

"What did he say that piece of shit's name was?"

I begin to become irate at his obvious game. "Come on, dude. That's Greg's business. Ask him yourself."

José slowly waves the lighter. "Just one more thing. Did I hear him mention John Gotti in that conversation?"

He's playing me for a punk, and I begin to feel my blood boil.

"Toss me the lighter, José."

We stare at each other a moment from across the abyss, then I advance.

"Ok, ok, ok. Here's your fucking lighter. Jesus fucking Christ. I'm just playing with you—besides, I want us to be friends."

José tosses the lighter and lets out a sigh. "I'll just ask DePalma later."

Then, like a chameleon, José's whole demeanor morphs into one of approachability.

"Hey! How about a game of chess tonight? I promise it won't end badly again. What the fuck? If DePalma, Gotti, and Cagnina think you're okay, you must be a stand-up guy. Right?"

"We have our moments."

"What's Gotti like?"

I look for a way out of this conversation. "You'll have to ask Greg, and our chess game will have to wait until tomorrow. My shift is ending for the night."

José thumbs at the door. "Then let's get out of this pisser. It smells like ass in here."

José wheels himself down the hallway beside me as I walk towards the elevator. "You know, Mark. I'm really not a bad guy. I'm a product of the streets. And, now that I'm stuck in this shithole forever, I overreact sometimes. But it's not personal, and I hope we can become friends."

José sounded like Greg, but with a forced and sarcastic sincerity.

"No worries. I'm edgy myself. I get out in a couple of weeks, and I don't want anything to fuck it up."

"Oh yeah. Greg mentioned that during mine and yours last fiasco." José looks at me quizzically. "Hey. If you're so worried about going home, why were you, just minutes before, willing to do more time over a Bic lighter?"

"I didn't want you to think I was a punk."

"Clearly..."

"And, who knows that I would have been caught?"

José begins to respond, but his thoughts are interrupted by Greg's voice booming down the dimly lit hallway.

"FUCK YOU, NICKY!!!"

José's wheelchair comes to an abrupt stop as he pulls his glasses from his shirt pocket, adjusts them on his face, and quickly wheels himself down the hallway. His voice trails behind him..."

"I gotta see thissss...!"

José stops again in the hallway's intersection with the foyer and takes a position by the Coke machine. He then pulls out a book from a bag hanging from the side of his wheelchair and pretends to read while waiting to use the phone. When I turn the corner into the foyer, I find Greg bellowing into the phone, which is situated directly across from the elevator door and only six feet from the guard's door.

As I move towards the elevator to escape this evening's pandemonium, Greg continues to scream into the phone, oblivious of anyone else's presence."

Blinded by rage, his face turns beet red with veins popping on the sides of his neck and head.

"Fuck you! You Goddamn cocksucker!!!"

I press the down button on the elevator as Greg's voice becomes louder with every sentence.

"What the fuck do you mean 'things have changed'? Nothing's fucking changed, you cocksucker. You still owe me my mother-fucking money. You hear me, Nicky? You think I'm a punk? You think I can't touch you while I'm in here? You'd better pay me my money—otherwise, it's your fucking ass!"

Greg becomes increasingly enraged as he listens to Nicky's response, which unhinges any further rational thought in the old man's mind.

"I made you, you cocksucker. And, if you think you can fuck me over, you can go fuck yourself, Nicky. You hear me? You're dead to me. Fuck you! Fuck you!"

Losing all emotional restraint, an enraged Greg slams the phone down on the receiver so hard that Mike finally comes out of his office. "For Christ sakes, DePalma. Pull it together, man.

You're going to have a heart attack. You do know all these phone lines are bugged, right?"

Greg glares at Mike. He begins to say something to Mike but thinks better of it. He then stomps down the hallway toward his room, cussing beneath his breath.

Mike grins at me as I stand in the open elevator and tries to make light of the situation. "Well, that's a hell of a way to end the evening. Someone's probably banging his old lady. Seen it a million times. Even happened to me when I was deployed to Iraq."

I can only give him a halfhearted smile before he returns to his office.

I glance towards José as I press the elevator's down button again. He is sitting silently wearing a silly grin while clinging to a black book as if it's the Gospel. He recognized that I noticed his odd behavior and speaks up.

"Answer me this, Kwai Chang Caine. Who said, 'In the midst of chaos, there is also opportunity?'

"Sun Tzu?"

As the elevator door finally begins to close, José raises the book and holds it over his head like an evangelical preacher, revealing its title, which is written in bold red letters: *The Art of War* by Sun Tzu.

"You're not as dumb as you look, Mr. Black."

CHAPTER 23

My suspicion that José is up to no good intensifies as he begins to show up whenever Greg and I are together. My apprehension that José may stab me in the back at least temporarily takes a back seat to my concern about being stabbed by an older gangbanger who arrived on our unit. Like José, he also was paralyzed from the waist down, and like José, received his injury when shot during an altercation on the street. This gangbanger made no attempt to hide his foul attitude and immediately began demanding respect from the other inmates. My first interaction with him occurred when he approached me in his wheelchair while I was mopping the floor.

"Hey, honkey! Give me a smoke."

I've seen black guys like him in prison before, and even had one demand the boots I was wearing. When I refused to give up my boots and stood my ground, he backed down, and we went our separate ways. I'm hoping this will be the case today.

"Do I owe you money?"

He moves closer and snarls, "You might be through with money if you don't give me a cigarette."

Because I'm leaving in a week, I know I should just give in and give him a cigarette—but that's just not who I am or ever will be.

To stop his advance, I pull the mop up to his eye level and jab it at him, flinging dirty water onto his clothing, while simultaneously grabbing the metal mop ringer out of the bucket. I raise it over my head and act like I'm going to hit him.

I snap back, "Back off. I don't need this shit today."

Startled, he wheels himself backwards, then points a crooked finger at me.

"You're fucking dead, cracker."

I move forward, and he backs up. He then turns and wheels himself down the hallway while still threatening to kill me.

"You're going home in a box, you motherfucking cracker. My homies are going to cut that lily-white ass up like a Christmas turkey."

As he rounds the corner, I try to think of something tough to say but only feel dread that is building in the pit of my stomach. After a couple of hours, I finish mopping the floor. As I'm putting away the cleaning supplies, Curtis walks up.

"Heard what happened with you and Tyrone."

"Is that his name? He didn't properly introduce himself."

Curtis stifles a chuckle. "He used to be a lieutenant in the Hoover Crips and still has a little pull, but since he got shot in a drive-by and landed in that wheelchair, he's not much to worry about. But, just watch it. He's trying to turn your little disagreement into a black versus white thing. I heard he's having a hard time pulling it off, though, because of your friends with so many of the blacks on the yard."

"Damn, Curtis. You trying to cheer me up? That's not what I want to hear days before getting out of this clusterfuck."

Curtis pats me on the shoulder. "Don't worry, brother. I have your back and will let you know if I hear of anything else going down."

Thinking all is well for the moment, I walk into the common area just in time to see Tyrone leave. He sneers at me and calls me something under his breath.

To ensure Tyrone doesn't come up from behind and stick me with a knife, I sit in the corner with my back against the wall as I try to relax. There is a nature program in progress on the television when I sit down. Moments later, Slim barges through the door and starts yelling at me, accusing me of changing the channel after he was momentarily called away by the guard. I explain that I just arrived and don't have any idea who changed the channel. But he moves aggressively towards me anyway, screaming that Tyrone told him that I changed the channel and also used the N-word to disrespect him.

I stand up and hold up my hand. "Hey! Back the fuck up, motherfucker!" I probably should have considered being slightly more diplomatic because the next thing I know, he's screaming in my face.

"You goddamn fuckin' cracker! We can bang out on the yard with knives or pipes. I don't give a fuck! You get your friends, and I'll get mine. We'll meet out on the yard tomorrow, and I'm going to send you home, alright—right back to your momma in a fucking body bag!" Slim then throws a gang sign, turns around, and slams the door behind him with a loud wham, leaving me to stand staring at the door thinking: *What friends?*

Great, I think to myself. *I'm six days from going home and now this.* As I leave the medical unit for the night, Greg comes up to me and puts his meaty hand on my shoulder. "Hey, Mark. Word's going around that someone's getting a little personal with you. You need some help? John said we're all in if you want our help."

His sincerity in my moment of need pulls at my heart strings, but I decline his offer, telling him I should probably handle it myself. Greg doesn't listen to a word I'm saying. He knows exactly what's at stake and, apparently, so does Rick. As soon as I'm back on my unit, Rick informs me that Curtis told one of his boys I'm in trouble. And because I'm only days from going home, he's willing to kick Slim's ass and risk doing more time. *Wow! I guess I do have friends.*

Rick slugs my arm. "Besides, you're my fucking favorite cracker."

"Right back at ya slick, and you're my favorite Special Forces honkey."

Rick's laughter reverberates against the concrete walls as we try to make light of the situation. Yet, I still feel nauseated by the knowledge that a group of inmates just around the corner have knives with my name on them.

The next day one, of the military guys gives me a homemade double-bladed knife that is razor-sharp. He and Rick then show me the basic military strategy on how to kill someone quickly with it. I feel empowered but conflicted—simultaneously amped and hollow inside, knowing that, at any time, I may be killed or may have to kill. After my knife tutorial, Rick decides I shouldn't walk to work on my own and personally escorts me to Greg's unit at shift time. My imagination runs wild with thoughts of gang members ambushing me in the hallway and leaving me in a pool of blood, never again to see my parents or the free world. Or alternatively, scenarios where Rambo Rick saves the day or I kill Slim in combat.

Once at the unit's elevator, we ride the lift in silence until Rick suddenly grabs my shoulder. "Listen. I got your back, so don't worry, and remember what we taught you..."

His thoughts are interrupted as the doors open to reveal José waiting for me in the foyer.

Rick glares at him. "We have a problem, or are you waiting for the show?"

José glares back at Rick but says nothing. He then wheels himself halfway down the hall before defiantly turning around and backing into the shadows to perch like an ever-watchful gargoyle."

"Looks like he came for the show," I announce.

Rick jabs me in the arm. "Well, then give them one they'll remember."

As I step off the elevator, I hear Rick's last words filter through the doors closing behind me. "Semper Fi, Motherfucker!"

I vigilantly head straight for the communal room, where I sit and watch TV as the Alligator Hunter, Steve Irwin, marvels at a venomous snake.

Just as Steve Irwin exclaims, "Crikey, mate. She's a beauty!" Slim walks through the door. Instinctively, I reach for the knife in my pocket as he dispiritedly asks my permission to enter. I'm shocked by his humble demeanor, but still firmly grasp the blade in my pocket. This could be a trick designed to get me to let my guard down.

Slim backs up a little while eyeing my hand in my pocket, then continues, "Mr. Black, I'm really sorry for yelling at you the other day. I was duped by my home boy, Tyrone. It looks like he lied to me, trying to juice me into fighting you. We'll deal with him later, but it looks like it was all a misunderstanding. I didn't mean nothing by it and just wanted to tell you I'm really, really, sorry. So, we're cool, right?"

My hand releases the blade. "Yeah, Slim, we're cool."

Curiosity gets the better of me. "Did Greg or John have anything to do with this?"

Suddenly, Slim looks scared. Holding up his hands, he stutters, "I can't say, but, but... I want you to know it will never happen again." He then backs out of the doorway, acting as if I have the plague.

Later that night, Greg comes up from behind and slaps me on the back while I'm sweeping the hallway. "I'm sorry, Mark, but we had to intervene. Couldn't take a chance of letting anything happen to somebody we care about in this fucked up place. You've helped us out, and we wanted to show our appreciation. It's not time for a funeral; it's time for you to go home, my friend."

Greg's right. I could have fought my own battle, but in prison, there are no winners in a knife fight. One combatant either dies or is severely injured, and the "winner" receives a life sentence for murder or additional years of confinement for assault with a deadly weapon. The loser, of course, returns from the hospital disabled and disfigured or leaves prison in a coffin and never sees the free world again.

I suddenly feel I owe my freedom and life to Greg DePalma and John Gotti for stopping Slim and his gang members from slaughtering me in a hallway or the yard.

"I really appreciate it, Greg. I really do. Please tell John thank you, too."

In typical DePalma fashion, he waves off my heartfelt appreciation. "Fuhgeddaboudit! Plus, John's taken a shine to ya."

Greg takes a kite out of his pocket. "Could you give this to John tonight when you see him?"

"You got it, brother."

Greg throws his hand up as he walks away. "Doesn't the world turn a little better when you can count on people?"

I put the kite in my pocket as I watch Greg walk away. I feel the knife touch my hand and think to myself, *You got that right, DePalma. The world will always turn a little better when you can count on people.*

Now, all I must do is make it five more days, and I'm out of this shit hole.

CHAPTER 24

I see John later that night when I deliver his dinner. Once the guard is out of earshot, I thank him for stepping in and looking out for my welfare. He gives me his usual "Fuhgeddaboudit," along with his notorious smile and hand wave. "What the fuck are they going to do to me? Give me another life sentence? Besides, it's time for you to go home, Mark."

As the guard walks over to the adjacent empty cell, John looks at me with the seriousness of a Mafia hitman and whispers, "I need you to do me a small favor."

He studies my face before continuing, "Listen. I'm stuck in this fucking box, and I need someone to be my eyes and ears out on the unit and on the yard. I wouldn't even ask you to get involved, but Greg said I could trust you, and I think the feds are going to try and fuck me one last time by hurting my son."

We hear the guard turn the lock on the adjacent cell as I nod my head yes, understanding that I owe this man my life.

"Anything I can do, buddy."

John's cancer-riddled face firms into a grimace of determination as the guard opens the door to the adjacent cell. "I told my son the fucking feds will never stop trying to fuck him over, no matter how straight a line he walks. But I'll be damned if let them fuck him over while I'm still alive. I've put my time in, so if I have to break a few more rules to save John Jr., so fucking be it."

John slams his fist into his palm. "I'll be damned if those motherfuckers get my son as long as I'm still breathing." His face cringes and, for a moment, I think he's going to cry either out of anger or the helplessness of being held in solitary confinement. Either way, he's in one fucked-up situation.

We hear the guard close and lock the adjacent cell door.

"Listen, Mark. This won't affect you leaving. And, if you do me this solid before you leave, I promise I'll pay you back one day." Like an aging prizefighter, he raises his fist in defiance. "And John Gotti always keeps his fucking word."

The guard walks back towards John's door, coughs, and tells me, "Wrap it up in there. I have shit to do."

John rolls his eyes, then whispers while pointing his finger at the floor between him and me. "This stays just between us until I can figure what the fuck is going on. Ya got me? No one else. Not even Greg."

I feel a little conflicted because of my friendship with Greg, but pat John on the shoulder to reassure him as I leave. "Hey. Don't worry about it. I got your back."

John looks lost in the moment, and his eyes water. "It's fucking appreciated. I mean that."

I glance back at John and joke, "Fuhgeddaboudit."

John simpers, looking pleased with himself as the guard shuts the heavy iron door in his face.

Later that evening, I swing by Sammy's room to play a game of chess. As I approach, I hear a loud and contemptuous discussion coming out of Sammy's door.

Greg's voice rages, "I want that fucking cocksucker dead! You hear me!"

José's low, monotonic voice pipes in, taking me by surprise. I stop in my tracks a couple of yards from the doorway. "Listen. I'm down for this, but my guy has got to know this is no bullshit, and it comes straight from the top. We got to get John Jr. involved and to meet my guy, or I don't think I can make this fucking happen."

Greg pauses momentarily. "I'll have to get John's okay on that, but I don't think it will be a problem. We can't let some cocksucker punk us out because we're in prison. It sends the wrong message. Am I fucking right?"

I hear Sam and José give Greg an affirmative.

Greg again raises his angry voice, "Fuck Nicky! Fucking prick! Who the fuck does he think he is, anyway? I made that guy, and now he's going to treat me like this? Fuck him!"

I hear Sammy grunt. "These guys know what they're doin' and will burn any bridge back to us. Right?"

José speaks a little louder and with an attitude that drips of pride and confidence. "Gentleman, I think my record speaks for itself. I'm a professional. And, like I said, once I get the okay to whack this piece of shit from the Gottis, I give you my word that son-of-a-bitch will be tortured and dead within a few days. As a personal favor from me to you, Mr. DePalma, I'll make sure they give Nicky your regards before they blow his low-life wig off."

Hesitation fills Greg's voice. "No torture. And I guaran-fucking-tee everyone will get the message not to fuck with Greg DePalma. Nicky's a made man and, although he owes me money, he not a fucking rat-like Gravano. We do have fucking rules."

Sammy murmurs with agreement, "That's how I've always played it, but that fucking cocksucker has got to go with two in the head."

José derides the old man's comments. "Suit yourself. It's your show, Mr. DePalma."

Satisfaction and disappointment spill from Greg's mouth, "I sure wish the fuck I could see Nicky's face when they whack that fucker."

Sammy laughs. "They all look the fucking same. Like they just walked in and caught their wife fucking their best friend, and I've had the privilege of seeing both." Everyone in the room breaks out in a thunderous roar of laughter until Greg and Sammy break out coughing.

I take a couple of steps forward into the doorway and lean against the doorjamb. "What's so funny?"

José glances at me with a mixture of surprise, malice, and annoyance. "How long you been standing there?"

Brushing off José's question, Sammy waves me inside. "Come on in, Mark. I was just telling Greg and José about the face people make just before they get whacked. Did I ever tell you about the look Clyde Lee had when I opened up on him as he was talking in a phone booth? Fucking priceless!"

"Nope, you never have."

Sammy punches José in the arm. "Listen to this fucking story."

Just as Sammy begins his story, a newly arrived inmate, who the other convicts and guards dubbed "Helmet Head," comes waltzing down the hallway. Helmet Head acquired his name because he is prone to epileptic seizures and wears a modified bike helmet to lessen the likelihood of a significant head injury when he falls to the floor in an epileptic fit. It looks like he's having one right in front of me.

From down the freshly polished hallway, Helmet Head's 5'3" frame lurches towards me like a zombie with outstretched arms. His eyes flutter wildly behind his black glasses' thick lenses, then roll back into their sockets with abrupt erratic motions that cause the thick black glasses to shift and sit crooked across his face. Gnarled fingers claw empty air until they meet my shirt, ripping the buttons from the material. His dead weight pulls me downward as I try to keep him from hitting the floor too hard. I suddenly feel a sharp pain in my lower back and wince at the same time that his sour breath assaults my senses.

Realizing I'm in pain, Greg rushes to my aid. Sammy and José dispassionately sit on the sidelines watching Helmet Head's epileptic convulsion.

"For Christ sakes! That guy came outta nowhere. You alright?" Greg asks.

"I think I'm good for now. Watch this guy. I need to get the guard to call the medics."

As I head down the hall towards the guard's station, I look back and see Helmet Head writhing on the ground at Greg's feet. José and Sammy are laughing uncontrollably in the background as Greg throws his hands in the air and shouts down the hallway. "What the fuck do you want me to do?"

CHAPTER 25

After the medics cart Helmet Head to the infirmary, I notify Mike that I hurt my back, and he sends me there, too. The medic there tells me I pulled my back and prescribes Flexeril and physical therapy before sending me back to my unit for the rest of the night to recoup.

When I return to work the next day, Mike tells me to take it easy and that he will have the other orderlies take over any strenuous work. I thank him, then I head straight towards Sammy's room to play a game of chess. As I walk up to Sammy's door, I once again hear José adamantly declaring that John Jr. must be involved to authorize a hit on a made man.

"Listen, Mr. Cagnina. You have to get Greg to get John Jr. involved before I can move forward with this. We do understand each other, right?"

Sammy grunts. "I don't tell Greg what to fucking do, and Greg sure as fuck doesn't tell John what to do. Why don't you..."

As I walk through the door, José purses his lips.

"Hey, guys. Am I interrupting something?"

José glares at me like he'd love to flay me alive. "You're always interrupting something."

"Glad to be of service."

José's jaw clenches. Before he can respond, I address Sammy. "You up for a game of chess today?"

Sammy looks like a beached whale as he lies back on his bed wearing his bright yellow pajamas, and he exhales with a hoot. "I sure as fuck am. I need to relax and take my mind off a few things."

Sammy squints at José. "Well José, I promised Mark a game of chess. So, let's continue this conversation later."

José gives a humorless smile and condemns the situation. "Hmph. Well, we wouldn't want to interrupt a fucking game of chess when business is on the table, now would we?" In a huff, he turns and wheels himself out the door, then abruptly spins his wheelchair around and gives Sammy one last reminder. "Just remember what I said, or it's no deal."

Sammy shoots back, "Don't get your panties in a bind. I'll talk to Greg and see what's up."

Without another word, José turns in the opposite direction and wheels himself down the hallway. Sammy turns to me. "Jesus, that guy is wound up tighter than a frog's pussy. He needs to learn how to relax."

Sammy heaves his heavy body to the edge of the bed and strains to reach the chess board beneath his bed. Fuck. I'm fat. Guess it's too late to go on a diet now. Mind getting the chess board from under the bed for an old man?"

I retrieve the chess board and place it on a portable tray beside his bed. I then move a chair from the corner of the room and place it on the opposing side of the table so I may face him. I sit down and grab two different colored pawns and shake them between my hands. After separating one into each hand, I present my closed fists to Sammy.

"Pick one."

Sammy chose my left hand, and I turned it over and opened it, revealing a black pawn. As I begin to set up the chess pieces, I ponder José's adamant need to have John and John Jr. involved in his plans in context with John's deep concern regarding the feds screwing him one more time before he dies. It's easily deduced that José, Greg, and perhaps Sammy are hatching a plan to whack someone who owes Greg money named Nicky, and José needs John or John Jr.'s nod to unleash another merciless killer.

I put out my feelers. "So, what was so funny before Helmet Head took a dive?"

Sammy scratches his head. "Besides him pulling you to the ground like the twos of you were going to make love?"

I snicker. "Wow. You do have a dirty mind."

Sammy laughs until he coughs. "You don't know the half of it."

Sammy rubs his chin and grins. "I don't know. I forget... Oh, yeah, oh yeah, I know what we were talkin' about. We were talkin' about killin' people. You ever kill anybody, Mark?"

I'm surprised, and my reaction is vehement. "No!"

My shocked expression gives Sammy a belly laugh. "You should see your face. I'm just fuckin' with ya."

Once I set up the last chess piece, Sammy waves his finger over the board and chuckles. "Make your move, gunslinger."

As I slide a pawn forward, I blurt out, "I don't trust José. Do you, Sammy?"

Sammy jumps his knight forward and blows off my concerns. "You worry too much, and he doesn't trust you either. So, I guess you guys are even."

I take my queen and place it on C6. "I know José isn't a big fan of mine, but I'm not a rat."

Sammy moves his other knight into the field of play. "Neither is he, and if I thought you was a rat, we wouldn't be sitting here playing chess. Him and Greg have a deal going, which I'm sure you're aware of unless you're deaf, dumb, and full of shit. I know Greg has a big mouth, and he talks to you. Hell, Greg said John talks to you."

Staring at the board, I scratch my head, then lift my gaze to look into Sammy's eyes. "Well, I am one of the only people he sees."

"Hmph." Sammy sighs. "I don't blame John or Greg. It is what it is. And like I said, the end game isn't pretty for guys like us, nor is it for the weak. But John's strong, and he'll wear it to the end with his chin up knowing he didn't rat anybody out—unlike that fucking cunt Gravano."

Frowning, I lift my knight and move it into battle.

"I could have snitched on my friends, too, and avoided prison but didn't, and now I sit here."

Sincerity is etched into Sammy's face. "I know. It's why Greg, John, and I respect you. And, even though I like you and don't particularly like José because we're cut from a different cloth, we work with what we have here. So, everyone's a little fucking edgy right now. Lei Capisce?

When I cock my head. Sammy says, "Do you understand?"

"Yeah, yeah. I completely understand. But there's something I can't put my finger on with José and..."

Sam advances a pawn and cuts me off in midsentence. "Did I ever tell you I was a cop?"

I move my bishop diagonally across the board. "Yeah, I think it was mentioned before."

"After being a cop and living the life I have, I can read people pretty fucking good."

"So, what's your read on José?"

Sammy studies the board before moving his king's pawn forward to challenge the centerpieces.

"Let's dance!"

Sam leans forward in anticipation of my next move. "As far as a bogyman, your right. José is a fucking sociopath with an above-average IQ. So, he's extremely dangerous, methodical, and without remorse regarding those who get in his way. That being said, you need to watch yourself and make sure your two paths don't cross before you leave. I would like to see you get the fuck out of this place in one piece, if you get my drift."

"I do, and I've thought the same. So, if he's a sociopath, why do you guys want to hang out with him?"

Sammy retorts, "I like sociopaths and psychopaths. They get shit done. Hell, I've worked with them most of my life on both sides of the law. Besides, José idolizes me and Greg and John. And..."

I scrunch my face in confusion. "Idolizes?"

Sammy drills me like a cop. "Don't tell me you didn't know Greg, John, and I are in the Mafia."

"Yeah, I know, but it's not why I hang out with you guys."

"Clearly. That's why John and Greg like you. You don't have any hidden fucking agendas like most of these parasites."

"Why would José idolize the Mafia and try to act like one? He's not even Italian."

Sammy twirls his hands in the air indicting his surroundings and guffaws. "Beats the fuck outta me—the retirement sucks big Tijuana donkey dicks. But, before they come a-knockin,' it's a helluva ride.

Sammy leans back against a pillow on the bed's headrest, puts his feet up on the bed, and steeples his hands on his huge chest. "Did I ever tell you how I was caught after playing a never-ending cat-and-mouse game with the cops?

Leaning back in my chair, I ready myself for one of Sammy's stories. "No, I don't think you have."

"See, Mark, in them days, when the cops were bustin' my balls, what I would do is buy a house adjacent to my main house. Then, I'd build a tunnel running between the two with escape holes hidden beneath washing machines. Every time the cops would try to corner me, I'd make good my escape—every fucking time. It would drive those poor bastards crazy."

Sammy exhales a big hearty laugh, which crescendos into a coughing fit, undoubtedly from the good ol' days of hard living. The tenor of his voice then turns melancholy. "Yeah, that plan saved my skin more than once, but in the last house I lived in, the tunnel wasn't complete when the cops stormed my house.

I got no place to run... so I pull out my Thompson machine gun and start blastin' away." Sammy starts chuckling, reliving his last moments of freedom. "They return fire until I finally run out of fuckin' bullets. When they tell me to come out, I tell 'em to come in and fucking get me."

Sammy shrugs like there was no other choice. "Then those fuckers fill the house with tear gas and force my surrender. Now, here I sit in this piss hole."

Suddenly, an excited Greg DePalma wheels himself through the door in his wheelchair. "Hey Mark, you got a minute? I need you to wheel me out to the yard to talk to John."

Raising his eyebrows, Sammy looks at Greg, "About that. You might want to talk to José before you talk to John."

Nodding his head, Greg smiles knowingly. "Yeah, he caught me in the hall. I'm going to see what I can fucking do right now."

I gesture towards the chessboard. "You wanna finish this chess game later, Sammy?"

Sammy shoos me out of his room like an old woman. "Go! Go! We'll do it again some other time. I was kicking your ass, anyway."

I rib Sammy back as I wheel Greg out of the door, "In your dreams, old man."

Sammy gives me the finger for a goodbye.

As I wheel Greg down the hallway towards the elevator door, I again contemplate about John's concerns that the Feds want to fuck him over one last time along with José's insistence that John Jr. be involved in this assassination plot. Usually, under these circumstances, one would—or maybe should—just mind his own business and not compromise his chances of going home by getting involved in any Gambino prison drama. But daily interaction with certain inmates makes them become the closest thing you have to family. You develop feelings for these people, with loyalty and willingness to help them when you should probably walk away.

Greg, who wears his feelings and thoughts on his sleeve, continues his rant, "If Nicky thinks he's going to get away with this shit..."

As Greg rambles on, I weigh my loyalty between Greg versus Gotti, comparing and contrasting my relationship to each with those of the many other gang members I'd befriended in prison. To an outsider, gangs seem complex and volatile, but from my experience, regardless of name or color, they all seem to follow two principles—respect and a loyalty to hierarchy. I assume the Mafia is no different. The dilemma that comes from befriending a gang member is that no matter how close the friendship with you, it will never override his loyalty to his leader. If the boss gets mad at you and gives the order, your newly found friend will stab you in a heartbeat. Not being a Mafia aficionado, I'm really not sure who is in charge between Greg and John. And with just four days left before going home, I didn't want to be on the wrong side of the knife's blade when it came to Greg's relational hierarchy to John. So, I ask Greg point-blank his thoughts without spilling Gotti's agenda. "Hey, Greg. I need to ask you something pertaining to our friendship and your gig in the Mafia."

Greg tries to twist his head around to look at me. "That's a fucking weird way to start a conversation. What's your concern?"

"Well, John asked me to do him a favor, and I was wondering who has the last word when it comes to you and John."

Greg gives me a WTF look. "Why? You gonna put two in the back of my head?"

"What???" I ask, genuinely confused.

Greg laughs in amusement. "Ah, nothing. I'm just breakin' balls." Greg clears his throat and takes on a serious tone. "I hope to fuck this doesn't have anything to do with me. Does it? I know you guys talk..."

Greg studies my face, and I tell him the truth.

"I don't know if it will or not. That's why I'm asking."

Greg shakes his head. "Aw, for fuck sakes, Mark. Listen. I'm not gonna even ask what John and you talk about. That's between you two. Plus, I know you won't fucking tell me anyway, will ya?"

Greg gives me a moment of silence to spill the beans.

174

I sigh out of frustration. "Look, Greg. I don't want to step on anyone's toes before I leave, and you know I consider both you and John friends. I'm just not sure where you guys stand in this thing of yours, and I..."

Staring forward with an intensity of purpose, Greg holds his hand up to silence me and belts out his credo. "Here's the fucking deal. John's the boss, and whatever he says fucking goes. Capiche? I don't always fucking agree with what he fucking says or does, but we all hitched our fortunes to John's star when he made his move against Paulie. I've never looked back, and I don't intend to now. I'm in this for the long-haul, and it's all I've ever wanted it to be. Let me tell you something, Mark. I've had some shitty times and some really good times in my life, and through it all, I don't regret shit. I wish you could have been there back in the day before it turned into a clusterfuck. The fucking fame, power, and money are unlike anything you've ever fuckin' felt in your whole goddamn life. I lived through it fucking all. You know how many people die in their graves without ever realizing their dream? Billions! I'm not one of those motherfuckers and never will be. Like Frank said, 'I did it my fucking way, and so did John.'"

As we continue down the hall, I interrupt him to summarize my understanding. "So, whatever John says goes. Right?"

Greg's voice turns gruff. "Look! John's the boss, and regardless of what I fucking think, he's got the last say. He's the boss, and I don't break the rules. Capiche?"

I respect Greg's loyalty. "I do. Who's Paulie? Another rat like Gravano?

Greg strains his neck to look at me again. He feigns irritation. "You know, when you get out of here, you should look some of this shit up. You remember that picture of me standing by Sinatra? Big Paulie is the big guy standing next to me. I set that whole gig up with Sinatra for Paulie's brother Carlo when I was running the Westchester. And, no, Paulie wasn't a rat. He just wasn't one of us either, and he had to go. And now John's the boss. But one thing is for sure—we all had a helluva time that night."

Rounding the corner, I kid Greg. "That's what Sammy said. But that the retirement sucks."

Greg starts laughing, "He's got that fucking right."

Once we reach the elevator, I notice that the food carrier has already been brought to our floor, but Slim is nowhere in sight. I walk past Greg and press the elevator's down button. As I turn around, I notice that Greg is studying my face.

"So, what did John say?"

Just as I'm about to open my mouth, Mike walks out of his office.

"Don't go anywhere. It's almost chow time, and I need you to pass out trays. Inmate Miller is on a visit."

"Who?"

Greg taps me on the leg. "That Slim's last name. Jeez, you need to pay more attention around here."

Mike nods his head affirmatively, tells Greg to get to his room, and then his thunderous voice bellows through the unit. "Chow time!"

Wheeling himself towards his room, Greg hollers back over his shoulder.

"Don't forget about me after lunch!"

As I watch the old man turn the corner in his wheelchair, I realize that, until his dying day, his loyalty will always be with John. Like Curtis said, Greg is old School. For as long as Greg DePalma lives, John's the boss. And regardless of what John thinks or says, Greg will always jump on board, regardless of his personal feelings.

Now that I have a clear understanding with respect to who has the last word, I know I must get a kite to John before Greg talks to him to inform John regarding my distrust of José and his repeated insistence on having John Jr. involved in the death of Nicky, the deadbeat.

CHAPTER 26

One thing you never want to do in prison is disrespect another inmate, especially if they are in a gang. Besides getting beaten down and stabbed for being a snitch, I've seen more guys die or beaten to a pulp in prison over disrespect than any other perceived offense. And now that I know John is the boss, I intend to keep my word and help him save his son, if possible. Besides, like I've said before, if it wasn't for John, I probably wouldn't be walking out of here into a new life in a few days. I feel I owe him this last return favor before I leave.

Just before Mike and I take John his lunch tray, I try to buy time in order to write John a kite in private.

I look at Mike and ask permission to use the bathroom while feigning a desperate demeanor, "Hey, Boss. You think I can take a five-minute bathroom break before we head to lockup?"

Mike briefly studies my frantic face before asking, "Can't you wait 10 minutes?" In response, I start jumping around like I'm going to be incontinent. Mike frowns and waves me down the hall and gives his best John Wayne impression, "Ah, go ahead. Just hurry. We're burnin' daylight, pilgrim."

I rush to the bathroom and into a stall, lock the door, sit on the commode, pull out pen and paper and start writing. I keep it simple:

I DON'T trust José. He continuously insists that your son be involved in Greg's deal in order to proceed. Greg is coming to talk to you after lunch. Caution!!!

I fold the three-inch piece of paper into a triangle and wrap it in saran wrap before shoving it into my pocket. I then walk to the food carrier, grab John's tray, open the serving lid, and cram the kite into a pile of mashed potatoes. Just as I put the tray back into the food carrier and place the cloche over the plate, Mike comes out of his office.

"Ready to go?"

I feel my heart beating a little faster after almost being busted. Trying to act nonchalantly, I hold John's food tray up.

"I have Gotti's food tray right here, boss, and I'm ready to go."

Mike smiles as he signals me to follow him towards solitary confinement.

Once we arrive at the SHU, Mike inserts the huge key into the front door's keylock. Through the wall of steel bars, I see John's face suddenly appear in his door's small plexiglass window. He looks directly at me with a cocked eyebrow as if to say," What *do you got?*"

As Mike pushes the massive barred door open into the small barred concrete cage attached to John's tiny cell, I give John a thumbs up from behind Mike's back and point to the tray with the concealed kite. The door's immense weight produces a grinding squeak that fills the hallway with sounds reminiscent of a mausoleum or crypt. As we walk into the cage, Mike walks up to John's door and inserts another key into a lock that opens a small slot in the middle of the door called a bean hole.

I've been told that the bean hole received its name because, before prison reform, inmates were often only fed beans while left in their cells to contemplate their crimes. The slot was used to pass a plate of beans or facilitate any other interactions between the guard and inmate. Today, I hand John his well-balanced meal with a kite smothered in mashed potatoes through the bean hole. After retrieving his meal on the other side of the steel door, John seems to stare straight into my soul through the small window. "I fucking appreciate it more than you'll ever know."

Mike tells John he should write a letter of appreciation about his delicious cuisine to the Federal Bureau of Prisons.

John gives a half-grin to Mike. "Maybe I fucking will, right after I write a letter of appreciation to that two-faced prick, Giuliani."

Mike gives a nervous chuckle as I bid farewell, "Guess we'll see you for dinner." Although John has the heart of a lion and acts as if he doesn't have a care in the world, I can tell he has a lot on his mind.

"Doesn't look like I'm going any fucking where soon. See ya at dinner, Mark."

After lunch is over, Slim comes back from his visit, giving me the opportunity to push Greg out on the yard and beneath John's window. John waves at me through a dirty, barred-and-steel-grated window, which is bolted onto the red brick structure. I wave back, then tell Greg that I'm going to walk around the track and smoke a cigarette while he talks to John. As I walk, I watch as Greg and John talk, and I can tell it's not going well for Greg. With a humbled but agitated face, I see him raise his arms almost in a posture of supplication to his king, looking all the part of a man with his hat in hand, asking the Emperor for a favor.

After about 20 minutes, I see a guard walk over to Greg and wave him away from the window. A very irritated Greg DePalma wheels himself onto the track as I walk up.

"Everything alright?"

Greg's disgusted face tells the story. "Fuck no!"

Greg studies my face. "Did you say anything to John about José?"

I dodge Greg's question, having already decided I was going to help John save his son from whatever José had up his sleeve. Besides, I knew Greg was hell-bent for revenge and no longer wanted to hear the truth or reason. He just wants Nicky dead, no matter the consequences. And unfortunately, on the street or in here, that type of attitude unaccompanied by logic and careful consideration could bring down everyone involved.

I look at Greg and emphatically state, "Would it matter if I did?"

Greg squints at me. "So, that was your moral dilemma earlier on, about where the buck stops with me and John?"

I know Greg can tell if I'm bullshitting him, so I again just tell him the truth. "Well, John told me not to say anything. So, if I tell you what he said, is it going to get back to him?"

Greg humphs. "It depends."

I look at Greg incredulously and pull a cigarette out of my pocket. "What kind of fucking answer is that?"

Greg becomes irritated. "The only fucking answer you're going to get! You gonna fucking tell me or not?"

Lighting my cigarette while being a little irritated with myself for getting involved in this prison intrigue, I glare at Greg. "Yeah, I will. He asked me to be his eyes and ears on the floor, and I wondered if telling him the truth would conflict with our friendship. Hell, I don't know what's going to happen out here before I leave in a couple of days, but I didn't want it to fuck up our friendship." I cock my head. "Why, do you want me to lie to him?"

Greg's eyes grow big as he becomes flustered. "What? No. Well... ah, fuck no! I don't want you to lie to John!" I tilt my head again. "Well, that's why I asked you."

"Ahhh, fuck." Greg sighs. "Just try to stay outta my way on this José thing."

"So, you do want me to lie to John."

Greg becomes clearly agitated. "Just fucking forget about it for now, will ya?"

I can't let it go. "So, we're still friends?"

Greg looks at me like I'm crazy. "Get the fuck outta here. You think I save my enemies?" He points to an unoccupied picnic table. "Let's smoke a cigarette and get some sun before we go back to the unit."

As I push Greg to the picnic table, I look down at his bad combover and realize how much I admire this old man—not because he's in the Mafia. I could care less about that. It's his unwavering loyalty to his friends that I most admire. Loyalty is an admirable trait in theory, but difficult to maintain unwaveringly in practice.

For most, loyalty is blatantly contextual and rarely reciprocal. Their loyalty only lasts while it's beneficial to them. The minute it doesn't fit neatly into their paradigm or becomes time or effort-intensive, they turn into nebulous sheets caught in the wind of indecisiveness. They can't be counted on to honor promises in times of trouble, although they would expect you to do so if the circumstances were reversed.

For a very few, it means being there for someone without regard for the circumstances. It is, in essence, what marriage should be: "For better, for worse, for richer, for poorer, in sickness and health, until death do us part." Most will fall short, but not Greg DePalma.

Railing about the Feds was a passion point; being treated disrespectfully was a passion point; but, loyalty... *oh, **loyalty**...* that was **the** passion point for not just Greg, but John as well. I park Greg to the side of the picnic table and sit beside him as we look out into the center of the yard.

Greg lights his cigarette, then goes off on this very subject, "You know what really fuckin' frustrates me about the whole situation I'm in? The disrespect and disloyalty. Is it so goddamned hard to keep your fucking word?" Greg enquires through a puff of smoke.

I light my cigarette. "I guess for most it is. I can count on one hand the people I can trust, and one of them is my mom."

"She sounds like a good Italian mother. You're a lucky one, Mark."

Greg hit the nail on the head of a sad truth. Some convicts can't even rely on their mothers to come to see them on their birthdays or send a card on Christmas. Over the last seven years, my mom came every two weeks, rain or shine, sent money for commissary, wrote every three days, and when I needed her to go beyond the call of duty and bring another inmate's mother to visit her son in prison, she didn't waver. Inmates who literally have no one outside of prison who cares about them often turn to other inmates for help. The Italian wannabes, Luigi and Mario, who bum smokes off Greg, are an example.

Greg interjects to break the silence, "I don't even think people understand just how much it hurts when someone you trust proves disloyal to the family. Sammy was a goddamned pussy for ratting John out. Hell, John's probably talked shit about me, too, but he NEVER gave me up, and he's always had my fucking back. You know, through the years I've fucked up. I got a loud mouth. I admit it, but I never fucked anybody over, and that's why I'm still alive and why I'm still here in this place. If you fuck up, you get smacked. If you become a snitch or go against your family, you get whacked."

I stare at Greg in disbelief. "Sammy ratted John out?"

Greg stares at me like a cannoli that had morphed into a taco.

"What??? Goddammit, Mark. You're going to have to look some of this shit up when you get out. Not our Sammy—Sammy the Bull. One of our former associates and a real motherfucking, cocksucking rat."

I give a low whistle. "Glad it wasn't our Sammy."

Greg gives me an irritated look. "Get the fuck outta here."

"You know, Mark, when you get outta here, you need to come see me in New York. I'll take you to one of my favorite restaurants in Port Chester and introduce you to some friends of ours."

"That would be nice, Greg."

Greg slaps my leg. "Remember that picture I showed you of me and Sinatra. Well, that was at a time we ran everything in New York."

"You couldn't take a shit without our say-so. I know you don't believe me, but at one time, we were like fucking kings." Now the Feds have our guys running with their tails between their legs where their balls used to be."

I snort a laugh.

Greg continues with his rant as he taps the ash from his cigarette, "You know what really hurts me right in the nutsack? I would've gladly gone down for that goddamned rat either here or on the street. I know I talk too much sometimes, but I've always been a standup guy, played by the rules, and never even thought about ratting out one of my associates. Nobody wants to play by the rules anymore, and it's all turning into one big clusterfuck. What does your military friend say about death, not dishonor?"

I correct him. "Death before dishonor."

Greg huffs. "You know what happens when someone in the military is charged with desertion? They're supposed to face a firing squad. They fight for country; we fight for our family. It's no fucking different. And when you're called to serve, you go—even if your kid is in the hospital or your wife's in labor. These rules aren't democratic. They're orders with fucking rules."

Greg takes a drag off his cigarette. "You take an oath just like in the military. And you know what's supposed to happen when you break an oath in our business, Mark? You get whacked. That's fucking what."

Greg clenches his jaw. "If I ever run into that son-of-a-bitch, he's dead, right after I torture his fucking ass. He is not one of us anymore."

Greg looks at me like he's said too much before gazing into the ether with a combination of sentimentality, anger, love, pride, and fear. "I'll never go out like that bitch. Fucking motherfucker.

I don't know Mark. Maybe all I'll be known is for all my fuck-ups because I didn't become a rat and tell my side of it."

Greg's voice trails off, growing softer as he reminisces on people who he thought he could trust. "Motherfuckers... broke John's and my hearts, I tell you."

Taking another drag off his cigarette, he regains his composure. "I don't care what those other pussies do. I'll be loyal to John and this thing of ours until they put me in the ground. I swear to fucking God, Mark."

Greg stares right at me with sincerity that is nearly palpable. I grabbed him by the shoulder and felt a tired old man beneath the bravado. "I know you will, Greg. I know you will."

The truth of the matter is that I didn't fully comprehend what Greg or John were talking about most of the time. It would only be much later, after my release from prison, that I would realize the Sammy who Greg was talking about was Sammy "The Bull" Gravano, who turned federal witness against Gotti—or that John was the head of the Gambino crime family, that Greg DePalma was his capo, that Sam Cagnina ran with the Trafficante family, or that José Reyes was one of the biggest and most violent drug lords of New York City.

Greg naturally assumes I should be familiar with all the people he mentions from watching the news or reading tabloids, but I'm clueless. I knew from other inmates and my dad that the Feds had busted John, and he was supposed to be a big shot in the Mafia. Other than what I'd seen and read from the fictional accounts from the movie, *the Godfather,* I knew little of the Gambino crime syndicate.

Crushing my cigarette out into the side of the picnic table, I sigh. "To be honest, Greg, I don't know if I could go through all this again. I never snitched because out of principle. I was taught that you don't snitch on your friends, no matter what. But no one I protected has ever written, sent money, or even come to see me. I don't believe in the black gang's 'I gotta get mines' credo even if it means walking over the bodies of your friends and family, but what is the point of protecting people if no one has your back once you save theirs?"

The original catalyst that sent me to prison was smoking and possessing pot. If busted and facing prosecution, all you have to do to get out of your legal predicaments is become a snitch for law enforcement and rat out all of your pot-smoking buddies, which in my case was nearly everyone I knew. I was twice offered such a deal to get out of my legal problems and avoid jail, but I declined because I thought the people I was protecting were my friends—"friends" that I would later discover had snitched me out or would never write, come see me, or send money.

Most people don't know or believe that the DEA, FBI, and other law enforcement agencies will often bust you and get their claws into you via an informant or by planting evidence on you to gain a conviction. I personally experienced this four times. Accordingly, it isn't a stretch of the imagination to expect the FBI to do anything, whether illegal or unethical, to bust Gotti one last time before he dies. Maybe John's current paranoia is justified, or maybe it wasn't. Regardless, Greg was right when noting that the days of either side playing by the rules disintegrated into chaos years ago. "Good" cops look the other way while dirty cops break the rules to gain a bust in order to further their careers or line their pockets with dirty money.

The current situation where rules no longer apply has created a new breed of criminal loyal only to himself and who now feels free to kill indiscriminately comforted by the knowledge that if a big fish like Gotti is on the line, a deal may be struck to wipe away his sins against the community. I've seen these individuals in the wings of prison and on the street waiting to replace the old guard who played by the rules, like John, Greg, and Sammy. And whether they are corporate thugs or so-called friends, they are some of the greediest, most vicious, backstabbing people I've ever met, who only fly their flags of loyalty whenever the wind favors their own ship.

I spit at the ground in disgust. "I don't know, Greg. Every time I thought I could count on family or friends, they would either stab me in the back or walk away without a word. Yet, they still want me to be a stand-up guy and have their backs when they're in a bad spot."

Greg gives an understanding response, "Hmmm... have you ever seen the Godfather movie? And I mean the first one, because the rest are crap, in my opinion. But it's when Amerigo Bonasera comes to Don Corleone with hat in hand asking retribution for his daughter?"

"You mean the wedding scene where he asks Don Corleone for help, but up until that point had never put forth an effort to befriend the Godfather?"

"Yeah, that's the part. Do you know why Coppola put that into the film right at the beginning?

I shake my head. "Not a clue."

"Because every made man can relate to that scenario of some fuck who, when times were good for him, didn't give us the respect deserved, then suddenly wants our family to step in when the wheels fall off, and the people they thought they could count on aren't reliable."

I jab Greg's arm. "Why did you help me?"

"Well, for one thing, you have never asked for anything, you helped when asked, and I've always known where you stood. Besides, I like helping my friends when I can and have helped everyone from Frank Sinatra to the guy on the street corner selling cannolis. Mark, I know it hurts and pisses you fucking off when people don't understand the value of loyalty but take it from an old fuck like me—it's less about them and more about you. Loyalty and standing by your word aren't just about what others think. They are measures of self-worth, part of becoming a man. At the very least, you can look back and know you did the man in the mirror right. Fuck those disloyal pricks. Celebrate the ones who've stayed true like you, me, John, Sammy, John Jr., and a whole lot of others that refuse to die on their knees sucking the Fed's cock."

I chuckle at the seeming contradiction of Greg illustrating a noble truth while flowering the explanation with profanity. "Well, I've never thought about it like that before."

Flipping my cigarette into a can that sits at the foot of the picnic table, I thumb towards John's cell. "Speaking of John Jr., John showed me a picture of him. He looks like a standup guy."

Greg nudges my arm. "You got that fucking right, and John has every right to be proud of the man he's become."

I know Greg is in the Mafia and has probably done some ruthless shit in his life and, by societal standards, is a criminal. But our lives have intersected at a place where talk of loyalty and friendship are cheap, and his words ring of truth—a truth that escapes most people because they can neither conceive the sacrifice or the ideology that form the foundation of true loyalty. But Greg and John understood—so did Sammy and my soldier friend, Rick Randall, who would always have his brothers' backs in battle. Later, after I was released from prison, the loyalty Greg and Rick spoke of would be paramount in my distinguishing true friends from those who cut and ran when our friendship proved a burden or inconvenient.

One could argue that the police and the feds demonstrate this type of loyalty too when they refuse to snitch on a dirty cop. I've personally seen plenty of times where law enforcement officers in every branch, except the FBI, observe another brother in blue break the law or violate someone's rights but remain silent to maintain their "thin blue line." The difference between law enforcement and Greg is that DePalma didn't play both sides of the fence. What you saw is what you got. And what you got was someone who not only played by the rules no matter where they lead, but he would give his life to defend those rules with unwavering loyalty to this thing of his we call the Mafia.

Greg takes one last drag and flips his cigarette towards the butt can and misses. "Are you ready to head back to the unit?" Nodding, I stand to stretch and notice John staring at us from behind his dirty barred window. Greg seems oblivious to John's shadowy face in the window. Saying nothing, I walk behind Greg and begin to push his wheelchair along the running track towards his unit while I listen to him continue to rant about all rats having a special place waiting for them in hell. I don't know anything about the Mafia's afterlife, but I do know one thing for sure—John is watching us and, if possible, I'm not going let José or the Feds shove a knife in him one more time or take his son before he dies.

CHAPTER 27

Once I'm back, Mike has me sweep around the unit just before dinner. As I push the dust mop through the halls, I pass Curtis's room and see him sitting at a table filling out his commissary list.

Leaning against the door frame, I kid him, "Are you buying me an ice cream tomorrow as a going-away present?"

Curtis looks up and smiles. "Word? Shouldn't that ice cream be moving my way for all the inside dope I've provided to save your lily-white ass?"

"Well, there's no denying you've saved my lily-white ass on more than one occasion. What flavor may I bestow upon you for services rendered?"

Curtis guffaws and taps a pencil on the table. "Well, I did have my heart of hearts set on a Rocky Road."

I snap my fingers. "My favorite, too. Allow me to fulfill your heart's desire."

"If I didn't know you better, I'd think you were trying to pimp me out."

We both laugh.

Tapping his pencil on the table, he looks at me with a suddenly serious expression. "Speaking of solid intel, I was just getting ready to come see you with something that may be of interest to you and your Mafia pals." Turning his chair towards me, Curtis strokes his chin. "Yo. I know Mr. DePalma and José are gearing up for a hit out on the streets, and I think one of my niggers may have seen something that everyone may be interested in. My…"

I cut him off and try to negate Greg's involvement. "I don't know how you know all this, but Greg doesn't have anything to do with…"

Curtis raises his hand for me to stop talking. "Yo, bro, I get it. You and Mr. DePalma are friends, but don't play me like a dumb motherfucker. Besides, three hours ago, one of my niggers was cleaning out a cell adjacent to Gotti's when Mr. DePalma rolled up ranting and raving about a street hit. And guess what? My boy heard their whole fucking conversation. Check it out. My nigger said Mr. DePalma told Gotti he needed his son involved with José in order to make a hit on Nicky. That, I'm going to assume, is the same Nicky Mr. DePalma was yelling at the other night on the phone."

My heart sinks. "You heard about that, huh?"

Curtis chortles. "Who the fuck didn't hear it? And don't take this wrong, but my nigger also said when things got heated, he heard your name mentioned concerning Gotti's decisions. After their discussion, Mr. DePalma was seen talkin' to you out on the yard. So, I'm startin' to think you're involved to make sure Nicky is through with money."

Without pausing, I emphatically state, "Hey! I'm not involved on any hit. I'm just looking out for my friends."

Curtis's face contorts into a smirk. "Word? Hold up homes, I'm just reporting the daily news, and your so-called friends are only loyal to the Costa Nostra and money—nothing else. FYI, my nigger, all your friends are stone-cold killers, especially José. And, I just don't wanna see you get caught up in some fucked-up bullshit days from you going home. Can you feel me, brother?"

"I'm sorry, Curtis. I do understand. So, what conversation did your boy hear between Greg and John?"

With the self-confidence of a man who has his hand on the pulse within the prison and on the streets, he beams. "It was a mad discussion, no doubt, with Mr. DePalma telling Gotti that José was a solid motherfucker. Then, he begged Gotti to sanction a hit on Nicky and allow John Jr. to meet José's hit man. Mr. DePalma even tried to use this hit on Nicky as a steppingstone for future hits on the Albanians, who are moving in on the Gambino's turf in New York. But my boy said Gotti shot his ass down in a ball of flames on any involvement by John Jr. He told Mr. DePalma that he is the boss and believes the Feds are going to try and fuck him one last time before he dies by using his son in one of the FBI's sting operations. Gotti vowed to protect his son until his dying breath. Then, get this my nigger; Mr. DePalma asked if you had swayed Gotti's decisions.

My boy said Gotti's feathers got mad-ruffled. He told DePalma that he loved him, but he was the fucking boss and not to question any of his decisions when it came to his son, and anything between you and him was between you and him. Before Mr. DePalma could answer back, a guard came up and told Mr. DePalma that this was the last warning to move away from Gotti's window."

I affirm Greg's nasty disposition. "You're right; the old man wasn't happy after his conversation with John. What's the deal with the Albanians? Do I have any worries there? I didn't even know they were a thing."

He takes a long pause. "The Albanians aren't really a threat in here, but on the street, they're for real. Word on the street is the Albanians are moving in on Gotti's territory, yet Gotti won't give the word to retaliate."

"Why not?"

Curtis shifts in his chair. "Why not, indeed. ...??"

He looks at me quizzically, stroking his chin. "I can't help but wonder if Gotti's sudden paranoia concerning José and his kid is also why he isn't giving the word to hit the Albanians or help Mr. DePalma whack Nicky. I'm also thinkin' you're getting yourself involved whether you like it or not. Remember when you first got here, and everyone warned you to keep DePalma at arm's length? This is the reason. But, since you seem intent on having some crazy rabbit-ass sense of loyalty, I have more solid intel that is going to help you and your goombahs. So, why don't the fuck you just tell me what's going on with you, Gotti, and Mr. DePalma before it's too late? Besides, don't you think I deserve information if information is given?"

"You're right. Something does feel strange with José, and I personally don't trust him. But I promised John that..."

Curtis holds up his hand. "Bitch, please. What I'm about to tell you can help Mr. DePalma and Gotti. Do you want to dance or not?"

I weigh my options and loyalties to John and Greg but ultimately need Curtis's network of eyes and ears to fulfill John's request to bring him any relevant information. "All right. John told me the exact same thing you heard. He thinks the feds are going to try and fuck him through his son, and he said he wasn't going to let that happen. He's crazy about his John Jr. and doesn't want John Jr.'s life to end in a shit hole like his is. A couple of weeks ago, he asked me to be his eyes and ears on the units until he can figure out what's going on. Today, just before Greg met with him, I sent him a kite and told him that José had aggressively pushed Greg to have John Jr. meet with the hitman to sanction Nicky's assassination. I also mentioned that I don't trust José because I get a weird vibe that he has a hidden agenda."

Curtis frowns. "Maybe more of a hidden agenda than you think. Now I understand why you helped John without telling Mr. DePalma. The feds are some vindictive bitches who will work with the scum of the earth to stab a motherfucker in the heart. I've never met Gotti, but I heard he really loves his son."

"Absolutely. And if I can help him before I go, I will. It seems like a small request to fulfill for a dying man stuck in that medieval isolation tank."

Leaning back in his chair, Curtis reflects. "You have that one right, homes. That's some fucked up vindictive shit to do to anyone not causing any problems. Hell, only a psychopath would torture their victims like that... and then go after his son. That's some cold-ass shit, my nigger. Yo, one thing's for sure. It's all good under the hood with you and Gotti. He must really like you if he's willing to yell at Mr. DePalma on your behalf."

"Well, I didn't mean for that to happen. I really like Greg and feel like I owe him, too, but I guess it is what it is."

"Yes, it is. I wouldn't worry too much about Mr. DePalma. He knows Gotti's the boss, and he plays by the rules. Hell, I think Mr. DePalma actually likes you. Did you know before you got here, Mr. DePalma never hung around any other inmates besides his Mafia friends? If you weren't Italian or Mafia, you weren't shit—and Cagnina? Hell, he acts like everyone besides the Costa Nostra has the plague. So, my man, what's your end game?"

I sigh. "Short term, I guess loyalty to those who are loyal to me and trying to do the right thing by them..." Thinking of home, I sigh and scuff my foot on the ground. "...but at the end of the day, I just want to get out of here in one piece so I can finally go back to whatever is left of my life."

Curtis sighs back. "All the luck making it back into the world. Your loyalty is admirable, homes, but it's going to be a hard thing to do, especially in here with everyone running game and with pieces of the puzzle still missing."

"Well, at least I can try. What about you, Curtis? What's your end game, and what pieces of the puzzle do you think are still missing?"

"Unfortunately, you're looking at it, homes. With a 10-year sentence for tax evasion and, at my age with this diabetes, I don't think I'm going to make it outta here except in a box. I guess earlier, like Mr. DePalma and the rest of these guys, it was all about the money and myself. But, as the sun goes down on my life, if I can do some good before it ends, like you, I guess I'll try."

Raising one finger in the air, he continues with an intriguing bit of news. "Speaking of doing some good and missing puzzle pieces, like I said before, I just happen to bounce into some information that you and your goombahs may find of interest. Although I haven't pieced everything together yet, my gut feeling tells me Gotti's paranoia concerning José and the feds may not be all in his mind."

Curtis's ability to spy on almost every aspect of prison life here at Springfield is based on one simple fact—the prison system runs primarily on inmate slave labor by providing each guard on the units, administrators, and even religious personnel a minimum of three inmates to assist them during their shifts. With most of the inmate population being black, at least one of the three inmates on any given crew is a homie that sings to Curtis. Since I've known this old pimp, I've never known him to be wrong.

"You definitely have my interest, brother. Please continue."

Curtis then implicates José in a shadowy rendezvous in the physical therapy unit. "Yesterday in physical therapy, an old-timer was cleaning equipment in a back-storage unit when the guard yelled for everyone to leave the unit. My nigger didn't hear that order because he was listening to a sports channel through his earphones, so he continued cleaning. After about ten minutes, he emerged into the main area, and who do you think is sitting in his wheelchair talking to a couple of men in suits?"

I gulp. "José?"

"That's an affirmative. When they see the old man, they all have this horrified look on their faces, but quickly gain their composure and call for the guard, who runs the old man out of physical therapy."

"Wow!" I exclaim. "Did he hear them say anything?"

"Not a thing because he was wearing his earphones, but he did say the two crackers talking with José weren't guards or administrators and looked like federal agents. He also thinks José had a binder full of papers on his lap."

Curtis continues to piece together the puzzle. "And, get this. Two of my niggers working the yard out front saw these same crackers flash a badge as they drove through the front entrance, like they were on a mission from God. Then, another one of my homies, who was unloading supplies from a truck, saw these same fuckers walk into the back entrance of the medical unit with a briefcase and a duffel bag."

I'm blown away. "Damn! You think José is working for the Feds?"

He nervously taps his pencil on the desk. "Shit. I don't know what to think anymore. José could have snitched a long time ago, but fuck—anything is possible when you're facing a couple of life sentences, and Gotti is involved. If something is going on, this is just the beginning of the storm, so watch yourself. That reminds me. Did you hear about Peter? He..."

Before he can finish his sentence, José rolls up and mocks me, "Am I interrupting anything?"

Curtis's eyes go wide, and I feel my body stiffen.

"Not at all. I was just telling Curtis I was going to buy him an ice cream as a going-away present."

José studies our faces. "That's awful white of you. What about me?"

"Limited funds, my man. Plus, I know you have money."

With a curled lip, José runs his thumb over his well-manicured fingers and taunts, "More money than you'll ever fucking have."

He looks at me with dead eyes. "You mind if I talk to your friend in private for a minute?" He motions to Curtis. I nod at Curtis, and he nods back.

"It's okay, Mark. We'll talk later. Just don't forget that ice cream tomorrow."

While pushing the dust mop down the hallway towards Sammy's room, I notice that the paper towel dispenser by the microwave is empty. I lean the dust mop's handle against the wall and step into a utility closet where cleaning supplies are kept. As I grab a packet of paper towels and proceed to fill the dispenser, I hear Greg's irate voice coming from Sammy's room. "What else can we offer José since John isn't on board? I can't believe he's gonna let Nicky walk away with this shit! And what about the fucking Albanians? I want these motherfucking cocksuckers clipped."

Looking around to make sure no one else is present, I think to myself. "*Good Lord, DePalma.*"

CHAPTER 28

I continue to hear Greg's venomous words tumble out into the hallway as I walk towards Sammy's room. Reaching the doorway, I find Sammy on the bed, wearing his standard yellow pajamas, lecturing Greg, who sits in a chair.

"Hey! Let's lower your fucking voice, huh?"

From the doorway, my frowning face adds its two cents. "Dude, I can hear you all the way down the hall."

Greg knocks Sammy's chair over as he stands up and shakes his fists. "I can tell you both one motherfucking thing! I don't give a fuck who hears me. I'm not going to let some cocksucker disrespect me while I'm in prison. You hear me! And you..." Greg shakes his big finger at me. "...I know John's listening to you. You're fucking my shit up."

Greg's anger puts me on guard as I take a step back into the hallway. "Greg, we've already had this discussion. Do you want me to lie to John or not?"

Greg glares at me as I stand my ground, waiting for his answer. Sammy glances back and forth between Greg and me with an irritated mug. It's a very uncomfortable moment between friends, until Sammy breaks the tension. "Leave Mark outta this, will ya

Greg? John's his own man and don't listen to anybody but John. Let's think about all this shit and talk about it later. Ok, Greg?"

Greg protests. "How much more of this shit am I supposed to let slide down my back before I get some justice here? If this was a few months back, I wouldn't even have to ask twice to have that fucker whacked. What the fuck happened to the fucking rules? Come on. You know this isn't right. Help me out here, Sammy."

Sammy again tells Greg they will talk later, resulting in an irritated Greg DePalma huffing off into the hallway. He stands before me, sizing me up. Gaining his composure, Greg's stare softens, and he sighs as he runs his hand through his thinning hair.

"Goddamn it. Sammy's right." He exhales. "And I don't say this very fucking often, but I'm sorry. You're only doing what John asked, and I gotta trust his judgment. Let's just forget about this for now."

He extends his hand, which I eagerly shake with sincerity.

"Don't worry about it. This place has a way of pushing each of us over the edge."

Greg pats me on the shoulder and tells me I'm a good kid, then shuffles down the hallway mumbling under his breath. "You got that fucking right."

Sammy stares at me and squints in scrutiny. "I can count on you to keep your lip buttoned on this, right?"

Walking back into Sammy's room, I sarcastically assure him it's in the vault. "Seriously? I'm the least of your worries; however, I would suggest Greg lower his voice a little. Jeez!"

Sam wheezes. "You fucking think? I love Greg, but he has always had a loud mouth. But a more loyal paisan, you'll never find. I trust Greg with my life and am honored to call him friend. Hell, he's family."

I pick up the chair Greg was sitting in, place it in the corner of the room, and sit down with an exhausted demeanor.

"I sure wish I could count on my family as much as you guys count on each other. Greg never mentioned that you two were related."

Sammy leans back on his bed, causing the springs to creak under his massive girth.

"Oh, I didn't mean blood relatives, who may or may not be there when you need them the most. I'm talking about true family—those who are willing to lay their life down for you and be there in a moment's notice, whether it be blood or otherwise. That's the only shit that counts at the end of the day. Everyone else is just a player."

I ask, "So, you think I'm a player?"

Sammy cocks an eyebrow. "Personally, I'm not sure what you are, but you're not a player. Let's just say you have grown on me, Greg, and John, and I'll miss our chess games when you're gone."

Before I can tell Sammy that I feel the same about him, José rolls in with a fury and blurts out, "I just talked to DePalma. So, Gotti's not fucking interested now? I thought we..."

Sammy quickly holds his hand out like a traffic cop and rolls his eyes and head in my direction, where I sit in José's blind spot.

José turns his head to find me sitting in the corner of the room with my raised eyebrow.

"I'm not interrupting anything, am I?"

José's jaw clenches, and a vein in his neck pops into view as his hand begins to lift the wheelchair's armrest makeshift weapon.

Sammy hollers and comes flying off his bed. "HEY! HEY! HEY! CUT THE FUCKING SHIT! José quickly lets the armrest go and leans back into his wheelchair, regaining his composure. His facial expression transitions to a cold, frosty demeanor as he releases the wheelchair handle and straightens out his shirt. "Of course, Mr. Cagnina. This is your home. My bad."

Sammy sits back down on the bed and reinforces José's observation. "Goddamn right it is." Shaking his head, Sammy looks at me. "José and I have some business to attend to, you mind? We'll talk later."

José presses his fist to his lips and stares at me through his wireframed glasses like a predator ready to pounce, given the right opportunity.

I turn my attention towards Sam and tell him it's all good and that I need to sweep the rest of the hallway, anyway. Moving past José into the hallway, I try a little levity to placate the situation. "Well, I guess I'll leave you two swinging dicks alone to discuss business."

José gives a sardonic grin. "If your girlfriend was here, that would make three."

Sammy begins to chuckle.

I keep my composure and fire back, "Thanks for the warning. I wondered why she was only sending headshots."

"Well, now you fucking know."

Sammy laughs uncontrollably until he starts coughing.

As I walk away, José utters a veiled threat, "And tell your Uncle Tom friend to stay the fuck out of my business."

Without further comment, I continue to walk down the hallway, grab the dust mop from against the wall, and push it towards the rear of the unit where Peter is housed with other medical inmates. Peter's unit is a huge windowed hospital room where 20 or more hospital beds are separated by medical cubicle curtains. When I walk past Peter's cubicle, his bed is stripped bare, and the area is vacant. In the next cubicle, there is a bedridden inmate on oxygen who is working a crossword puzzle.

"Excuse me. Do you know where Peter went?"

The grizzled old inmate raises a tired, wrinkled, tattooed arm and thumbs towards Peter's vacant cubicle. "Damnedest thing I've ever seen. The guards bum-rushed him in the middle of the night and were specifically interested in all of Peter's identity theft material. They didn't even let him put on his glasses as they escorted that poor blind fuck right off the unit. When Peter asked where he was going, they said he'd find out when he got there. That's what he gets for fucking with the feds—I warned him. But, if you ask me, I think somebody snitched him out for teaching identity theft, and now old Petey is on his way to diesel therapy."

Diesel therapy is an inmate's worst nightmare, worse than solitary confinement. It's a punishment of perpetual transportation by the Bureau of Prisons for any inmate deemed a problem child or threat to a high priority federal case. It's designed to break an inmate by shutting down all access to friends, family, and most importantly, his attorney. It is a never-ending human shell game, during which the Bureau perpetually and repeatedly transports an inmate, in the middle of the night, to another federal prison's solitary confinement unit, often thousands of miles away from his family. The journey involves a multitude of transfer center's solitary confinements with all the inmate's personal property perpetually trailing behind, simulating that the inmate is forever lost within the system.

Once the inmate's family or lawyer finds them within the prison system and tries to make contact, the inmate is again shuttled away to, maybe Alaska, then perhaps Hawaii, or Puerto Rico, making it virtually impossible for anyone to locate him with certainty. Diesel therapy is one of the techniques used to discourage most guys doing time from fucking with the feds or the prison administration. Even inmates in solitary confinement, including John Gotti, keep their outbursts in check in order to avoid this fate.

While at a transfer center, I met a black guy in the Nation of Islam who had been on diesel therapy for nearly two years after filing multiple grievances against the Bureau for religious rights violations. He told me that, at the beginning, he would spend two weeks in solitary confinement at the Supermax near Florence, Colorado, but once his people begin to write and send money, and just before his personal property and legal documents reached him, he'd be sent off for another two-weeks at a federal prison in Guaynabo, Puerto Rico. He named several other prisons he'd been processed through and stated that he'd been transferred so many times that his canteen money and personal property had never reached him. Now, it looked like poor Peter was on the same nonstop journey to nowhere.

I pressed the older inmate for more information, "How do you know the guards were specifically looking for Peter's identification theft material?"

The inmate gave a grizzled grin. "Because I fucking heard them through these paper-thin curtains. Three guards dressed in black came in here in the middle of the night. I heard one of them say they had to find every scrap of Peter's identification theft material. They even ripped open his mattress and found where he had stashed some Xerox copies."

The old-timer crossed his tattooed arms, and with a smug look said, "How the hell do you think they knew to look there? I'll tell you how—a snitch. But they didn't get everything."

"Why is that?" I ask.

The old man laughs. "Because his last student took a binder full of material to study the other day."

"Who was that?" I inquire.

"That Puerto Rican kid in the wheelchair that dresses nice. I can't remember his name."

"Jay?"

The geezer rubs his whiskered chin. "Yeah, yeah, I think that's it."

I thank him for this intriguing piece of information, then continue to sweep the hallways while pondering Peter's abrupt departure and the link between the missing binder taken by José and the one seen sitting on José's lap while he spoke with the two unknown, suited men. A guard's voice bellows down the hallway, disrupting my thoughts. "Chow time!"

As I make my way to the elevator lobby where the food cart has been delivered, Curtis sees me pass his room and sticks his head out into the hallway.

"Psst! Mark, Greg is looking for you, and we have got to talk." I give him the thumbs up and continue down the hallway, where I run straight into Greg's smiling face, who shoves a kite into my hand.

"Hey, Mark. Sorry for breakin' balls earlier. It was nothing personal."

"I know it wasn't."

Greg points to my hand. "Give that to John, will ya? I gotta get to my room. But we'll talk later. Ok?"

As Greg turns to shuffle down the hallway, I put the kite in my pocket. "I got you covered, buddy."

Greg's voice trails behind him. "I appreciate it, Mark. You're a standup guy."

After handing out food trays to the other inmates, Mike and I walk to the SHU with John's tray.

Curious, I ask Mike about Peter. "What happened to Peter? I heard they came and got him in the middle of the night. Did he break some prison protocol?

Mike shrugs his shoulder. "Don't know. It's above my pay grade."

I'm genuinely surprised by Mike's answer and muse; *Wow, I've never heard that one before.*

Once at the SHU, Mike opens the front gate with his back to me. John's grinning face magically appears in the small Plexiglas window.

"How's everybody fucking doing today?"

Mike delivers a platitude, "Another day, another dollar."

John cracks a smile. "What the fuck do you know? Me, too."

I wink at John as I balance the food tray in one hand, while quickly retrieving Greg's kite from my trouser front pocket with my other hand. Pressing the kite to the bottom of the tray, I ready myself to deliver the tray and kite. After Mike unlocks the bean hole, he steps aside to let me hand John his dinner tray, then turns and walks toward the adjacent cell for a quick inspection. I slide John's tray through the bean hole allowing the kite to drop to the floor on the other side. Hearing Mike unlock the adjacent cell door, John nods his head, and we both lean down to the bean hole for discretion.

I put my ear to the bean hole and hear from a Mafia boss still in complete command. "Listen, Mark. I got your back on this, so you keep feeding me information and don't fucking listen to nothin' no one tells you out there. Fuck them. I'm Cosa Nostra 'til I die, and this shit hole doesn't change a fucking thing. You fucking hear me? I'm still the fucking boss."

I nod my head and whisper a motto I'll utter to the end of my days, "You may not like what I tell you, but I will never lie to you."

John reflects from hard lessons learned. "It's appreciated. I respect a man who's willing to put all his cards on the table. I'm getting fucking sick and tired of motherfucking, ass-kissing, wise guy wannabe's trying to play their last card to fuck over John Gotti to beat their time. Fucking rats. Why don't they grow a pair and be fucking men?"

After what Curtis told me about Sammy the Bull's betrayal, I completely understand John's ruminations. I, too, had been snitched out by a so-called friend who I'd helped when he was homeless. However, unbeknownst to me, he was busted for meth while down the street from my house and, to escape his meth charges, he was willing to plant his girlfriend's gun under my mattress and tell the DEA that I was selling pot. Now, here I sit doing time with a thousand other shmucks who were ratted out by someone they trusted. This type of betrayal forever leaves a bad taste in your mouth and gives a clear understanding that law enforcement will work with Mephistopheles himself in order to score a conviction. If law enforcement is willing to use a homeless snitch to violate my rights to gain a conviction, what chance does

John Gotti have that there isn't a snitch waiting in the wings to take him down?

"I totally understand, John."

Through the adjacent cell's window, Mike apparently witnessed an inmate violate prison policy on the yard. Pounding on the screen, he yells. "Hey, inmate!"

A confidential tone mixed with determination and resolve bleeds through the iron door's metal slot. "You also fucking understand that I have other people out there feeding me information besides you, and the only thing that matters before I die is that these rat motherfuckers don't frame my son in some bullshit FBI sting."

Mike yells again. "Yeah, you! Pick that cigarette butt up off the ground and throw it in the butt can before I come out there and write your ass up."

After looking over my shoulder, I lean into the hole. "I think I have something for you, but I'm not sure exactly what it means."

John cocks his head as I see his eyes go wide and his temper flare. "Don't you leave me here holding my fucking cock."

His voice shakes with a quiet rage, and through clenched teeth, he demands. "I want every fucking thing you have. You understand me? I know you're a smart guy and can figure things out. I'm fuckin countin' on you..."

From the adjacent cell, we hear Mike lock the cell door from behind us with a mechanical finality: THUNK.

Before Mike can pull the key from the keyhole, John and my conversation ramps into high gear as our volume diminishes. "I promise I'll do what I can."

"Take it up a notch if you have to. And remember, John Gotti never forgets who fucked him over or helped him—fucking ever."

From behind my back, I hear Mike's keys jangle. "Let's go. I got other shit to do."

John steps away from the door with his tray as Mike locks the bean hole. Through the plexiglass window, John juts his jaw out and, with a cocked eyebrow, points his finger at me and mouths. *"I'm counting on you."*

CHAPTER 29

As Mike and I walk back to the elevator lobby, he quips, "Quite a character, wouldn't you say?"

"Yeah, you'd think the SHU and cancer would break him, but not John. He's going to walk the walk and talk the talk 'til the bitter end. Still, it's distressing to see someone like him caged like an animal, waiting to die there alone."

"Listen. I've worked here for a while, and every inmate I've ever talked to said that's his greatest fear—to die alone in prison."

I glance at Mike. "We must listen to the same grapevine. I've heard the same."

"Hey, Mike. You don't mind me talking to Gotti a little when I clean his room? Like I said, I kinda feel sorry for him."

"If I thought you were out of bounds, I would have said something." Mike turns the corner into the elevator lobby, walks to his office, then turns and stands in front of the office door with his thumbs in the front pockets of his pants. "Look. I'm not a bleeding heart, and I don't feel sorry for Gotti. He's a mobster, and this is where mobsters come to die. But, I'm not a heartless prick either where I'm going to deny a man a little human dignity."

Mike unhooks his thumbs from his pants pockets and puts his hands on his waist like a drill sergeant. "That being said, just don't get involved in their nefarious bullshit. You're days from going home, and you have never struck me as someone who belongs here."

"Well, I am for getting out of this shit hole. No offense."

Mike grins. "None taken."

He points to the food carrier. "There's an extra food tray in there if you want it."

I thank him and grab three meal trays from the food carrier, then walk into the common area to find Slim waiting for me.

Slim lifts his head "Sup?"

I joke as I set the food trays on the worn card table, "I'll tell you what's up. An extra meal tray, courtesy of our friendly guard. Would you like to partake of Springfield's latest delicacies?"

Rubbing his hands together like a hungry miser, Slim beams. "Does Snoop Dog like weed? Hit me up, M'man."

While eating Springfield's latest sensation, Slim again tells me how sorry he is that his homie tried to trick me off. As I jab a green bean onto my spork, I tell him that I'm too close to the door not to let bygones be bygones. Besides, I'd heard through the prison grapevine that he'd received a beating for his indiscretions."

Slim nods his head. "You got that right, Homes. That nigger got the black knocked off of him."

He throws a gang sign. "Crip's don't play that shit in here."

Leaning back in his chair, he waves his spork towards me. "Listen, my nigger. I'd like to make what happened between us right if you're down for beating this piss hole one more time before you leave." Slim leans in. "I just got some inside information that could help us to be the first in line for commissary tomorrow."

"Really? First in line for commissary?"

Commissary is a weekly bitch of necessity and inconvenience, where hundreds of eager convicts rush toward the commissary after count clears, only to stand in a two-hour line before being told that the last Rocky Road ice cream sold 30 minutes ago. So, I'm more than a little intrigued.

"Tell me more."

Slim's persona suddenly changes into one of excitement and stratagem as he lays out a plan to beat the guards and the long commissary line. It begins with one of his homeboys who works for the lieutenant and who recently delivered a work order to maintenance regarding a faulty security camera—one that is directly above the elevator door as it opens onto the basement floor, 45 ft. away from the commissary's entrance. To further sweeten the deal, another of Slim's homies conveniently lost the camera's replacement parts, forcing the Bureau to reorder the replacement part and delaying its arrival until next week.

"Listen, my nigger. With that camera outta commission, all we gotta do is take the elevator down to the basement three minutes before count clears, then walk 20 feet to the next hallway intersection to make sure there's no heat. Once count clears, we bounce around the corner and sprint another 25 feet to the commissary entrance. Mark, we could be the first motherfuckers in line after count clears! All we need to do is make it past Mike's door, and we're home free. And, since your Mike's main orderly, I know you have his schedule and habits down so we can slip by him to access the elevator. What do you think? You in?"

Personally, I think it's a doable plan that will allow us to easily beat the commissary's two-hour wait time. Also, if I can invite Greg for one last hurrah to make up for throwing a monkey wrench in his plans with John Jr., it might be just what the doctor ordered.

I rub my chin. "You're right. I do have Mike's schedule down and, with that camera out on the basement floor, it sounds like a foolproof gig. But, if you don't mind, I'd like Greg to ride in the car with us to make up for a few misunderstandings we had lately."

"Sure. I don't mind, but it can only be Greg—no one else can know about this shit."

"I promise. Only Greg."

Slim high-fives me. "My nigger!"

After Slim and I finish our meals, we stack our empty trays in the middle of the card table. Slim then slouches into his chair and turns his attention to a TV program as I reflect on John's emotionally charged request that I give him all information at my disposal. Excusing myself to the bathroom, I write John another kite that is just over a page long, detailing everything I've heard or seen, from José being pissed when John pulled the plug on John Jr.'s involvement to Sammy and Greg exploring alternate scenarios to placate him. I also detail my third-source account of José being seen in physical therapy with two men in suits, Peter's mysterious and untimely demise into diesel therapy, and José's growing hostility towards my general presence on the unit.

Fifteen minutes later, I'm at the SHU emptying John's trash. As I kneel down to replace John's trash can liner, I find two kites at the bottom of the wastepaper basket, with "Mark" written on one and "Greg" written on the other. I shove them into my sock and place my own kite on the bottom of the basket before replacing the trashcan liner. I hear a low, edgy voice from behind me that has a sense of urgency. "Mark, I know you're leaving in a couple of days, but I feel I'm running out of time. I..."

Mike is just outside the door. I eyeball the wastepaper basket and mouth, "I have you covered, John."

As I pick up the food trays, I hear Mike walk to the other cell to answer an incoming walkie-talkie communication. John nods in understanding and points to a picture of his son. He again affirms his love for John Jr. and his concern over a growing conspiracy theory to hurt him. "That boy's my heart and one of the only kids of mine that ever fucking understood what this life meant to me. I'm starting to fucking think, more and more, that some cocksucker is going to use his love for me to stab me in the back..."

I realized I'm throwing gasoline on John's fevered thoughts, but it's the truth, and I have no regrets. I again ogle the wastepaper basket. "I think you're right."

Cocking his head, John's eyes widen, but, before he can say anything, Mike sticks his head in the room.

"Let's go. I need you to take the food carrier back down to the kitchen."

John stands up. "I thought you'd never fucking ask. I've been dying to stretch my legs all day."

Mike laughs. "Wish I could, Gotti. Let's go, Mark. You have orderly stuff to do."

As we walk back, I can tell Mike is preoccupied and ask if anything is wrong.

"Nah, I just have some paperwork to attend to. Why don't you sweep the unit until I need you?"

"Don't you want me to take the food carrier down to the kitchen?"

"No. Unless I say otherwise, I really need for you to stay close to the unit until further notice."

"You got it, boss."

While Mike is busy with paperwork, I grab a dust broom and head to Greg's room to see if he wants to take a quick smoke. I knock on his door and find him sitting at a small desk filling out his commissary list. Glancing my way, Greg lifts his hand. "I was wondering if you were going to come get me before you hit the head for a smoke."

"Ye of little faith."

"That's what everyone keeps tellin' me."

We both laugh. I walk closer to Greg and slam my fist into my open hand. "Something just dropped in my lap that will cut our wait time at the commissary down to zero."

Greg immediately stops what he is doing, places the pencil on the desk, and turns in my direction.

"You have my attention, paisan. I'm all about zero wait time."

I nod towards the door. "Let's talk on the way to the head. No telling how long Mike will be preoccupied."

As we walk to the bathroom, I give Greg the details of Slim's plan to beat the commissary line while I also stress the importance that he can be the only one who knows our plans. Greg's house shoes loudly flippity-flop down the hallway as he puts his arm around my shoulder.

"I appreciate you thinkin' about me, and I understand your concerns. Too many swinging dicks in a hole always fucks up a good thing. What time are you going to take the elevator down to the basement?"

I explain as I hold the bathroom door open for him. "We're playing it by ear. Everything revolves around Mike's movements on this unit and those of any guards patrolling the basement's hallway below. But, I'm thinking, be at the elevator immediately after count and pretend to be waiting to use the phone. Once Mike is preoccupied, Slim and I will go down to the basement after first making sure the coast is clear. If we don't come back in two minutes, follow us down. I'll meet you and push you around the corner, right into the commissary."

"That's a fucking good plan, Mark. Let me buy everyone an ice cream for allowing me to ride."

I protest, "Before I leave, and to make up for any misunderstandings, I'd really like for you to let me do this without compensation."

"I appreciate that, Mark."

Reaching our smoking spot at the back of the bathroom, Greg pulls out his half a cigarette wrapped in cellophane from a cigarette pack, unfurls the wrap to retrieve the butt, and places it in his mouth. "Did you get a chance to talk to John? How's he doin'?"

"Yeah, I did. He's preoccupied with his son and people fucking him over."

"That's what I've been hearing, too. Hopefully, we can remedy that if everyone demonstrates a little bit more faith." Greg points at himself. "In this guy."

I pull a cigarette pack from my pocket and retrieve a cigarette and Greg's kite from it. Placing the cigarette in my mouth, I hand Greg John's kite, while I keep my kite hidden, to be opened later in private. Greg's face contorts in anger as he reads John's kite. He balls the kite in his fist and throws it in the urinal as if its contents contained mafia kryptonite.

"For fucking Christ sakes, now everything is on fucking hold until I can convince John otherwise."

Squinting at me, Greg cocks his head and tries to enlist an ally in his cause to whack Nicky. "Look, Mark. My personal feeling aside, I just want you to fucking know, Nicky is not only spitting in my face. He's spitting in everybody's face. It makes us look weak, and now other cocksuckers are bulldogging John's favorite restaurant without buying a bullet. This disrespect has gotta stop, and if not addressed is going to set a bad example for the rest of us."

Greg lights his butt, then lights the cigarette dangling from my mouth, and solicits, "Let me ask you this. Do you think that fuck would be walking around in here if he owed a store in here a couple of grand?"

His question is a no-brainer. In prison, a store is someone who loans out commissary items for a high rate of return in some form of prison currency. An inmate can be stabbed over a couple packs of cigarettes owed to a creditor, and nobody would blink an eye—especially if the inmate openly avoids paying the debt, like this Nicky fellow Greg described. It's a sign of disrespect to the creditor, who then must answer this disrespect with unmitigated violence. Otherwise, the creditor is considered to be a punk and weak and, in prison, the weak are eaten alive. I suppose it's the same in Greg's world.

"Not long. Listen, Greg. I completely understand where you're coming from, but what if I told you that José might be a snitch and John's paranoia may be justified...?"

Greg rolls his eyes, and he cuts me off. "What the fuck are you talking about 'may and might be?' If I flinched every time those words were mentioned, I'd never get anything fucking done. That can't be true about José, and I don't want to hear nothing more about it. You fucking understand me? You're playing with fire, even insinuating José is a snitch, and you're getting ready to cross a line that I may not be able to help ya out of. And who the fuck told you José is a snitch?"

"Nobody has told me José is a snitch, but Curtis said José had been seen in physical therapy with two guys in suits."

Greg rubs his cleanly shaven chin. "I respect Curtis, and he does have a lot of birds singing in his ear. But I can tell you right here and now, whatever his homies told him is a bunch of bullshit."

Greg emphasizes "homies" in a sarcastic tone, and I realize he stopped listening to anything that disparages José or interferes with his own plans.

I try to disengage from this topic by bending a knee. "Don't shoot the messenger, and you're right, Greg. I'm sorry I brought it up."

"Hey, forget about it. You did what you were asked, and I can't slight a man for that."

Flipping his cigarette into the urinal, he turns and rushes towards the bathroom door. "We'll talk later, Mark. I gotta go talk to Sammy and John."

Taking a drag from my cigarette, I wave goodbye through a haze of bluish smoke.

After returning the food carrier to the kitchen, I hit the yard for a quick walk around the track. Unexpectedly, I see Greg in his wheelchair under John's window. I notice another inmate from the orderly's unit standing near a tree, waiting for Greg, indicating that Greg chose someone else, besides me, to push him into the yard this time. I also assume that John already read my kite, and whatever is being said isn't sitting well with Greg. As I walk past John's cell, he sees me from his window, smiles, and waves. Greg turns to glare at me, then turns back towards John with voice raised saying something that I can only assume has to do with me. As I walk past their position, I hear John's voice raise angrily, cutting off any further opposition from Greg, whose voice goes silent under his superior's authority.

After returning to the unit, I'm sitting in the communal lounge watching TV when a beaten-down Greg DePalma comes through the door. He doesn't mince words. "Well, it looks like you screwed me with John."

"I'm sorry. I only did want John asked, and I..." Greg holds up his hand.

"It's okay. John's the boss, and you're right. You did what John asked, and we're proud of ya. And, to show there are no hard feelings, before you leave, John wants me to give you a phone number to call when you're out of this shit hole to show our appreciation."

I'm relieved that John has smoothed over any harsh feelings between Greg and me. "So, you're not mad?"

Greg shrugs his shoulders. "It doesn't matter what I fucking feel, and it ain't over 'til the fat lady sings. Besides, like I said before, you did what you were told, and I still believe in rules. And, if John Jr. happened to be hurt because of something I did, Jesus fucking Christ! I don't think I could live with myself—if John even gave me that choice."

Greg gives a nervous laugh and mimes a gun with his hand to shoot himself in the head, then slugs me in the arm while grinning. "But that cocksucker still has to go."

All of a sudden, Mike and another guard's voices boom down the hallways. "Everyone in their rooms! Orderlies front and center. We are evacuating the unit!"

Greg ponders prison protocols. "I wonder what the fuck that's about?'

"Beats the fuck outta me, but I gotta go. Talk later. Ok?"

"You got it, paisan."

I leave Greg and meet Slim at the elevator lobby, where Mike is talking to three guards who I have never seen before. They turn and give Slim and me a hard look.

Breaking the uneasy tension, Mike points to Slim and me. "These inmates are with me."

The guards turn back to Mike and whisper as they point down the corridors. They then shake hands and fan out down the darkened hallways. Over the intercom, a steely, authoritarian voice commands, "Inmates, stay in your rooms to be evacuated off the unit in an orderly fashion. Repeat: Stay in your rooms for evacuation."

Mike turns towards us. "There is a gas leak on this unit, and we are evacuating to the gym. Help the other inmates where needed."

I sniff the air. "I don't smell any gas."

From down the hallway, I hear Sammy's angry voice, "I don't smell shit! And I'm not fucking leaving this room, so go fuck yourself."

Slim smells the air, hunching his shoulders in bewilderment. "Nothin' here, Boss."

Mike looks at our confused faces. "Hell, I don't smell anything either. I'm just following orders, and I suggest that you do the same. Inmates, standby until needed. Are we clear?"

We both obediently nod our heads and stand by the elevator awaiting further orders. As Mike returns to his office, Slim curses under his breath, "This is fucking po-po bullshit," while Sammy continues his defiant protests.

Later, I heard that the lieutenant personally came to Sammy's room and told him he would either be evacuated from his room with the other inmates, or the CERT team would physically remove him, and he would spend the next 90 days in the SHU. When I see a disgruntled Sam Cagnina walk into the gym wearing his bright yellow pajamas, I assume he decided to fight the man another day.

The inmates' gym looks like any other small-town gym with its shiny wooden floors, basketball hoops at either end, and traditional metal bleachers stationed courtside. The newly evacuated are placed on the court according to their room assignments, while the guards sit on the bleachers to keep an eye on the corralled inmates. This gym floor arrangement separates Greg from Sammy. Since there is no sign of John, I presume he was moved to another SHU elsewhere in the prison, ostensibly to avoid the deadly gas leak. To fight the boredom, most inmates play cards, read, or sleep as the sun begins to set on Springfield's penitentiary. Slim and I are free to walk around the gym to attend to the geriatric needs of the inmates. Sammy waves me over as I pass him and whispers under his breath, "I think you're right, Mark. Something is fuckin' not right here. Let talk once this is over."

"That's what I've been trying to tell everyone."

From across the gym, I notice Curtis urgently waving me over to his position. Sammy rubs his head and laments, "Probably should go over there and find out what he knows."

"Probably so."

As I amble over to Curtis, I feel the uncomfortable sensation of someone's stare scorching my backside. Quickly glancing around, I spot José across the gym with a smug look and book in hand, sitting in his wheelchair with his eyes steadily following my every movement. Brushing off his steely gaze, I nonchalantly stroll over to Curtis, bend down on one knee, and whisper, "What's up, buddy?"

Curtis bows his head to move closer to my ear. "I think we're being watched."

Rolling my eyes towards José, I respond to the obvious, "Yeah. Tell me something I don't know."

"This has gone beyond José, and I'm almost positive the Feds are involved."

As I look on the other side of the gym, I'm momentarily distracted by watching Greg applying his expressive Italian hand gestures while talking with his roommate.

Curtis elbows my arm to regain my attention. "Listen, homes. I gotta talk to Mr. DePalma, quick. I just saw and heard some things in today's confusion that he probably needs to hear straight from my mouth."

"I can walk over there now and tell him. But you should know, I told Greg what you told me about José and the men in suits, and he didn't believe a word of it."

Curtis squirms. "I didn't think he would, and it's why I need to talk to him. The heat is here, my nigger. And, it's why I don't think you should be involved with this anymore."

"What???"

"You heard me, my brother from another mother, walk away from this shit and bounce home. This has turned into a game without old school rules, filled with rats and players. You dig? José is up to bat, and he doesn't take any prisoners. You go tell Mr. DePalma I need to speak to him, and then step off."

I prod for more information. "I don't mean to get all up in your business, but if José is so dangerous, why don't you walk away from this unmitigated disaster?"

"My nigger, I was born on an electric mile, and I can see the red light up ahead. But, before this red-eyed flight ends, I owe a homie and a couple of my girls a little get back."

Suddenly, a guard bellows over the crowd of inmates. "Grab your junk, everyone back to the unit! Orderlies, assist anyone who needs help!"

Turning towards the guard and inmates, I see Greg wave his hand and holler. "Hey Mark, can ya help an old man!"

I wave back at Greg and yell, "Be there in just a second."

Curtis remarks on this unlikely affiliation. "You're lucky that Mr. DePalma has got your back, but remember, at the end of the day, he is only loyal to Costa Nostra."

"If you feel that way about Greg, why do you call him Mr. DePalma? I've noticed you don't offer any other inmate that type of respect."

Curtis doesn't hesitate. "Unlike his Mafioso friends, Mr. DePalma has never treated or called me a nigger or ever slighted me in a business deal. Hell, he had Diana Ross open the Westchester

Theater and play golf with Willie Mayes. Mr. DePalma is a righteous dude, and I give respect where respect is given."

"He's mentioned that theater before and said it hosted some wild times."

"You don't know the half of it, my friend."

"I guess Greg knows José from the street."

Curtis gives nothing away while gazing at Greg. "Something like that. Go help Mr. DePalma and tell him I need to talk to him ASAP."

"Will do."

As I turn to walk away, Curtis suddenly grabs my shoulder. "And tell him that there weren't any gas leaks."

"I wish you'd tell me what's going on."

Curtis squeezes my shoulder as a sign of friendship. "It's time for you to go home brother, just don't forget to bring my Rocky Road tomorrow."

"It's already written down on my commissary list."

Curtis high-fives me. "M'man!"

I'm not blind or deaf to what these inmates represent to society, but like Greg, Gotti, and Sammy, I'd grown to like and respect Curtis a little more each day. Little do I know that this will be the last time I see my old friend alive.

CHAPTER 30

Like a ravenous lion stalking its prey on the plains of the Serengeti, I feel José's laser-point focus follow my every movement as I walk across the polished floors towards Greg. His eyes never blink, nor does his gaze falter as I wheel Greg, with his larger-than-life personality, out the gymnasium's door. As I wheel Greg through the prison's basement corridors and away from José's watchful gaze, I look down on his combover and whisper softly, "Greg, Curtis needs to speak to you ASAP."

"What about?"

"He wouldn't tell me, but I think it has to do with José. He also said there wasn't any gas leak."

"What? How the fuck does he know all that?"

"I don't know. He wouldn't tell me; he said because it was time for me to go home."

"Well, there's something everyone can agree on."

Understanding Greg's appreciation for those who show respect, I try to paint Curtis in a favorable light by recounting Curtis's reason for addressing him as Mr. DePalma.

Shaking his head, he huffs. "Although I appreciate his respect, we're associates because money doesn't see color." Greg glances over his shoulder with a wise guy smile. "But neither do bullets."

"Come on, Greg. You're a pussycat."

Giving a wicked grin, he unexpectedly professes, "I like to hurt people who deserve it."

"That's what I've heard."

"Who told you that? Curtis?"

"If it involved a sledgehammer and a rat. Then, yeah."

"Damn, that pimp has his canaries singing everywhere. Well, Curtis has always had his ear to the ground. I suppose it wouldn't hurt to hear what he has to say, but if it's got to do with José being a rat, I don't fucking want to hear about it."

I reiterate the urgency and push Curtis's agenda. "Still, probably wouldn't hurt."

A snarl escapes Greg's mouth. "We'll fucking see."

Before and after our arrival to his room, we keep our conversation light. He reminds me before I leave, "Don't forget about me tomorrow when we screw the Screws one last time before you leave."

"I wouldn't miss it for the world." After all the hard feelings of late, I meant that.

Once I'm back at the elevator lobby, I stick my head into Mike's office and ask him if there's anything else I can do before I leave. He instructs me to make one more round on the unit with the dust mop.

Suddenly, he changes his mind, waving me into his office.

"Hey, come in here for a minute. I want to talk to you."

I immediately think I'm in trouble. "What's up, Mike?"

Mike sizes me up. "I didn't know you were here on explosives and weapon charges. You don't strike me as a Jessie James."

"Who told you that?"

"Me and a few of the guards were talking amongst ourselves. So, what gives?"

Sitting down in front of Mike's desk, I quickly run down my previous life of being overmedicated by psychiatrists since childhood and how the side effects from these insidious medications caused extreme paranoia and psychotic tendencies that landed me in boys' homes, mental institutions, and finally, prison—where a prison psychiatrist finally determined I'd been overmedicated. Mike stares strangely at the man before him who he doesn't recognize as either mentally ill or criminal. But his face contorts into confusion when I divulge that these psychoses manifested into bizarre beliefs that everybody from the CIA to shadow people was after me."

Mike stutters. "S-S-S-Shadow people?"

"Ironically, that's what they looked like to me. They appeared as something resembling Grim Reapers, but without arms or scythes. More than that, though, I felt their auras, their very essence as soulless, indifferent, black holes of ambiguity that somehow latched onto my life as it spiraled out of control."

"When and where in the hell did you see these soulless fucks at?"

"Well, it's not something I usually discuss, but I began seeing these apparitions shortly after psychiatrists administered a regimen of psychoactive medications around age 14. It all started just before my arrest in 1995, with a petrifying experience in the hills of California. A girl and I were asleep on a moonless night in a secluded cabin on Mt. Herman, with only a single night light burning in the corner of our bedroom. Around midnight, I was startled awake by a presence in the room. I tried to sit up but couldn't move my body—only my eyes."

As I continue my tale, Mike's jaw begins to drop.

"Glancing around the bedroom, I witnessed what looked to be a small humanoid shape approximately five feet tall standing utterly motionless at the end of the bed. It appeared to be draped in a completely black cloak and had no face or visible arms. Even though I couldn't see its face, I knew it was staring at us through vacant eyes. Rolling my eyes to the side, I saw my girlfriend staring up at the ceiling, murmuring, 'What's happening?' Like I said, at that time, I thought everyone, including aliens, was after me. I had a gun on the nightstand beside me for such an occasion. Through sheer will, I managed to slowly reach, lift, and point the gun at this shadow being, at which time it immediately dematerialized."

As I describe my unspeakable night, Mike becomes visibly shaken. And his knee begins to jackhammer up and down, and his face appears painfully nervous. I ask the obvious, "What's wrong, Mike?"

His knee stops. "I've seen one of those fuckers, too."

Then, for the next ten minutes, our unit guard tells me a horror story about one night when he and his wife were asleep in their bedroom. He was awakened by one of these shadow creatures and chased it through their house, gun in hand, as it moved across the walls like Spiderman. For the next hour, the guard and I bond in the realm of the paranormal, discussing a variety of stories others have told us about the shadow people and what their existence could possibly mean. After this lengthy conversation, Mike leans back in his chair, taps his watch, and gives a heartfelt half-grin.

"Well, I guess that concludes our session of getting ass-fucked in the *Twilight Zone.*

We both laugh before his voice suddenly assumes a more serious tone. "Listen. I was also told you're leaving the day after tomorrow. If so, I want you to keep your distance from DePalma and focus on going home. Trust me on this. Ok?"

The hair on my arms rises from my skin as a feeling of déjà vu washes over me, stemming from an earlier incident in which someone else warned me that a bust was imminent. But, at that time, in my drugged-out state, I disregarded the information causing me to experience peril and prison time.

I nod my head. "Okay, Mike. I appreciate the heads-up."

Mike twirls his hand and instructs me to complete the round with the dust mop before I leave.

"Will do, Mike. And, thanks for looking out."

Mike gives me a thumbs-up as I walk out of his office back into the elevator lobby to find José silently sitting in his wheelchair near the pop machine, with a closed book in his lap. As I nonchalantly walk past José's position and drift down the hallway, his head swivels to follow my movements. Either to intimidate or annoy me, he begins tapping the book rhythmically to synchronize with my footsteps.

As I pick up my pace, José's voice drips with innuendo from down the corridor, "That was an awfully long time to converse with a guard. Was there anything in particular you and your friend were talkin' about?"

My voice echoes down the dimly lit hallway. "Shadow people."

From behind, I hear José's astonished voice. "What the fuck did you say?"

Laughing under my breath, I turn the corner to the utility closet. Once there, I grab a dust mop and push it towards Sammy's room. I find him reading a book. Before I can speak, Sammy looks over his glasses and puts his finger up to his lips.

"Let's walk down to the microwave for a minute; I was just going to heat my coffee up."

Sammy pushes his great girth off the bed, slips on his house shoes, then grabs my elbow as he walks by.

As we walk down the hallway, Sammy confides, "I think those cocksuckers moved us out to bug this unit. Don't say shit in my, Greg, or John's room. You understand?"

"I've heard the same."

"Who the fuck told you that?"

"Curtis."

"The old pimp that Greg knew from the street?"

"Yes. He said he felt the same and wants to talk to Greg ASAP."

Sammy squints his eyes. "What the fuck about?"

"I don't know. He wouldn't tell me and told me to go home."

"Greg did say that old pimp had more connections than an investigative reporter at the New York times. And, yeah, I would suggest the same at this point—go the fuck home. I feel the hair on the back of my neck begin to stand. In the middle of the hallway, Sammy unexpectedly stops. "So, what did your friend say about José?"

At this point, I sense that I should just keep my mouth shut and keep pushing the broom down the hallway, but over the last year, these convicts have had my back when blood and friends did not. On one hand, I did need to put this all behind me and go home; but, on the other hand, what kind of man walks away from friends who proved themselves in the shittiest of times? I pat Sammy's shoulder and lay out everything I've been told in order to give him a fighting chance against any unknown confederacy. "Okay, here's what I know..."

Sammy listens intently, bringing his fist to his mouth when I tell him of John and my kites that, for all intents and purposes, derailed John Jr. from meeting with José's emissary. When I reveal Curtis's intel on José, his eyes flash, and he rubs his chin.

"Hmmm...interesting."

Stopping at the microwave table, I lean against its counter. "So, what do you think? Is everyone paranoid except Greg, or do you think there something to all of this?"

Glancing around to be certain the area is clear of any low-lying snitches, Sammy lowers his voice. "Well, from what Greg has been telling me, I kinda figured you'd told John something to derail José's plans with John Jr., but who knows who else talks to John? Like I said before, John makes his own decisions, and it looks like he's decided that John Jr. is off the table. Hell, John has paid his dues, and if he wants his kid outta this thing of ours, so fucking be it. You know, Greg really loves his kids too, but he hasn't been as lucky as John. Fuck, his wife is still breakin' his balls in here over their son."

"I didn't know Greg had kids. What happened?'

"Let's just say his wife hates the business we're in, and Greg has a lot on his mind."

"I'm really sorry to hear that."

Sammy crosses his arms across his massive chest and continues his original train of thought. "As far as Curtis goes, I've heard he has a score to settle with José; so, he may have ulterior motives. For all we know, *he* might be working with the feds. Who's to fucking know at this point? Do you?"

With an incredulous frown, I deliver a joke to give Curtis the benefit of the doubt. "I wouldn't know. They took my Magic 8 Ball when they stripped searched me. But that aside, do you really think Curtis has just been feeding me a line of bullshit to screw over José? If so, why me?"

Sammy smiles. "I'm going to miss your candor. And, why not you? Look. I've been in this business for a while, and you don't always know what's going on until it's already over. But then again, if we were pussies every time business needed to be handled, nothing would get done, and people might get the idea they can take over."

"Aren't you leery of José?"

"I'm fucking leery of everybody, and I fucking think they bugged our unit. But, if José is working with the feds to trap Gotti, I think you've kicked any plans for that in the nuts. Still, I suppose at this point, it wouldn't hurt to give José a red herring until everything plays out. Then, if he's really legit, bring him into future business ventures..."

"I'm glad I'm going home. Figuring out who's the snitch is getting exhausting."

"Oh, I'm just thinkin' out loud," Sammy declares. "And, I appreciate you tellin' me what the fuck is going on. Hell, Curtis may know something that he's not telling anyone else except you, and he's giving you a heads up before the feds come to town because you're friends."

I again feel an uneasiness and mutter, "The guard sort of said the same thing and told me to keep my distance from Greg and go home."

Sammy's tone changes to one of suspicion. "When were you talkin' to the guard?

"Just before I came to see you."

"What the fuck were you talkin' to the guard about?"

I gulp inaudibly. "Shadow people."

Sammy's face contorts. "Are you fucking crazy? Greg told me you were taking crazy pills and seeing a shrink at one time, and now you're talking to the guards?"

Talking to a guard for anything other than basic necessities is forbidden in this world—if you do, you're either an ass-kisser, a snitch, or both to the man. Although I understand the mentality behind this convicts' decree, unless you're in a gang, I personally find this maladaptive behavior to be detrimental when doing time. You do not want the guards to become your enemy, either.

I interrupt Sammy and try to explain my conversation with the guard along with my story of being misdiagnosed by psychiatrists, but Sammy stifles any excuses by raising his hand and blowing out an exhaustive sigh. "That's enough of the shadow people. Anything that can materialize on this earth can bleed. Remember that. Is there anything else I need to know about?"

Sammy's demeanor signals that his cop's suspicious mentality is now on point, and I realize he is not interested in any stories of the shadow people. Understanding that anything I say will only make matters worse, I capitulate any further explanation. "Not really."

Sammy walks past me with an air of ambivalence. "I've got a lot of thinking to do, Mark, but I'd take everyone's advice and forget about this bullshit and go home."

Back on my unit later that night, I wait until everyone's asleep in my dorm before stepping into the orderly's white tiled bathroom and walking past two empty shower stalls to a row of exposed toilets. Walking under bright fluorescent lights to the end commode, I put my foot on the toilet's seat and retrieve John's kite from my sock, then sit down and pretend to defecate—prepared to flush any contraband down the toilet on a moment's notice. Once I determine that no sleepy inmate will walk in unannounced, I open the kite. It read:

Pasian,

First off, I appreciate your helping a dying man save his son from these rat motherfuckers. My son is his own man now and has decided to go his own way, and I suggest you do the same before these cocksuckers try to pull your ass into this klusterfuck too. Heads up. I'm hearing people say you might be a snitch. I don't believe shit, but we'll know soon enough who's the fucking rat. Destroy this kite after you read it. If my associates are correct, this is the last kite between us before shit hits the fan.

You're a stand-up guy and welcome to sit at my table anytime. Hang tough, and I'll see you on the other side.

John Gotti

Transfixed by the words "a snitch," I quickly gain my composure, tear the kite into small pieces, and flush it down the toilet. I stand and walk seven feet to an opposing wall where stainless-steel mirrors are attached above a row of sinks.

Staring into my obscured stainless-steel reflection, I hear myself whisper, "A snitch."

In prison, being denounced as a snitch is a label that can result in a beat down or even murder. Without John identifying my accuser, my mind races in an attempt to determine the culprit's name with one thing for certain. *Curtis will know this backstabber, and I'll demand that name tomorrow when I deliver his Rocky Road.*

Laying in my bunk that night, my exhausted mind is filled with conspiracy theories but finally shuts down into an uneasy sleep with one single pervasive thought: *One more day and a wake-up, and I'm out of here.*

CHAPTER 31

My morning is occupied with the completion of the final paperwork for my release the next day, returning the Bureau of Prisons' property, and giving personal items away to friends who I will be leaving behind forever. After seven long years, it's hard to fathom that I will finally be released from this concrete and razor-wired world. Still harder to believe is what I've endured through these chaotic and violent years without being stabbed, beaten, or molested—in large part due to the intervention of people who have been kind to me like Gotti, Greg, Rick, and others who I met along prison life's jagged edge. Besides having a mild case of PTSD, it appears that, if all goes well until 9:00 a.m. tomorrow morning, I should walk into the arms of my parents virtually unscathed. Unfortunately, given John's cryptic implications that I've been branded a snitch by an unknown accuser, a sharp shiv could interrupt my peaceful plan and cut off my last step to freedom.

Despite the vague and dangerous accusation, my mood is upbeat and generous. My generosity and goodwill will first materialize in the form of ice cream for Curtis and Rick for having my back through the years. Of course, I must take the opportunity to burn one last memory with Greg DePalma before I leave as I eagerly anticipate a final canteen caper with Greg and Slim.

As I take care of last-minute business, I laugh to myself at the irony that this allegiance was even possible—only weeks before, Slim threatened to send me home in a box, with John and Greg undoubtedly threatening him with the same fate; however, if necessary to beat over a thousand impatient, desperate, violent inmates to a one-line checkout lane at the canteen, improbable alliances will be formed.

Holding my laundry bag, the inmates' official shopping bag within all penitentiaries, I arrive for my last day of work right before count. Slim is waiting impatiently for me by the Coke machine as the elevator's doors slide open. We huddle and quickly put our plan into motion, telling the guard we need to clean and wax the elevator. Slim walks out of the guard's office and presses the elevator's hold button, locking it into place, while I hustle to the cleaning closet to retrieve the buffer and stop by Greg's room to let him know we have a green light. Pushing the buffer to Greg's door, I find him sitting in his wheelchair, filling out his commissary list.

"Hey, Greg. You ready to do this thing?"

"Sonny, I've been prepared for this before you were just a gleam in your daddy's eye. So, what's our plan?"

After laughing at his risqué though trite pun, we get down to business.

"A minute ago, we locked the elevator onto this floor. In a few minutes, Slim and I will be riding the elevator down to the basement. I need you to head that way in about five minutes. Once you're at the bottom, I'll come get you and push you into the canteen when count clears."

Checking his watch, Greg gives me a thumbs-up. "Sounds like a hell of a plan. Thanks, Mark. I'll get you back for this."

Striding out of the door, I tell him over my shoulder, "It's not necessary, buddy."

Back at the elevator landing, I find Slim chatting up another Crip gangbanger. He informs me that his homie will distract the guard by whatever means necessary while we, and later Greg, ride the lift to the basement floor. Slim promised him a pint of ice cream for being a lookout for the guard, which in prison is called a "jigger." I nod my head to signal my approval and accept my obligation for a share of the ice cream. The gangbanger doesn't reciprocate my gesture or acknowledge my existence, signifying to a non-compatriot that "Your approval is not needed." Slim and I step into the brightly lit lift and focus on our mission, ignoring any societal boundaries I may have transgressed. He presses the elevator's worn down button, and the cables, pulleys, and machinery that propel this vintage lift come to life.

As the doors begin to come together, Slim flashes a gang sign to his fellow Crip. "Don't let me down, my nigger."

The young black kid forms a C with his right hand, which is the sign of the Crips. "I gotcha back, Cuz."

With gang pleasantries and protocols afforded, the stainless-steel doors close, sealing our decision to break prison rules and risk a write-up in order to beat the system one last time. The aging elevator creaks and groans against the weight of the elevator car that slowly descends towards the basement floor. Curious, I ask Slim why he didn't invite his friend to join us in our escapades. Slim confesses that the kid was scared of getting a write-up.

"He just started doin' time a few months ago and has already had a few write-ups for being stupid. He told me he just couldn't risk getting busted again because he would go to the hole. Before you arrived, I was talkin' to DePalma, and he thought you had some pretty big balls doing this the day before you leave. And I gotta admit, if I had a blunt, I'd burn one with ya G."

I wave off any gangster accolades by confessing, "Like I said before, this is about a last hurrah with Greg to make up for past misunderstandings."

"I told DePalma that's why you were doing this, and he said he was going to have your back when you got out. That's some sweet shit! You gonna take him up on it?"

I shake my head with indecisiveness. "At this point, I don't know, Slim."

Slim cracks a knowing grin. "Man, I would. But I understand with all the shit that's goin' down lately. I heard some faceless fuck dropped a dime on ya by sayin' you was a snitch workin' for the feds, but my niggers in the hood don't believe jack shit. Good thing you're leaving these backstabbing posers behind in the dust, huh?"

"You got that right, brother."

As the elevator car screeches languidly towards the bottom, I'm more than miffed that Slim has already heard I've been accused of being a rat working for the feds, which means by extension, the entirety of the Springfield penitentiary will soon know, and everybody knows what happens to rats in prison. Now, with everything in question, including this canteen caper, my stomach unexpectedly churns, and it feels like acid drips into my empty intestines.

"Who told you I was being accused of being a snitch?"

Slim doesn't hesitate. "Curtis broke that shit down to me."

The elevator car shudders to the end of its journey. In anticipation of what lies below, Slim licks the moisture off his top lip and grips his laundry bag much tighter, while I try to control my breath to steady nervousness brought on by this newest information. The lift stops with a screeching halt followed by a metallic rasp as its heavy doors slide open to reveal the basement landing. To confirm that our nemesis is actually temporarily preoccupied, we apprehensively raise our gazes toward the ceiling's security camera's dead eye. Then, with a nod and a grin acknowledging that homies in the hood successfully executed their roles in this operation, we silently and safely slip onto the basement's polished concrete hallway floors, defeating a million-dollar security system through unexpected teamwork and convict audacity.

Stealthily moving along the 80-foot corridor, we listen for the echo of any unexpected footsteps. Hearing no sentries wandering the hallways, we proceed to the T-junction and cautiously peer around its corners, scanning the vacant hallways. To the left lies the orderlies' living area and 20-feet to the right, the canteen entrance. Slim glances at his watch and cracks a nervous smile. He nods towards the canteen. "Count should clear in any minute. Get ready to jet around this corner as soon as they sound the bell."

"I can't go without Greg. He's in a wheelchair, and I promised I'd push him into the commissary."

Irritation washes over Slim's face. "Where the fuck is he?"

The elevator's door closes behind us, and the hall lantern light indicates the elevator car is traveling back up to Greg's unit.

I nudge Slim's elbow. "It looks like he's on his way now."

Slim and I keep watching up and down the dimly lit corridors until the elevator car reaches the basement landing.

When the elevator's doors pop open, Slim glances over his shoulder and curses at an unbelievably moronic sight. "Ahhh, hell no!!"

Whirling toward Slim's contention, I'm dumbstruck to see Greg wheel himself out of the elevator car with José, Luigi, and Mario in tow.

It feels like I've been sucker-punched in the stomach, and the wind has been knocked out of me. I give a forced whisper. "Awww, for fuck sakes."

Greg turns to José, who sports a sarcastic grin. He then gives a flamboyant wave towards Slim and my stunned faces. "See, what did I tell ya? We got people on the inside to make our lives a little easier." Greg calls out for my assistance. "Hey, Mark. Come and help me out here, will ya?"

Luigi ingratiates himself to Greg. "I'll push ya, Mr. DePalma. You don't need Mark to do that. I can push ya with no problem."

With a grimace, Slim pleads, "This wasn't part of our deal. Don't fucking trick me off here, Mark. They're going to get us fucking busted. We gotta do something."

Slim franticly ogles around the corner towards the canteen, then gazes back at Greg and his entourage as they move closer to our position and suggests, "Tell 'em the Lieutenant is coming down the hall."

It's not every day you get to pun the Mafia and a drug kingpin and live to tell about it, but today was going to have to be that day; Greg violated the convict's code by breaking his word and is endangering our operation. Undoubtedly, his motive for this affront is to lure José into his inner circle in order to get Nicky whacked. Although my friendship with Greg far outweighs any alliance I have with Slim, I gave my word to Slim that Greg would attend this jaunt alone and, in here, your word is all you have. More to the point, however, is that there was no way in hell that was okay with me that José and, especially, Luigi and Mario were included in today's operation.

Suddenly, I rubberneck around the corridor's corner, then jump back with a startled expression and yell at Greg, José, Luigi, and Mario with fanatic bark, "The lieutenant is coming! The lieutenant is coming!"

Six feet outside the elevator's door, they each stop in their tracks and go wide-eyed with confusion and fear. I then dash in their direction with a panicked expression as if the Lieutenant is, indeed, striding down the hallway towards us, giving us only moments to escape. Slim follows my lead by tagging behind with the same bogus trepidation. Greg is three feet in the lead, with Luigi and Mario paralyzed with fear beside José's wheelchair. José is the first to gain his composure. What happens in the next few seconds is unbelievably comical.

José abruptly spins his wheelchair into a 180-maneuver knocking over Luigi and Mario. They both squeal from their injuries and roll to the side of the elevator doors like dogs hit by a car. José leaves Mario and Luigi in their agony and rushes back inside the elevator car before executing another 180 turn, positioning himself to face everyone else attempting to make their escape.

With Slim and I now bearing down on Greg, he is certain that the jig is up and spins his wheelchair into the opposite direction. Luigi and Mario strain to stand as José waves Greg forward with a command.

"Hurry up, DePalma! Hurry!"

Like characters from a cartoon, Greg straight arms the wheel-chair's wheels forward, which again knocks down Luigi while running over Mario's foot. Mario shrieks in pain, grabs his painful foot, then attempts to hop on one leg towards the elevator.

Again, José yells at Greg as his hand simultaneously begins to press the up button triggering the elevator's doors to close together. "Fucking hurry. I'm leaving!"

Greg continues to straight-arm his wheels aggressively, propelling the wheelchair across the elevator car's threshold with such momentum that it crashes into the back of the elevator, almost throwing him into the wall. Thud! Slim and I continue to close the gap but slow down to witness Mario hop on one leg into the elevator car and collapse near Greg, while Luigi crawls through the elevator's doors as they close. Unable to turn around, Greg cries out at the back wall of the elevator, "Wait for Mark, José!"

Instead of complying with Greg's request, José pulls his hand away from the control buttons, raises both hands with palms to the air and, with a scornful smile, lets the elevator doors shut in our faces. Luigi screams in pain and fear as his foot is caught between the elevator doors.

Through the crack of the elevator door, I hear José sneer, "Fuck that guy!"

Stopping short of the elevator landing, the last thing Slim and I see or hear is Luigi's shrieks of horror as his trapped foot rises slowly between the elevator doors towards the top of the lift. His screams intensify and harmonize with Mario's manic bellows, "I got you. Fucking pull!!!" Then, with one last whimper and a grunt, we hear a heavy thud somewhere in the elevator car as the doors slam shut as Luigi's empty shoe tumbles to the floor.

Slim places his hand over his mouth to stifle a teenage giggle, but his chuckles are contagious, and we both burst out laughing. I hear José's muffled voice come from inside the elevator, questioning his reality. "What the fuck is so funny down there? They just got busted by the Lieutenant, didn't they?"

We hear the elevator's doors slide open on a floor above, followed by Mike's mad, irritating, capricious temper flare out of control. "Who the fuck is yelling out here? Hey! Why are you guys inside the elevator? Count has not cleared. Get the hell outta there and get in your goddamn rooms until further notice!"

Whatever was said after that is drowned out by Slim's snickers and a gravelly voice that booms across the intercom. "COUNT CLEAR!" With the green light finally given, Slim and I high-five each other and bolt down the empty hallway to be the very first convicts at the canteen.

With my laundry bag chock-full of ice creams and slung over my back like St. Nick, I make it back to Greg's unit to give Curtis his ice cream. I find Curtis's door open to a dark room. Hoping to surprise the old pimp, I peer around the door's jamb and see a figure sitting in the dark. Assuming it's Curtis who's fallen asleep, I flip on the light switch, but then stand stiffly in the doorway, stunned. Sitting in his wheelchair with that stupid smile slashed across his face is José.

"Expecting someone else?"

CHAPTER 32

I feel my heart beat faster, and I stumble with my words. "Where's Curtis?"

"He's fucking dead, and I got his room. Does that fucking answer your question?"

Glancing around Curtis's room, I find it completely void of his personal property, save the lingering scent of his cheap cologne. Before I can gain my composure, José quotes Sun Tzu: "Let your plans be dark and as impenetrable as night, and when you move, fall like a fucking thunderbolt."

Then he sarcastically quips, "It doesn't look like your little bird will be singing in anybody's ear anymore." I feel as if all hope has been sucked from the room into a bottomless abyss. Although I can't imagine what excruciating expression falls across my face, witnessing my obvious misery seems to provide José with the utmost sense of pleasure. "You act surprised that someone who snitches to the feds got whacked in prison."

"Curtis isn't a snitch."

"You mean Curtis wasn't a snitch. And, since DePalma, Cagnina, and Gotti now think he is, in my world, that's all that fucking counts." José scoffs. "You should know how these things work in prison by now."

To stress that a thought is in progress, he drums his temple with his index and middle finger in a staccato rhythm. "Oh, I almost forgot. There's also a nasty rumor bouncing around that you are working with the feds and were talking to the guard. I suppose it all does make sense with you and Curtis being homies and all."

With a calm, eerily cool demeanor, José's hand shifts from his head to curl rhythmically around the wheelchair's weaponized handle. "It would be a real crying shame if you didn't make it home because somebody thought you're a rat."

"Are you threatening me?"

José's fingers tighten their grip around the wheelchair's handle's hidden knives. "If it's unavoidable, I suppose so. I hate fucking rats."

Instinctively, I respond with a defensive position by shifting my weight to my back foot and tightening my grip around the end of my netted laundry bag, readying myself to pummel José with its weighted mass of ice cream and cigarettes. Then, almost instantaneously, I realize the gravity of the situation and that my personal freedom is at stake. To defuse the situation, I place my gym bag on the floor, hoping to downplay any escalating threats. "Look, José. I don't know what's going on, but I can assure you Curtis and I are not snitching. And..."

José snorts derisively, interrupting my train of thought. "Oh, so you do know my real name isn't Jay? And, here's a news flash, slick—you can't assure me of shit."

Leaning back in his chair with confidence that comes only from a place of power, he drops his façade and admits to the deaths of those who have crossed him before. "If you know my name, then you know I'm in here for seven murders. And, I can assure you, that's just the tip of the iceberg of the fuckers I've smoked. Now, DePalma, Gotti, and Cagnini think you're a solid motherfucker and have let it be known you're hands off." He shrugs his shoulders in indifference. "I suppose for now I'll have to live with these terms but, as you have noticed, that isn't going to include your friends. You and Curtis should have realized long ago this chess game would end badly if you continued to battle against me."

Pursing my lips, I hold my tongue.

"Nevertheless, since you seem to be constantly in the fucking way, and given that I can't kill you, it leaves us in a precarious situation which has unfortunately escalated into a dispassionate relationship. What do you suppose Machiavelli's opinions would be under these circumstances?

"I believe it's something to the effect that it's better to be feared than loved if both cannot be acquired."

His hands come together in a sarcastic clap. "Very good, Kwai Chang. You know, if you weren't in the fucking way, we could probably be friends, but I sense that's going to be an impossibility."

Casually, José's hand slips into his trousers' pocket; as he withdraws a slip of paper, I take a step back in apprehension.

Knitting his eyebrows together, he taunts me, "Is it just me, or does it feel edgy in here?"

"It's uncomfortable."

Across the divide, José hands me a typed slip of paper. "Prison can be an uncomfortable place, and Gotti and DePalma won't always have your back. They're old and dying, and even Gotti wasn't able to keep a nigger from punching him in the eye. If the boogeyman comes to town, do you really think they could save you in time?"

Retrieving the slip of paper from his hand, I immediately recognize it as a Bureau timesheet that calculates how much time is left on an inmate's sentence. José's release date is designated as "Deceased," indicating his only way out of prison is in a body bag. And, if nobody claims his corpse, he'll be buried in a nondescript cemetery for unclaimed inmates. It also implies that, like Andreas at El Reno in Oklahoma, who beat down the black gangbanger in the TV room, José has nothing left to lose.

"As you can see, I've burned all my bridges long ago. Any thoughts on your dwindling options before you walk into the flames?"

A 16th-century quote comes to my mind. "Never contend with a man who has nothing to lose."

"That would appear to be sound advice for someone hours from the door. Who said that?"

"Baltasar Gracián, a 16th century Spanish Jesuit."

"Too bad Curtis didn't take that old fuck's advice, but his personal grudges obscured his reasoning, and now I fear his itch will never be scratched."

"He told me you two had a falling out. Care to elaborate?"

"Not really, but it's always personal. You know, before Curtis died, he mentioned that he didn't divulge to you any information that he was going to tell DePalma. Was that the truth?"

"It's the truth. Yesterday while at the gym, Curtis said he needed to talk to Greg, but for my safety, he refused to disclose any further information on the matter."

He studies my facial expressions for any deception before responding. "Well, at least the pimp saved you from further heartache. You should also know he never had a chance to talk to Greg."

Beneath my feet, the floor suddenly feels unstable—an unusual sensation that triggers an urgency to run before it's too late. Overwhelmed by the aftermath of today's events, I let out a heavy sigh and retrieve the laundry bag from the floor, sling it over my shoulder, and accept this game's untenable stalemate.

Thinking José built a bridge of fear and freedom for me to traverse, I quote Sun Tzu to establish motive, "Build your opponent a golden bridge to retreat across."

I then capitulate to corroborate an exit strategy. "Listen, José. I'm going to take Sun Tzu and everyone else's suggestions and take my ass home tomorrow. I don't mean to be rude, but I have a few things I need to attend to before I leave. It's been nice to know you."

With a smug demeanor, José waves farewell and returns a quote by Sun Tzu that drips with malicious intent. "Adiós, Kwai Chang! 'Can you imagine what I would do if I could do all I can?'"

Then, unexpectedly and without provocation, he wheels towards me while withdrawing his wheelchair handle's makeshift weapon. Momentarily confused, I step back and ready myself for José's assault when, from out of nowhere, I hear Rick's gravelly voice come from behind.

"That will be enough!"

As I'm pushed aside, Rick's foot violently slams against José's wheelchair, bringing it to a screeching halt. José lurches forward as Rick simultaneously pins both of his arms to the wheelchair's handles. He struggles against Rick's more powerful physique as he rattles off prison protocol, "You're not supposed to be on this unit."

Six inches from José's face, Rick growls through clenched teeth. "In about 5 seconds, it's not gonna matter because I'm getting ready to break all kinds of things."

Without turning around, Rick belts out a command drenched in venom and finality, "Shut the door behind you, will ya, Mark? This is going to get a little uncomfortable."

Frantically, José struggles to rubberneck around Rick's muscular torso only to catch a glimpse of me raising my hands with palms to the air, mimicking his own behavior when he callously shut the elevator doors in my face. He gulps as I turn my gaze away from the coming mayhem to adjust the laundry bag on my shoulder and shut the door, leaving Rick and José to what will undoubtedly be an enlightening discussion.

As I walk to the common area to find Slim, I pass by Sammy's room, where I immediately sense that our relationship has soured. He eyeballs me with irritation as if I'm an unwelcomed vagrant on his front lawn. Putting a finger to his bulbous lips, he rolls off the bed and walks by me, shaking his head as he emphatically states, "No offense, but I don't think we can talk any longer until someone can figure out what the fuck is going on." He scoffs. "Fucking shadow people."

His indignation then unexpectedly subsides as he lays a fatherly hand on my shoulder. "Look, Mark. I like you, so I'm going to give you some advice that you should take and run with. You need to go home and stay away from places like this and people like these. You don't belong here, and you're not one of us. That being said, Greg is going to try and give you a phone number before you leave—don't take it. I know John is appreciative for what you've done, but he's hotter than a Thompson machine gun in a firefight, and there are too many unknown variables in these recent events, you included."

I look for a meaning beyond his words, but Sammy's face remains static, blank, unreadable. I know I should step back, but I ask anyway. "My friend Curtis is dead, and José said he acquired his room. I gotta ask, Sammy. Did José kill Curtis?"

"I've heard your friend has been taken out for being a rat. And, with José having something to prove to Greg, who fucking knows? But nobody gave José that room. He's just fucking with your head. Like I said before, unless you grow bigger balls than mine, you've met your match, gunslinger. Just so you know, José has also let it leak you were talkin' to the guard the other night..." a low sigh comingled with incredulity passed Sammy's lips as he shook his head in disbelief, "...about shadow people, which didn't do you any favors."

Sammy rubs the back of his thick neck. "At the end of the day, José is willing to cross certain lines to win that you would never consider crossing. It's during these times you need to learn when to step off and when to tell people no to protect your best interests."

Then, in pure gangster fashion, Sam Cagnina sticks out his big paw, shakes my hand, and imparts his last decision and advice: "That's what I'm going to do now. Goodbye, Mark. Get the fuck outta and here and go live the American dream without prison psychopaths plotting to undermine your freedom."

Then, without hesitation, he turns and walks away without saying another word.

I'm moments from being released. I should be ecstatic as I walk through the prison hallways for the last time. Instead, I find myself in a melancholic state over the fact that Sammy and others think I may be a snitch, a label that is an anathema to anyone who has ever served time.

I find Slim alone watching TV when I stroll into the common area. I reach into my laundry bag and hand him Curtis's ice cream in addition to the one promised to his gangbanger compatriot. He sets them on the worn card table and thanks me for the unexpected gift, then explains the lie he told to Greg and his motley crew regarding today's canteen debacle.

"Listen, Mark. To avoid any hard feelings, I've told everyone that the lieutenant was really headed our way. Then, just before we were busted, he got a call on his walkie-talkie and turned around and walked back towards the orderly's dorm. And, since José screwed us from getting back on the elevator, we held our position until count cleared, letting us be first in the commissary's line." Slim goes on to say that the reason he lied is that everyone caught on the elevator by the guard was forced to wait in their rooms for an additional 15 minutes after count cleared, making them last in the commissary line and pissed.

When he finished, I asked him what happened to Curtis, but he nervously waved my questions away with a frown.

"Bro, all this Mafia shit with your friends is off the fucking chain. Nobody knows what the fuck is going on anymore. Word has it is that Curtis was a snitch along with you, and that's why he got smoked. Hell, I even heard a rumor today that Mario and Luigi are working for the feds. Can you fucking believe that insane shit? Mario and Luigi? Anyway, with all this craziness going on, I've been told by my lieutenant to back the fuck away from all this shit until they can figure out what's what. Personally, I don't think anyone except José is working for the feds, but that's not my call. I'm just a soldier, and I'm not risking a beat down for not following orders. Speaking of soldiers, one of my niggers spotted your special forces dog on the unit. I think he snuck in to visit his dying military buddy."

Surprised that Rick has a friend on this unit, I ask for details.

"They brought him in yesterday and put him in the room a couple of doors down from Curtis."

Slim quickly grabs the two ice creams off the card table. "I gotta jet this ice cream to my homie before it melts.

He turns as he approaches the door and, with a mischievous smile and shoulder shrug, reports, "The guard said you're leaving early tomorrow, and it's all me tonight. So... I guess this is it, my nigger. Maybe someday we'll see each other on the other side. Later, Mark."

With another piece of the puzzle locked into place regarding how Rick was able to make his seemingly insuperable entry into Curtis's room, I gaze through the rusted picture window for the last time at the view of the desolate killing fields lined with shimmering razor wire and ominous guard towers that have blocked my freedom for seven years. I open my ice cream container and enjoy one of prison's little pleasures as I turn my thoughts towards home. As the last cold, satisfying, scoop of ice cream slides down my throat, Greg waltzes into the common area sporting his bathrobe, feigning disappointment and hurt feelings.

"You ain't going to say goodbye before you leave?"

"Well, I thought I'd lie low before heading to the door tomorrow. It's starting to feel like everyone's either on edge or mad at me today."

"That's probably a good idea until you're out the door. But, I'm not mad at ya, and neither is John. It's just part of the game, Mark. It's nothing personal."

"Well, it's sure starting to feel personal. What about Sammy?"

Greg adjusts his bathrobe. "I'm feeling a little uneasy talking out here in the open. Let's walk to the bathroom for a smoke."

For a moment, I feel like I'm being set up but decide to trust my old friend and believe in John's promise. As our feet echo down the hallway, Greg puts his hand on my shoulder and expounds that they're playing it extra careful due to a snitch being in our midst. And, since John is out of the equation with respect to José's requests, Sammy decided to blow smoke-up José's ass by telling him that this hit on Nicky is a personal favor to Vincent Gigante. He also threw in a few other enticements to help flesh out whether José is the real deal. Once everything is proven to be on the up and up, and my paranoid feelings are dispelled as bullshit, they can continue on with business as usual with José. Greg also mentioned that John received an anonymously penned kite reporting that I was talking to a guard about shadow people and that José told Sammy the same thing.

"Yeah, that's true. Sammy didn't seem to think much of the shadow people discussion. You and John probably think I'm crazy after hearing that insane narrative, huh? But, it's the truth."

Greg squeezes my shoulder and reassures me, "I don't know what John thinks about that shit, but I believe ya."

I'm astonished at this remark and glance at his facial expression to verify he isn't teasing me, only to find a sober appearance.

"Really?"

"Yeah, really. I would never admit to this in a million years, except to John, but one time Liz wanted me to spend the night specifically to protect her from those evil fuckers."

Again, I'm genuinely astonished. "Elizabeth Taylor?"

"Really. Believe me, I've seen some crazy shit in my life and thought it had prepared me for almost anything, but what we saw that night, or what we believed we saw, was a fucking incomprehensible nightmare I'll never forget. Except for a few people I can trust, I don't talk about it."

"Why not?"

Greg smiles and crosses himself in the Catholic tradition. "Well, a priest told me during confession they were demons and, if I occasionally say three "Hail Mary's" and don't talk about them, they will lose their power over us. So far, so fucking good. Besides, in our business, you can act crazy, but you can't be crazy, or nobody's going to take ya serious. Capiche?"

"Loud and clear. I wouldn't want to stop a winning streak, and I'm touched you trust me."

"Get the fuck outta here."

"So, you and John don't think I'm a snitch for talking to the guard."

"Nah, I believe you and told John the scoop on Liz to back your story. Besides, nothin' you've ever done over the past year has come back to haunt me or John. But make no mistake, I also have to play the cards I'm dealt, and I intend to play those fucking cards."

"What about Curtis?"

His hand comes off my shoulder, and his tone turns gruff. "What about Curtis? He played the game and lost. Plus, it lets us know who's willing to take this shit seriously. You do know that I can't let this shit go unchecked. Besides, José has a lot to prove, and somebody had to pay, although his connections on the street will be missed. Did I ever tell you about buying a $10,000 dollar mink coat for $50.00 off a crackhead friend of his? My wife loved it!"

I open the bathroom door for Greg to the faint smells of cleaning products, urine, and mildew.

"I think you did."

Greg's house shoes shuffle softly against the tile floor as he walks past me toward the urinals, mumbling with regret, "I hope you know I tried to hold the elevator for you. It broke my heart when José disrespected you and me by leaving you and Slim holding your dicks down there."

Following Greg's lumbering frame, I disclose, "I heard you tell José to hold the elevator, and don't worry, we did okay down there after José abandoned us."

Greg mumbles again. "I heard."

Reaching the urinals at the back of the restroom, we both pull cigarettes out of our shirt pockets. Lighting Greg's customary butt, I study his downcast face, which I surmise is crestfallen because he allowed José to abandon a friend.

"Does it really bother you that José screwed me over?"

"Yeah. It fucking does because it could have cost you your freedom, and I shouldn't have brought those fucksticks with me. I'm sorry."

It's during this moment of heartfelt remorse that I decide to tell Greg the truth about what actually went on down in the basement.

"Aw, don't beat yourself up. I have something to tell you, but you can't tell anyone. Ok?"

Greg listens to my story with serious intent until he learns the guard was fictitious; then, his expression changes into one of surprise. While I recount José knocking Luigi and Mario to the floor and him straight-arming through them on his way back to the elevator, his mouth spreads into a comical grin. But, it's when I begin to paint the scene of Luigi and Mario tripping all over themselves to escape the fictitious lieutenant that Greg's initial giggle escalates into explosive laughter that echoes along the tiled bathroom's interior and spills into the hallway as I give witness to Luigi's shoe dropping to the floor minus a foot. He grabs my shoulder, grasping for support. "Jesus fucking Christ! That was fucking funny!" Then with a satirical grin, he tightens his grip on my shoulder. "But hey, don't you ever tell anybody that story or do that again. I got a fucking reputation to keep."

I keep it light. "As do we all."

Greg reaches into his pocket to retrieve a kite, which he hands to me with his right hand as he tightens the grip on his cigarette with his left and takes an exaggerated drag. "Hey. Here is a number I want you to call when you get out. We want to help you." I thought—just as Sammy foretold. As recommended by Sammy, I tell him I appreciate the overture but that I'd rather go it alone under the circumstances. His face goes red as he shakes the kite in my face, searching my eyes for deception. "Why won't you take the fucking number? Is José right? Are ya a snitch?" Immediately, he realizes his misstep and takes responsibility. "I'm sorry, Mark. That was fucked up."

"That's okay. Sammy told me you were going to try and give me a number and not to take it. After these latest events, I've decided just to go home without any further involvement. If I'm wrong about José, I'll find a way to get in touch with you and pay for a meal at your favorite restaurant."

"I'll take that bet, and if I'm wrong, I'll buy you a meal at a 5-star Italian restaurant in the Big Apple. Who knows? Maybe you're fucking right, and you saved John from getting fucked by the feds. I certainly wouldn't put it past the bastards."

Taking a drag, I exhale a nicotine-laden plume with nostalgic mentation. "At the end of the day, I hope my loyalty to our friendship has helped us and saved John's son from the rats."

"I'll always feel the same. When it's all said and done, it's down to who was loyal—nothing else matters in this life."

Greg pulls a billfold from his back pocket, flips it open, and takes out a picture of a guy with the looks of a movie star. Handing me the picture, he laments, "That's one of my boys. Even though I love John Jr., that kid is my heart."

"He certainly has your good looks."

"That's the DePalma shine."

I hand the photo back to him and remind him that, in addition to buying me dinner when he loses the bet, having his son is another reason for eventually leaving this place."

"Get the fuck outta here. You'll be buying me that dinner, and I can't fucking wait."

For a moment, my mood turns melancholic. "I sincerely hope so, Greg. I sincerely hope so."

Greg strokes the stubble on his chin. "John said we'd know who the snitch was within the year. Hopefully, we got him. No disrespect."

I tell him, "None taken," but I don't mean it. I'll never believe Curtis was a snitch.

As we inhale the last drags off our cigarettes, Greg tells me the names of a lawyer and a famous New York artist." "When you lose that fucking bet, you give one of those guys a call. You hear me?"

Even though I have no idea whether I will call or not, I reassure the old mobster. "You got it, buddy."

As we walk out of the bathroom, we hear the guard's voice echo down the polished hallway, instructing me to go to the elevator lobby, where I will leave this unit for the last time. "BLACK! TO THE ELEVATOR LOBBY!"

Greg pulls me in for a hug, shakes my hand, and gives me a heartfelt grin. "Well, I guess this is it, you fuck."

"I reckon so, old man."

Greg stands watching me amble towards the lobby with his hand in the air. Before I turn the corner, I ask, "Greg, do you have any last pearls of wisdom to share?"

He smiles the DePalma grin. "To stay outta places like these. Oh, and one other thing—John said stay solid, and thanks for helpin' out."

His last words trail behind me as he turns back towards his room. "You're a good kid, Mark. See ya back in the world, my friend."

I sleep restlessly on my unit that night, knowing that this will be my last night in prison. Around five in the morning, I'm startled awake by a nudge on my arm. In the darkness, I try to focus on the image kneeling beside my bed.

It's Rick.

"Hey, brother. I gotta work till 8 a.m., but I did want to see you before you left for your new life in the world."

I sit up in bed. "I was hoping we could say goodbye before I left. I want to thank you for always being there for me."

"Captain Save-a-Whore. That's me."

We both expel a hushed laugh.

"Listen. I spoke with José, and he was just scaring you, so you'd back off from helping Gotti or DePalma. I was able to extract a little intel that he's working on something with your Mafia friends, which you don't need to be involved in."

"What about my friend Curtis? Did José kill him?"

"I don't know. At this point, it appears everyone, including your Mafia buddies, is throwing as much sand in the air as possible. No one knows what the truth is anymore. Personally, I can't tell who's lying in that group of goombahs, but I do know one thing—I have your back, and you're going to walk out of this shit hole in a couple of hours."

Rick hugs me with a handshake.

"Semper Fi motherfucker."

"Semper Fi and thanks, brother."

Rick smiles and slips back into the darkness as I slip back into an agitated sleep with one thought. *You're going to walk out of this shit hole in a couple of hours.*

When I wake up at 6 a.m., there is a flurry of activity that ends with a guard bellowing the most sanguine phrase to a prisoner's ears. "BLACK! BUNK AND JUNK."

I strip my bed and gather any personal items that may be useful for my new life at a halfway house. I'm directed to a room where my release will be administered. As I walk down the corridor towards my freedom, I can't believe my eyes when I see José rapidly coming towards me in his wheelchair.

He nods his head. "What's up? It took a couple of packs of cigarettes and my personal charm to convince the orderly to allow me in this area, but I couldn't let you leave without saying goodbye."

Out of habit, I take a defensive stance as he rolls up. Sensing no animosity from his demeanor, however, I relax my posture.

"Contrary to what you might think, I've grown quite fond of matching wits with you, but as you have also unmasked, I don't play fair."

Adjusting himself in the wheelchair, José recounts his interaction with Rick, "But, then again, apparently neither does your military friend, who was very persuasive in us reaching the understanding that we both have endured enough pain for a lifetime. Personally, I wasn't looking forward to tearing off your wings just before you learn to fly again. But I do have one question to ask before you leave—you do intend to leave all this behind for a sunnier day, right?"

"Well, it is reassuring to learn that you no longer wish to tear off my wings. And, as I said before, I'm through here. I just want to meet my destiny down this hallway."

He glances at the inaccessible release room and the promise of freedom it holds. "Don't we all."

Almost as if he can read my mind, his lips curl into an enigmatic grin. "I hope you don't judge me too harshly for these recent monstrosities. I'll always do whatever it takes to survive. And, mark my words—you'll do the same once released. I won't think any less of you, either, because it's all part of the game, from which nobody gets out of alive—just ask Curtis."

I frown. "What about Greg, Sammy, and John?"

"Poor Kwai Chang, still concerned with people that don't care about you? That's going to be a problem when you're free. Let me leave you with a quote to contemplate on your journey back home. 'The promise given was a necessity of the past: the word broken is a necessity of the present,' Niccolò fucking Machiavelli."

Then, with an upward nod of pure confidence, he wheels right past me with his words echoing down the morning's sunlit hallway.

"Goodbye, Black. Enjoy the world and grab everything you can. It only lasts a moment."

CHAPTER 33

About one year after my release, on June 10, 2002, John Gotti died at Springfield's federal penitentiary. Although saddened to hear of his death, I was also relieved to know that his suffering finally ended—considering his living conditions and his cancer's fulminant course. A few days later, the nightly news aired his elaborate funeral highlighted by over 40 black limousines and 19 open-aired flower cars that meandered through Queens to his final resting place. Four news helicopters circled over sidewalks flooded with throngs of admirers, some sporting signs reading "John Gotti Forever," alongside undercover agents, news reporters, and the paparazzi—John would have been proud.

Before my March 2000 release, John predicted that the snitch would be exposed within a year. His prediction was ultimately confirmed in May of 2001 when Greg DePalma, Sam Cagnina, and Richard Famiglietti, an acquaintance of Greg's who identified Nicky for the undercover hitman, were all indicted and charged with the attempted assassination of Nicky LaSorsa. I followed the news and learned that Nicky LaSorsa was a 66-year-old owner of an automobile showroom in the Bronx who had completed a five-year sentence on a drug conviction in the 70s. In 1992, he pled guilty to lying to the FBI about leasing an automobile to a murder suspect in 1989, and he was hit with another drug charge indictment in 1993. Nicky was a made man, which is why José ostensibly needed John's permission to whack him before the plug was pulled on John Jr.'s involvement.

Because Greg failed to heed the same warning signs revealed to John, he found himself sitting in a tense courtroom with Sammy on July 30, 2002, watching in astonishment as José testified against them as a government informant. Court journalists portrayed José Reyes as a ruthless, murdering, drug kingpin from New York, known by his street name El Feo, who made millions monthly in the cocaine trade. They also reported, as Curtis told me, that he was gunned down on his way to a birthday party by a rival gang member in 1992, rendering him a paraplegic. He then received a life sentence for his involvement in seven murders in 1996.

On that day, José sat calmly in the witness stand and testified that Greg solicited him to kill Nicky LaSorsa for reneging on weekly payments of $2,500. Court transcripts divulged that the feds had wired José's wheelchair and bugged Greg's unit's telephone, which Greg used to contact Richard Famiglietti with orders to meet and identify Nicky LaSorsa for José's undercover hitman. The newspaper and web pages identified Greg as a flamboyant caporegime in the Gambino crime family who rubbed elbows with the stars, including Frank Sinatra, with whom he played golf. Little was known about Sam Cagnina—the shadowy figure known as "The Fatman"—except that he was an ex-police officer who ran with the Trafficante family in Florida. He had murdered Ronald Yaras, the son of a Chicago mobster, and was also linked to nebulous JFK conspiracy theories.

With these court transcripts and a little hindsight, it became quite clear that Greg disregarded everything Curtis or I said and, instead, went full steam ahead with the hit on Nicky LaSorsa. Greg DePalma was heard over a bugged telephone reassuring Richard Famiglietti that the hitman could be trusted: "Whatever he tells you, it's all right. He's a good guy. Whatever he wants to do, just do it." Then Greg blurted out, "That fat fuck. I'll show him a thing or two."

However, as we know from my story that Richard Famiglietti was not José's first choice. Initially, he would only make a deal if John Jr. had been willing to meet the undercover hitman; because John heeded the warning about José's possible intentions, that arrangement never happened. Completely unknown to all those at Springfield's penitentiary, José had already flipped for the feds years ago, according to New York Post reporter John Lehmann: "He helped the feds locate a wanted person in the Dominican Republic but had been waiting three years for his prison sentence to be reduced when he decided to tip the feds off about the gangsters' plan."

After Lehmann's revelation that José already worked with the feds in an attempt to gain his freedom, there was little doubt that the late-night raid on Peter by the men in black, which resulted in his sudden disappearance into diesel therapy, had José's fingerprints all over it. Lehmann's revelations also seem to indicate that José had played everyone in a manipulative Machiavellian game—everyone except for John Gotti and me.

Although I never was a Mafia aficionado, when writing this last chapter, I was able to find several sites dedicated to information useful for use in its completion. Americanmafia.com gives information helpful in understanding why José adamantly wanted Greg to convince John to sanction John Jr.'s meeting with José's hitman. "Following the imprisonment of the Dapper Don in April 1992, the feds set as their next goal John A. "Junior" Gotti. On January 21, 1998, a massive indictment would bring down the younger Gotti along with 39 other reputed underworld figures, including DePalma and his son, Craig. The DePalmas were charged with putting out a contract on two Albanian men who, in 1995, murdered two employees at Scores, a popular topless nightclub in Manhattan." Rick Porrello's American Mafia.com; May 2002—Gregory DePalma—Revisited (Part One).

If Rick Porrello's American Mafia.com correctly reports that the feds' goal was to imprison John Jr., José's original scheme, it was likely an attempt to achieve this objective. I often wondered if John had granted Greg's request to involve John Jr., if John Jr. would have met the undercover hitman and fallen into the trap designed by José instead of Famiglietti. This question was answered in a 60 Minutes interview on April 11, 2010, during which John Gotti Jr. professed to Steven Kroft that he visited his father at Springfield's penitentiary and told him that he was leaving the Mafia, which included a virtual retelling of the same story John told me the day John Jr. left the visiting room with tears in his eyes. Most of the interview, however, consisted of descriptions of his unwavering admiration for his late father. That made clear; it would have made little difference whether John Jr. was in or out of the mob—had John had asked him to meet José's hitman, he would have done it. John Jr. appeared quite intelligent and measured during the 60 minutes interview, but he loved his father and was a loyal son. Fortunately, John did not allow the federal government to leverage this love and sense of duty to entrap him. Unfortunately, Greg allowed José's Machiavellian tactics to infect his reason, which resulted in a festering anger that consumed his thoughts and prevented him from considering anything other than protecting his honor—he failed to protect his son in the way John protected John Jr.

My kites and conversations fortunately instilled a healthy dose of suspicion into everyone, leading to a game of "Who's the snitch?" at Springfield. That reinforced Sammy's decision to intentionally play both sides until the snitch was revealed, which proved beneficial. Court documents echoed this sentiment, disclosing that Sam Cagnina cunningly mislead José by telling him the proposed assassination of Nicky was a favor to Vincent Gigante, and that he offered him lucrative drug delivery routes and a brownstone in New York to sweeten the deal. Other court documents indicated that, after I left Springfield, John held to his suspicions and kept the Gotti's completely out of the fray. With Sammy's proposal the only game in town, José took Cagnina's deal and promptly called agents at the DEA.

I felt incredible relief to be vindicated, even after the year that elapsed. As I suspected, José was the snitch in this sordid tale of lies and betrayal at Springfield. It felt equally amazing to know that I thwarted José's plan to help the feds trap and prosecute John Jr. before John died in prison. Richard Famiglietti unwittingly took the fall for Greg. He was charged with conspiracy to commit murder and given no bond. When Greg was charged, he accepted no blame and was reported to have cried out, "I love Cagnina, but look at the mess he has gotten me into!"

I suppose it could have been a lot worse had I not been there to fuel such an intense state of paranoia. As Rick described it, "At this point, it appears everyone, including your Mafia buddies, is throwing as much sand in the air as possible."

Nicky LaSorsa refused to testify at trial, and the sandstorm of BS blew with intensity through the jury. The jury foreman, Christopher Ebert, told reporters, "We did not believe José Reyes. We had just the tapes, and we didn't find them sufficiently strong in swaying us that there was a murder-for-hire conspiracy." Incredulous jury members found José's story so far-fetched that they acquitted Greg and Sammy of all charges. Richard Famiglietti was the only defendant convicted, receiving a 41-month sentence for his involvement with the agent posing as the hitman. Greg and Sammy had the last laugh, with John undoubtedly laughing the loudest from above, having trusted his instincts and saving his son shortly before his death.

José's unbelievable story to the courts was the truth, however, and the self-proclaimed Machiavellian prince had his life sentence commuted to 20 years as a result of his cooperation. At his resentencing hearing, José listened as Judge Shira Scheindlin expounded that, even though his murders and crimes were horrendous, it was "time to temper justice with mercy," before ruling that he should serve another eleven years and four months, which would make him 44-years-old upon his release in 2015. I hope he enjoys his freedom after winning the ultimate game of deception he played on both federal and criminal agents. Well played, José—Sun Tzu and Niccole Machiavelli would be proud.

Years later, after Greg's death, I began having a recurring dream. I find myself in an elegant restaurant with white linen tablecloths, fine china, and illustrious clientele. Greg is always the center of attention, sashaying through the tables, shaking hands, conversing, and laughing with movie stars, sports figures, and politicians, all dressed in stylish attire. He eventually notices me standing alone and signals me, with a wave of his hand, to follow him through a curtain at the back of the restaurant, which leads to a hidden room. He opens a nondescript door, and we walk into a darkened room filled with cigar and cigarette smoke mixed with raucous laughter that wafts over my senses. Once the smoke dissipates and my eyes adjust to the dim lighting, I realize I'm in an older Italian neighborhood's speakeasy that sports stained glass windows and an antique wooden bar made from rich mahogany. Men in expensive suits saddle up to the bar, drinking expensive bourbons and puffing on fine cigars that dangle from their smug, smiling lips. They slowly turn in our direction, revealing that the group consists of John, Sammy, and other made men in their prime. With smiles on their faces, they raise their glasses to Greg, toasting him and letting him know that he is finally home.

THE END

EPILOGUE

After their acquittals, Sammy and Greg both returned to prison to complete their previous sentences. Sammy was released from prison in June 2009, and he subsequently lived a quiet life with his family until his death. He developed a Facebook page that includes photos and is available at:
https://www.facebook.com/sam.cagnina.1.

Sammy died June 21, 2010. His family recognized his death with this Facebook post:

~ ~ ~

Today we lost a father, uncle, brother, grandfather, great grandfather, and friend. Sam Cagnina was a storyteller, mentor, and always had great advice. Eight days shy of being home one year, and full of life 'til the end. Please keep us in your thoughts & prayers. Rest in peace, Big Sam. 12/13/35-6/21/10.

~ ~ ~

Greg's satisfaction with his 2002 acquittal was marred by personal tragedy later that year. Craig, Greg's son with the movie star looks, attempted to commit suicide by hanging himself in a prison where he was serving an eight-year sentence on racketeering charges. He failed in taking his life but was left in a chronic vegetative state. It was unclear exactly why Craig chose to hang himself—competing theories included that he had testified to a grand jury in the Gold Club racketeering case against Michael "Mikey Scars" DiLeonardo or that he simply was unable to adjust to prison life.

I'm glad that I listened to Sammy and didn't take the phone number Greg provided to contact him out in the world. Greg was released in February 2003. Soon thereafter, he was again serving as a capo of the Gambino crime family, and his crew was infiltrated by Jack Falcone, an FBI agent whose real name was Joaquin Garcia. Garcia claimed Greg planned to induct him into the Gambino family as a made man, and he wore a wire that allowed federal authorities to listen in on many of the Gambino mobsters' conversations, which helped build a federal case against Greg and his associates.

The FBI pulled the plug on Operation Jack Falcone after DePalma, Garcia, and Gambino mobster Robert Vaccaro met another mobster at Bloomingdales in Westchester County. Garcia claimed Vaccaro thought the other mobster failed to give him proper respect, resulting in Vaccaro commencing to beat him in the head with a solid crystal candleholder. Garcia talked Greg into leaving with his crew, ending the melee. Garcia later explained that as an FBI agent, he could not, of course, join in the attack, whereas a mobster wanna-be would have participated without hesitation in order to demonstrate his loyalty to the crew. His failure to help in the assault led the FBI to assume Garcia's cover was blown and that he was in imminent danger. Accordingly, they ended the operation. Subsequently, on March 9, 2005, agents arrested Greg along with 32 other Gambino mobsters on racketeering charges.

This time, Greg was convicted. He died in a federal prison on November 18, 2009, at age 78. Craig never regained consciousness and died in December 2010 without verification whether or not he testified before a grand jury.

At Springfield, there was a talk by Greg and Curtis about the Albanians disrespecting Gotti and considering a takeover. Greg complained that the Gambino family would not retaliate due to the paranoia that I instilled in Gotti. This reluctance to retaliate against the Albanians and the connection to Gotti was confirmed in the trial of a New York Albanian gang, as reported by the *New York Times*. Hartocollis, A. (2005, December 20). Albanian Gang Portrayed as Aspiring Mafiosi. *The New York Times*, p. B3.

During the third month of the trial of six defendants accused of being members of a violent organized crime group called the Corporation, Jennifer Rodgers said that over the course of several years, Nikola Dedaj, a defendant whom she called the Albanian mob's chief enforcer, wrested control of territory formerly controlled by the five Italian crime families. "They make mistakes somewhere; we move in and take it," she quoted Mr. Dedaj as saying. Ms. Rodgers further told a jury in Federal District Court in Manhattan, "Members of the Albanian organization felt so sure of themselves that they claimed John Gotti's old table at Rao's, the exclusive East Harlem restaurant patronized by writers and reputed Italian crime family members."

The natural and interesting supposition is that the feds allowed the Albanians to go unchecked, hoping Gotti would react to their blatant disrespect, allowing them to ensnare John and the Gambinos once again. I am certain that the wariness and suspicion I created in the Springfield prison played an integral role in sparing John and associates from falling into this trap.

ABOUT THE AUTHOR

Following his release from prison, Mark focused on rebuilding his life. He settled in Tulsa, Oklahoma, where he completed a college degree and turned his attention to researching topics relating to personal experiences or of academic interest. He initially focused his writing skill to bring attention to and help fight psychiatric abuse by completing his first book, *Black Truth: Medicated in America*, which details how his own life was devastated by psychiatric mismanagement.

Black Truth: The Last Days of Gotti, is Mark's second installment relating to one of his life experiences, this time describing his interactions with mobsters while imprisoned together.

Today, Mark has wonderful relationships with those he loves while he continues to enjoy his freedom and pursue his passion for research and writing.

www.ingramcontent.com/pod-product-compliance
Lightning Source LLC
Chambersburg PA
CBHW061005280326
41935CB00009B/840